S0-CJP-851

STRAND PRICE
$5.00

Training for the New Millennium

Benjamins Translation Library

The Benjamins Translation Library aims to stimulate research and training in translation and interpreting studies. The Library provides a forum for a variety of approaches (which may sometimes be conflicting) in a socio-cultural, historical, theoretical, applied and pedagogical context. The Library includes scholarly works, reference works, post-graduate text books and readers in the English language.

EST Subseries

The European Society for Translation Studies (EST) Subseries is a publication channel within the Library to optimize EST's function as a forum for the translation and interpreting research community. It promotes new trends in research, gives more visibility to young scholars' work, publicizes new research methods, makes available documents from EST, and reissues classical works in translation studies which do not exist in English or which are now out of print.

General editor
Gideon Toury
Tel Aviv University

Associate editor
Miriam Shlesinger
Bar Ilan University

Advisory board

Marilyn Gaddis Rose
Binghamton University

Yves Gambier
Turku University

Daniel Gile
Université Lumière Lyon 2 and ISIT Paris

Ulrich Heid
University of Stuttgart

Eva Hung
Chinese University of Hong Kong

W. John Hutchins
University of East Anglia

Zuzana Jettmarová
Charles University of Prague

Werner Koller
Bergen University

Alet Kruger
UNISA

José Lambert
Catholic University of Leuven

Franz Pöchhacker
University of Vienna

Rosa Rabadán
University of León

Roda Roberts
University of Ottawa

Juan C. Sager
UMIST Manchester

Mary Snell-Hornby
University of Vienna

Sonja Tirkkonen-Condit
University of Joensuu

Lawrence Venuti
Temple University

Wolfram Wilss
University of Saarbrücken

Judith Woodsworth
Mt. Saint Vincent University Halifax

Sue Ellen Wright
Kent State University

Volume 60

Training for the New Millennium: Pedagogies for translation and interpreting
Edited by Martha Tennent

Training for the New Millennium

Pedagogies for translation and interpreting

Edited by

Martha Tennent

John Benjamins Publishing Company

Amsterdam / Philadelphia

TM   The paper used in this publication meets the minimum requirements
of American National Standard for Information Sciences – Permanence
of Paper for Printed Library Materials, ANSI z39.48-1984.

Library of Congress Cataloging-in-Publication Data

Training for the New Millennium : Pedagogies for translation and interpreting /
edited by Martha Tennent.
       p.   cm. (Benjamins Translation Library, ISSN 0929–7316 ; v. 60)
Includes bibliographical references and indexes.
       1. Translators--Training of. 2. Translating and interpreting--Study
and teaching. I. Tennent, Martha. II. Benjamins translation library ; v. 60.
III. Benjamins translation library.

       P306.5.T717 2005
418'.0071'1--dc22   2005062369
ISBN 90 272 1666 5 (Eur.) / 1 58811 609 3 (US) (Hb; alk. paper)

© 2005 – John Benjamins B.V.
No part of this book may be reproduced in any form, by print, photoprint, microfilm, or
any other means, without written permission from the publisher.

John Benjamins Publishing Co. · P.O. Box 36224 · 1020 ME Amsterdam · The Netherlands
John Benjamins North America · P.O. Box 27519 · Philadelphia PA 19118-0519 · USA

For Anne Tennent Cecil

la germaneta,
la que sap tota la història

Table of contents

I. Training programmes: The current situation and future prospects

II. Pedagogical strategies

Acknowledgments

This book is dedicated to my sister, Anne Cecil, who has accompanied me through most of the geographies of my life.

I would like to express my appreciation to all of my colleagues from the School of Translation at the University of Vic, particularly to those from the translation department. Sheila Waldeck, who read many of the chapters of this book and offered valuable suggestions, Carme Sanmartí and Luísa Cotoner deserve special mention for their support and friendship.

Mary Hamilton Stephens, the last of the formidable Hamilton women who studied and travelled the world, and Montserrat Cortés were a constant source of inspiration and encouragement. I am also grateful to two anonymous readers who offered constructive suggestions for improvement. Dolors Juanola, from whom I learned Catalan and many other things, helped pave the way – without her every knowing it – to the founding of the School of Translation at the University of Vic.

I am indebted, as always, to my daughter Maruxa Relaño, who grew up trilingually and was translating cultures by the time she could speak. She has taught me much about life and languages.

My greatest thanks and gratitude go to Larry Venuti, translator and translator theoretician, travelling literary companion and chef, for ... everything else.

List of contributors

Rosemary Arrojo is Professor of Comparative Literature and Director of the Center for Research in Translation, Binghamton University, Binghamton, New York.

Francesca Bartrina is Professor of Translation at the Facultat de Ciències Humanes, Traducció i Documentació, University of Vic, Spain.

Andrew Chesterman is Professor of Multilingual Communication, Department of General Linguistics, University of Helsinki, Finland.

Ann Corsellis is vice-chairman of the Council of the Institute of Linguists, London and a member of the board of directors of the National Register of Public Service (UK).

Michael Cronin is Professor and Dean of the Faculty of Humanities and Social Sciences, Dublin City University, Ireland.

Eva Espasa is Professor of Translation at the Facultat de Ciències Humanes, Traducció i Documentació, University of Vic, Spain.

Daniel Gile teaches at Université Lumière Lyon 2, France.

María González Davies is Professor of Translation at the Facultat de Ciències Humanes, Traducció i Documentació, University of Vic, Spain.

Eugene A. Nida is a linguist and translation scholar. A longtime language consultant for the American Bible Society and the United Bible Societies, his most recent book is *Fascinated by Languages*.

Helge Niska teaches translation and interpreting at the Institute for Interpretation and Translation Studies, Stockholm University, Stockholm, Sweden.

Christiane Nord is Research Fellow at Hochschule Magdeburg-Stendal/University of the Free State Bloemfontein, Magdeburg, Germany.

Richard Samson teaches translation and interpreting at the Facultat de Ciències Humanes, Traducció i Documentació, University of Vic, Spain, where he is also Webmaster for the University.

Martha Tennent was the founding dean of the School of Translation, Facultat de Ciències Humanes, Traducció i Documentació, University of Vic, Spain. She has been associated with translation and interpreting for many years and is now an independent scholar.

Margherita Ulrych is Professor of English and Translation Studies at Università Cattolica del Sacro Cuore, Milano/Catholic University of Milan, Italy.

Foreword

Eugene A. Nida

Present critical developments in European multilingualism have brought to the fore the growing importance of training translators and interpreters and the need for a more innovative, less teacher-centred approach. This volume would therefore seem all the more strategic now. It is the natural development of the Vic Forum which took place in the spring of 1999 and in which I had the pleasure of participating. The conference provided the site for valuable debate on new insights in communicating principles and procedures for translator/ interpreter training.

Of the twelve essays in this volume, I have selected a few that I would like to discuss in this brief foreword. Andrew Chesterman's article is on causality in translator training and provides a helpful way of examining and evaluating the static model, the dynamic model, and the causal model of interlingual communication. As a result, readers can view more objectively Nida's concept of dynamic equivalence, Pym's discussion of Aristotle's four classical causes, the skopos theory with its obvious causal dimensions, and Gutt's relevance-theoretical approach. There is thus no necessary conflict between hard empiricists and soft hermeneuticists, because translation research needs both kinds of hypotheses.

María González Davies is primarily concerned with improving the product, a clear reference to causality, by exploring alternatives in traditional translation training. She is particularly concerned that so few schools are involved with existing pedagogical approaches, and she pleads very effectively for more relevant and empirical research.

González is a highly creative expert teacher, and she spells out her concerns for transforming the traditional classroom setting into a hands-on workshop by (1) transforming the classroom into a discussion forum, (2) involving professional translators, (3) designing programs with specific aims, (4) respect for different learning styles, and (5) including real life situations. I have visited her classroom at various times, and I must admit that I have never experienced a more exciting and relevant manner of teaching.

Most people think that interpreting is always the same kind of activity, whether in a booth or a huge conference hall or in helping foreigners receive justice in court. But public service interpreting, as described effectively by Ann Corsellis, requires an even wider range of interlingual experience. Such interpreters must often interpret for emotionally frightened people who use typically local dialects that include words and idioms that never get into dictionaries.

Public service interpreters must not only understand languages thoroughly, but they need to know how to comprehend the scenarios in which their skills are so strategic, for example, a tourist reporting a stolen wallet in a police station, a pregnant woman visiting a medical clinic, parents and teachers talking about a child's learning problems, social workers discussing care of the elderly, and police arresting a vagrant. Here is where issues of fidelity, confidentiality, integrity, and professional impartiality are so crucial.

Daniel Gile always has something relevant to say because he knows from personal experience what he is talking about. His concern is primarily the operation in comprehension, which can only then be reformulated into another language. This means that a person needs to keep abreast of developments in his or her passive languages. Unfortunately, there is a serious lack of competent teachers for interpreting.

Gile recognises the importance of interpreters improving their speaking skills because they are paid not only to reproduce the meaning of an oral statement, but to do so in a manner that will be acceptable and convincing. Too many interpreters swallow their words, add too many hesitations, and even confuse an audience by waiting too long to produce their interpretation, which often comes out so fast that many listeners cannot comprehend what is meant.

Richard Samson has the extremely difficult task of teaching people how to use computers effectively in the process of translating. Unfortunately, some experienced teachers simply do not know enough about computer expertise to teach students who are often far ahead of their teachers in this area. The generation gap in computer knowledge will hopefully soon pass, but the effective application of computers to the task of interlingual communication will continue to concern us all for another generation.

But the essays that I have mentioned are by no means the only or even the most relevant ones. I have personally enjoyed reading all the chapters in this volume, and I congratulate Martha Tennent for putting together this first-class collection that expresses in many ways her own experience and insight into interlingual communication.

Introduction

Martha Tennent

This collection of essays originated at the Forum on translation pedagogy held in May 1999 at the University of Vic's School of Translation and Interpreting, Facultat de Ciències Humanes, Traducció i Documentació. Or more precisely, the essays presented here are a consequence of it. They are not conference papers, however, but were commissioned in response to some of the issues that arose during the Forum. These essays attest to important changes in translation practice and the assumptions which underpin them.

Under the title "Training translators and interpreters: New directions for the millennium", the Vic Forum brought together leading specialists from some twenty-five countries. But what, to my mind, made the Forum unique was its structure: the meeting was conceived as a platform for debate, a site for examining critically different positions regarding translator/interpreter training. In an effort not to privilege any one approach, the 31 invited speakers represented distinct and often diametrically opposed approaches: varieties of linguistics and empiricism, polysystem theory and functionalism, literary and cultural studies. Debate was stimulated by the request that panelists submit, a month in advance, written papers which were then book bound and posted to all participants. Panels were organised thematically, in the fashion typical of academic conferences. Yet on the assumption that panelists and participants had read the papers beforehand, panelists were restricted to an initial presentation of key points. After these presentations, the discussion was opened to the audience. Every effort was made to create panels that included scholars representing different positions. The number of participants in the Forum was also limited in order to encourage discussion.

What became apparent from the beginning were precisely the differences and divisions, which were, more often than not, irreconcilable. The epistemological dilemma that lies at the base of Translation Studies was evident in most of the debates, most particularly in the opposing poles of linguistics (primarily text linguistics and pragmatics) and cultural studies (primarily forms of ideological critique, including feminist and post-colonial theory, among others), which are commonly viewed as the central bifurcation within the discipline.

Some of the panelists perceived Translation Studies to be a science that must be submitted to the rules and protocols of scientific research. Andrew Chesterman argues in his report on the Vic Forum in *Across the Boundaries: Language and Culture* that the basic methodology of translator training should be empirical, and that many notions about hypothesis-testing and prediction can be adapted from an empirical human science such as sociology, much in line with the thinking of panelists Gideon Toury and Miriam Shlesinger. Sergio Viaggio, Chesterman notes, presented a view that was quite similar to applied science, based on a general model of verbal communication which was specified to address "mediated intercultural interlingual communication." Elaborated together with Mariano García Landa, this model distinguishes certain elements within the linguistic chain – although Viaggio made clear that translation cannot be treated simply as a branch of linguistics – and is represented by means of symbolic notations such as those commonly used in science.

Some panelists and participants, such as Roger Bell and Viggo Pedersen, approach Translation Studies from a linguistics point of view. One of Bell's main arguments was that in order to work towards developing a definition of translation one needs to devise a system of empirically-assessed criteria regarding communication, taking into account such issues as mode of communication and channel type (auditory, visual and tactile) and the distinction between mono-communication and bilingual communication (i.e. translation). If in the 1980s Bell considered translation theory to be part of applied linguistics – insofar as it applies the tools of linguistics to the solution of cultural problems such as the cross-cultural transfer of meaning – by the end of the 1990s he was advocating that translation theory be considered apart from applied linguistics, which would nonetheless be used to study and practice translation. Even those present at the Forum who strongly believe that Translation Studies should be grounded in linguistics grant that contemporary linguistics has changed considerably since the time when J.C. Catford confidently asserted that "the theory of translation is concerned with a certain type of relation between languages and is consequently a branch of Comparative Linguistics."

Other participants, such as Rosemary Arrojo, Sherry Simon, and Lawrence Venuti find their roots in literary theory and criticism and cultural studies. Cultural studies examines a broad range of forms and practices in their social and political situations. It questions essentialist notions of the neutrality of culture, as well as the privileging of elite over popular cultural products. It is interdisciplinary, drawing its research tools from various fields. Like other approaches to translation, cultural studies also benefits from an empirical processing of data, although with the important difference that it views the selection and processing of any data, not as value-free, but as reflecting certain social and institutional interests.

The methodological divisions in Translation Studies were especially evident during what was perhaps the most spirited debate in the Forum, sparked by the phonemic, experimental translations by Louis and Celia Zukofsky of Catullus that appeared in the 1960s (the opposing views were represented by, *inter alios*, Theo Hermans, Gideon Toury and Lawrence Venuti). These homophonic renderings stretch the entire concept of translation to accommodate a disjunctive modernist poetics rooted in sounds, images, cultural impact. By producing a hybrid text which emphasised a discursive heterogeneity – drawing on a whole range of colloquialisms, slang, jazz talk, scientific terms, archaisms – the Zukofskys' renderings challenged the prevalent translation standard for the classics. Some of the participants saw the renderings as too marginal and experimental to be seriously considered. If, as linguistics-oriented traditionalists maintained, the Zukofskys' Catullus transfers only sound and not clear meanings, how can it be viewed as translation? For them, a fluent translation should be defended, a practice that does not deviate from the dominant practice of translating into standard usage, but rather creates a seamless language in the target text that produces in the reader's mind the illusion of reading the text in its original language. The provocative opening lines of Theo Hermans' position paper at the Vic Forum begin: "... First: why do we laugh at Zukofsky but gawk at Venuti?" From there Hermans proceeds to discuss the concept of abusive fidelity defended by Venuti, i.e. a form of translation – to use Philip Lewis' definition – which "values experimentation, tampers with usage, seeks to match the polyvalencies or plurivocities or expressive stresses of the original by producing its own."

Some of the empirically oriented participants felt that one translation, the example of the Zukofskys' Catullus, was insufficient to construct theoretical concepts and translation "laws" in a research project. On the other hand were those, among them Venuti, who felt that the value of the translation – for research as well as training – lay precisely in the fact that it was a modernist experimental text that deviated from current language use and dominant translation practices: its very deviation created the occasion to theorise about the impact of modernism in translation and about the limitations of translation research and pedagogy.

Yet another debate led to the discussion of the Brazilian translator Haroldo de Campos' well-known cannibalistic metaphor for translation: his own translations, like the Zukofskys' Catallus, are far from "faithful" to the original, but rather exploit the transgressive potential afforded by the act of translating. Both debates voiced, implicitly or explicitly, the complexity of establishing what is a translation, what is an adaptation, what is simply another original inspired by a foreign work.

These and other debates during the Forum illustrate the current positioning of Translation Studies between theory based on linguistics and empirical phenomena, on the one hand, and a cultural-studies inspired theory, which uses empirical among other kinds of research, on the other. In view of this divergence, it is highly improbable that any one general theory of translation could be capacious enough, open enough to encompass all the variants and satisfy the different theoretical and methodological constituencies.

Hence, one might wonder: did any of the scholars change their views as a result of the confrontation at the Forum? The answer would have to be "probably not". Nevertheless, one of the remarkable things about the Forum was that scholars were willing to discuss what divided them and some even to seek areas where divergent approaches could be reconciled. At one point during the conference Theo Hermans defended translation as a cultural, and therefore historical phonemenon, embedded in values; he emphasised the uniqueness, the unrepeatability of translating events. Chesterman acknowledged, to a degree, their uniqueness but wished to look for generalities that were shared between the different translation events. His argument was: why reject that which can be shared?

One of the positive consequences of the Forum was that debates initiated there spilled over into a series of exchanges published in *Target*. Andrew Chesterman and Rosemary Arrojo published a joint paper reflecting areas of "shared ground" between the seemingly irreconcilable positions of empiricism and cultural studies. Their article, "Shared Ground in Translation Studies", lays out basic tenets about translation which can be accepted by both an empirical and a hermeneutic approach. These are presented in the form of a list of 30 theses grouped under three headings: "What is translation?", "Why is this (kind of) translation like this?" and "What consequences do translations have?", ending with a coda written by each author.

Their article was followed up by two contributions, the first by Kirsten Malmkjær, "Relative stability and stable relativity", a linguistics-oriented commentary which seems to sketch very little of "shared ground." "The essentialism vs non-essentialism dualism," Malmkjær writes, "went out of the epistemological window with Immanuel Kant." She proposes that "we stop assigning meanings to utterances, and give them to persons instead," ending her article with the statement: "I don't quite see how it is possible to discuss translations without adopting a non-destructivist view of linguistic relativity." Yet it remains true that the linguists and philosophers she cites are very different from the theorists and cultural historians cited by cultural-studies oriented scholars, who might question her insistence on "persons" as essentialist, too detached from the social and institutional situations in which utterances are exchanged.

The second response, by Rakefet Sela-Sheffy, "The suspended potential of culture research in TS," discusses the Chesterman-Arrojo article from a culture-oriented approach, viewing the issue of essentialism/non-essentialism as being anachronistic because "relativity, multiplicity and dependency of 'meaning' ... [have] become a common creed in the humanities." Sela-Sheffy refers to Toury's study of translation norms, which stresses a target-oriented approach where:

> factors in the receiving cultural arena are the critical ones in determining the nature, status and tempo of the work of translation. Being basically a practice of importing, manipulating and transforming cultural goods and models, *the business of translation constitutes in itself an extremely interesting field of cultural production.* It is therefore time to take on the new directions recently proposed for TS (Toury 1995; Simeoni 1998; Venuti 1995; Hermans 1999) and give a better chance to the study of the peculiarities of this domain as a vital field of production in a certain socio-cultural space. This includes the way the field is organized, the profile of its agents, the distribution and availability of its repertoire, its sources of authorization, its relations with other fields of production, and more.   (the author's emphasis)

Writing from the perspective of culture research, Sela-Sheffy points to the need to move away from the "cult of the Text" and proposes that the focus of Translation Studies be reversed: "Instead of viewing information about translations and translation institutions as marginal facts subjugated to explaining phenomena in translated texts, indications of translatorial decisions in end-products should be used as data for exploring cultural processes." One might wonder, however, about all the decisions made automatically by translators and hence possibly determined by their conscious, however that category might be defined. Sela-Sheffy's comments are more open than Malmkjær's, but they reveal that the work of theoretical synthesis has yet to begin, and that unanswered questions remain. If nothing else, the Vic Forum set a precedent by posing questions that are still being discussed.

*

I have thought it helpful to describe briefly the state of Translation Studies today, using as a point of departure the debates that took place at the Vic Forum. Some of these discussions – on translation and interpreting pedagogy, critical debates in translation theory, the impact of new technologies in translation, among others – have created the occasion for this book and marked the direction it would take. This is a book which is addressed to both translator/interpreter trainers and trainees; it describes and discusses materials, approaches, textbooks, curricula. It is intended to facilitate the acquisition of a great deal of practical information, whether on skills and techniques or on the array of training programmes available and their methodologies. It presents, on the one hand, a selection of very practically-oriented pedagogical strategies related to specific areas of translation and interpreting and, on the other hand, a variety of theories around which the practice of translation and interpreting can develop. The essays reflect both the changes in pedagogical emphasis and the relatively new areas that are coming to the fore, such as Public Service interpreting, audiovisual translation and computer-assisted translation.

The five essays in the second section of this book, *Pedagogical Strategies*, put forward clear, practical presentations on how to train translators/interpreters in a primarily student-centred environment. These should be helpful for the translator, but also for the translator trainer who has rarely received any instruction in translation pedagogy. Both Christiane Nord and María González Davies, explicitly or implicitly, point to the need to train teachers of translation. As Nord states in her essay, "So far, there is no institutional training for translator trainers. Teachers of Mathematics or Philosophy are trained in their respective Faculties, Language Teachers are trained in Modern Language Departments or Faculties of Second Language Acquisition, but persons applying for a position as translator trainer in a Faculty of Translation and Interpreting need no particular formal qualification, and if they needed one, they would not know where to get it."

Other issues discussed during the Forum and reflected in the essays in this volume have arisen in large measure due to the rapidly changing world and the varied disciplines from which Translation Studies has emerged. One is the need to keep abreast of technological changes, changes which affect the social fabric of the present generation and which will determine to a large measure the conditions under which the translator and interpreter work. New technologies, especially the Internet, offer unparalleled access to information, data banks and terminology that will facilitate the translator's work, provided he or she acquires the know-how to rapidly retrieve and assimilate them. Richard Samson's essay on computer-assisted translation offers valuable, practical information and proposals, as well as a detailed appendix of sample projects that both translators and translator trainers should find useful. He advocates the immediate implementation of a methodological approach to training that goes beyond mere computer literacy. Students need to develop skills in specialised tasks which are cross-curricular and "involve a paradigm shift that affects the whole of the educational system."

What I believe, made clear from the majority of the essays in this volume, is that theory is considered a necessary tool for more effective training. Theory provides a structure from which to analyse translations, whether written or oral – i.e. interpreting –, describe them and apply empirical data to strategies. Translation theory is usually derived from translation practice, and knowledge of theoretical concepts can in turn motivate specific practical decisions. But perhaps one of the most valuable reasons for providing students with a theoretical framework is to give rise to reflection on what translators are doing and why. Whether one teaches theory that is derived from the hermeneutic tradition or from a more empirical tradition, or both, students need to be given an understanding of the process of translation and their responsibility for the product. Cultural studies emphasises the fact that culture is the creation of values and that translation is the re-creation of values in a different context. Empiricists argue that if one is familiar with data that have been empirically proven one can use the results to produce more effective translations.

Theoretical assumptions can only be arrived at through research. By providing empirical data on what can contribute to better translator competence, for example, research can help bridge the gap between theory and practice and challenge the often dismissive attitude toward theory that many translators have. In this sense, research can make a valuable contribution to the development of new methodological tools. To give but a few examples: Gideon Toury's notion of norms and polysystem theory have led to research in the area of audiovisual translation, such as that presented in work by Fotios Karamitroglou in the field of subtitling, especially related to the standardisation of subtitling in the European Union. In the case of interpreting, research that has been carried on for some time – involving for example, factors relating to stress or the importance of speaker visibility – should lead to better performance by interpreters. Mona Baker and others have written extensively on research based on the use of computerised corpora of translation texts and the relation to linguistic behaviour; some of the results have been applied to improving the quality of machine translation. From a cultural-studies point of view, research based on case studies that highlight such questions as the formation of national identities can provide a greater historical understanding of the social functioning of translation. Translations into Catalan, for example, not only promoted the language by contributing to its normativisation, but equally important, they created a reading public which had only been marginal before, and they were therefore used to advance the concept of Catalan identity. In general, any kind of research – whether it be theoretical, which is more the processing of ideas, or empirical, which is more the processing of hypotheses and data – will contribute to greater knowledge and awareness of the area under study and perhaps to a reassessment of that area.

Whatever one's theoretical point of departure, the primary aim of theory in translator/interpreter training should be to enable trainees to evaluate their decision-making, raise the level of consciousness about their practice and about the range of choices available to them and contribute to a growing awareness that translation is a linguistic, social and cultural practice that takes place in a particular moment in history. With greater knowledge and awareness, translators can make more responsible choices. Once they are familiar with norms, conventions, laws (laws in the descriptive, rather than prescriptive, sense of what translators tend to do in certain situations, such as the often-mentioned tendency to standardise the source language, flattening or softening the style) and socio-cultural conditions, translators can choose to apply these norms, laws, etc. or resist them. They can, except in certain cases – such as technical or legal translations where there is a fixed terminology – choose to transgress. But translator trainees need to be taught what the effects of their strategies are, and this is taught by examining theoretical assumptions.

The relevance of theory to the practice of translation is, precisely, the basis of the essay by Francesca Bartrina. Her essay proposes and discusses a syllabus for a general course on translation theory which would cover such areas as linguistics and translation, translation as communication, domestication and foreignisation, textuality and translation, cognition and translation. Other theoretical positions reflected in this volume are Chesterman's causality, Arrojo's non-essentialism and Christiane Nord's functionalism.

Andrew Chesterman's chapter examines causality, a central concept in any empirical science, and the roles that causes and effects play in translation studies. If translation is approached in the manner defended by Chesterman, it is with the always present assumption that one should propose hypotheses (he examines four: interpretive, descriptive, explanatory, predictive), which can subsequently be tested, and the results – when applied – will help to produce better translations. Without the ability to propose and then test hypotheses, translation theory has reached, in Chesterman's opinion, a stalemate. His abiding premise is that translator trainers want tested, corroborated hypotheses to show that certain conditions will contribute to achieving desired effects.

Rosemary Arrojo's chapter supports her argument against an exclusively essentialist approach to translation, an approach that assumes the presence of stable semantic essences in language, so that the translator seeks to substitute the "stable" meaning in a source text with an "idealised" equivalent – an ideally neutral reproduction – in the target text. She examines the work of certain scholars whom she associates with a predominantly essentialist theoretical foundation, viz. Mona Baker, Hatim and Mason and Paul Kussmaul, yet maintains that they share valuable arguments which could be incorporated into a wider approach. Hatim and Mason, for example, embrace notions from other disciplines such as stylistics, rhetoric, discourse analysis, ethnomethodology. Paul Kussmaul, on the other hand, approaches translation from a linguistics point of view, yet recognises that translation is not simply a mechanical activity but an interpretive one, an activity he associates with creativity, emphasising the fact that readers of a translation have expectations, norms and values which are influenced by culture. Arrojo points out that despite the apparent defence by Mona Baker, Hatim and Mason and Kussmaul of a conception of translation which would take into account the intimate relationship between language, culture and ideology, still their approaches remain very much committed to essentialism and lack any research in theoretical concepts beyond their own discipline.

After examining the essentialist approach to translation, Arrojo illustrates how translator training could focus on "the consequences of a conception of language and text which takes the conventionality of meaning to its last consequences … a perspective generally associated with post-modern, post-structuralist, or even post-colonial notions of language, which have as a common ground a disbelief in the possibility of any level of neutral, purely objective meaning."

Translation pedagogy, prompted by advances in foreign-language peda-gogy, is moving more and more away from the traditional teacher-centred approach to a more communicative one. Whether we refer to this method-ology as "student-centred", "empowering the student" or "deschooling" – to use Michael Cronin's term in this book – effective learning will no doubt prove that traditional methodologies based on the magisterial class, i.e. the teacher dictating/the student note-taking, are no longer adequate because they do not sufficiently involve the student in the learning process. María González Davies points out in her essay that research in language teaching has shown that learning is "enhanced when it is negotiated and experiential, with the students taking an active role in the process." In an interactive context, where the teacher is more guide and counsellor than ultimate authority, students participate to a much greater degree and tend to be more motivated as they become more responsible for their decisions, and ultimately for the final product, the translation. The opening words to Kiraly's *A Social Constructivist Approach to Translator Education: Empowerment from Theory to Practice* record this pedagogical shift: "In recent years, it has become a commonplace in educational psychology that knowledge is constructed by learners, rather than being simply transmitted to them by their teachers. The implications of this viewpoint for the educational process are revolutionary, because it shifts the traditional focus of authority, responsibility and control in the educational process away from the teacher and towards the learner." As Samson points out in his essay, "Teachers are no longer the most important sources of knowledge for their students ... [who] no longer have too little but too much information available and need to know how to manage the situation, how to find what they want ... The skills they need are skills for managing change and learning on an on-going basis."

In the final essay of the book, Michael Cronin presents a critical assessment of contemporary approaches to translation pedagogy. Under the section "Translators as readers" Cronin touches on the history of reading, which is a "history of change", one that may well have long-term consequences for translation didactics. He refers to the assumption "made in much translation pedagogy ... that while theories may change and disciplinary models come into or drop out of vogue, students are always and everywhere the same. In other words, the student is an invariant, transhistorical subject who is, to all intents and purposes, indistinguishable from his or her counterpart in the seventeenth, eighteenth or nineteenth century." Cronin remarks on "the failure of translation pedagogy to take into account synchronic, geopolitical differences in the student body and teaching profession ... [and] the further issue of the diachronic evolution of students over time, which directly impacts on what theories will be appropriate in pedagogic settings."

Translation, whether written or oral, clearly does not occupy a neutral space. It is much more than a mere cross-cultural exchange, and the task of training aspiring translators/interpreters requires new directions, as well as revisions of traditional notions concerning their roles. From an empirical point of view, students need to be more aware of the tools they have at their disposal, such as how to gather, process and analyse information; they will of course assess the information differently according to the bent of their theoretical assumptions. Another issue is the explicit element of power and ideology that arises from the irrefutable fact that it is the client who pays for the translation; students need to acknowledge this and recognise that their translation choices will – may – be affected. Likewise, students are often not aware of the potential influence translations and translators can have in shaping cultures, forming national identities, chronicling ideological shifts. They need to recognise their contribution to these social effects of translations and accept their responsibility for what may well have political consequences.

References

Baker, M. (1995). "Corpora in translation studies: An overview and some suggestions for future research," *Target, 7*(2), 223–243.

Catford, J. C. (1965). *A Linguistic Theory of Translation: An Essay in Applied Linguistics, 20.* London: Oxford University Press.

Chesterman, A. & Arrojo, R. (2000). "Shared ground in Translation Studies". *Target, 12*(1), 151–160.

Karamitroglou, F. (1998). "A Proposed Set of Subtitling Standards in Europe". *Translation Journal, 2*(2).

Kiraly, D. (2000). *A Social Constructivist Approach to Translator Education: Empowerment from Theory to Practice, 1.* Manchester: St. Jerome.

Lewis, P. (2000). "The measure of translation effects". In L. Venuti (Ed.), *The Translation Studies Reader* (p. 270). London and New York: Routledge.

Malmkjær, K. (2000). "Relative stability and stable relativity." *Target, 12*(2), 341–345.

Sela-Sheffy, R. (2000). "The suspended potential of culture research in TS". *Target, 12*(2), 345–361.

PART I

Training programmes

The current situation and future prospects

Chapter 1

Training translators
Programmes, curricula, practices

Margherita Ulrych

1. Introduction

This chapter discusses the results of a survey aimed at investigating the state of the art in translator training practices at tertiary level at Universities and Translator and Interpreter (T&I) Institutions and assesses the degree to which their educational and professional goals are equipped to meet the challenges that prospective translators increasingly have to face in a rapidly evolving world. The object of the survey was to observe and report on the situations where translation is taught as an end in itself rather than as a means of learning a foreign language. In view of their long-standing experience with specifically designed programmes T&I institutions provide the natural setting for this kind of survey. Other centres of higher education, especially modern language faculties with established professionally oriented translation courses, have also been included in the present survey, however, to reflect the changing situation in translation pedagogy. The basic premise was, therefore, that "translation competence is most effectively developed at an academic institution" (Schäffner & Adab 2000:x) and the discriminating factor was the purpose underlying translation courses rather than the type of institution.

Traditionally, the main criticism levelled at modern language faculties is that they envisage translation as a language exercise and that they fail to provide any preparation for "real-life translation in a vocational context" (Klein-Braley 1996:23). In Klein-Braley's view this state of affairs is "potentially damaging since it inculcates approaches and techniques which hinder rather than help a person who needs translation skills of any kind as a professional qualification" (1996:17) and the author goes on to outline possible vocational goals for modern language faculties (1996:24): "Our aim must be to enable all-round

language professionals to tackle translation themselves for in-house and informational purposes, and also – and importantly – to supervise the translation
of texts for public and formal purposes." However, she concedes that modern language faculties can only offer "the bare bones and basic techniques"
of translation training and advises "further training at postgraduate level" for
those students wishing to "take up work as professional translators" (1996: 24).

In the same volume, Sewell (1996: 135–136) reports on a survey she carried
out in Great Britain into "'traditional' university courses in translation whose
aim is to promote linguistic proficiency". Sewell (1996: 137) found that nine-
teen of the twenty-one institutions which responded to her questionnaire did
indeed use translation "as a way of improving students' linguistic proficiency"
and that their policy largely mirrored the out-of-touch-with-reality conditions
outlined by Klein-Braley.

Nevertheless, as the present survey shows, the clear-cut distinction between T&I institutions and modern language and philology faculties described
by Snell-Hornby (1988: 8), Klein-Braley (1996) and Klein-Braley and Franklin
(1998) in relation to a predominantly German context is gradually disappear-
ing, especially when university teachers are aware of their language and literature students' future prospects as "editors, authors, scholars and professional
translators" (Dollerup 1994: 121–122). This awareness has often led to the setting up of special courses within the existing language curriculum, either at
the undergraduate stage or more frequently at postgraduate level, which envisage courses or modules that present translation as a skill in its own right
and the main learning goal. Schäffner (1998: 117), for instance, reports her
experience in the Department of Languages and European Studies at Aston
University, where, in accordance with the standard practice at undergraduate level in the United Kingdom, translation is mainly taught as part of the
language courses. In order to provide students with a translation programme
that better reflects the real-life conditions of translation, an additional elective course of Advanced Translation from German into English was introduced
in the final year of study. The approach is functional in the sense described by
Nord (1991, 1997), Kussmaul (1995), Vermeer (1996) and Reiss (2000) and the
aim is the development of professional translation skills, "structured around
specific text types … and focusing on characteristic features of these text types,
on general(isable) translation problems and translation strategies" (Schäffner
1998: 127).

This rather flexible situation in translator training was borne out by the
survey reported in this chapter, which was based on the results obtained
through first-hand contact with Institutions involved in translator training

based mainly in Europe and North America via a questionnaire. The survey was designed to investigate the state of the art of current translation teaching practices and the relative pedagogies in academic institutions and to attempt to identify common fundamental principles.[1] The first part of this chapter provides an overview of the way curricula and courses are structured and examines the underlying rationale: the choice and timing of specific components, the stages of progression and development of specific competences are all taken into account. The second part looks specifically at methodological issues in the light of the way respondents perceive translation. It covers matters such as the inclusion and sequencing of theoretical and practical components, class management, the time devoted to contact classes and self-access assignments, and the availability of modern technology such as hands-on practice with translation memory tools, on-line glossaries and terminological data-banks, and parallel/comparable computerised corpora. The final part of this chapter discusses these findings in relation to market needs and the rapidly changing profile of translators in the professional world. Evidence shows that the range of competence required of translators is expanding to encompass diverse kinds of interlingual and intercultural mediation and rewriting, once considered as lying beyond the confines of translation proper, and includes such activities as multilingual documentation, localisation, technical writing, editing and multimedia translation (Kingscott 1996; Mossop 2001). Thus, the training of translators has become a challenging pedagogical prospect. An important aspect of the questionnaire, which is included as an appendix to this chapter, was to glean whether the various institutions were aware of these changing attitudes and whether their courses envisaged a blend of educational and vocational ingredients in order better to meet real-life criteria.

2. The state of the art in translator training practices at tertiary level

A questionnaire was sent out to 65 institutions of higher education located mainly in Europe and North America and 41 responded.[2] The initial questions of the questionnaire aimed to contextualise the institution in terms of whether it was specifically T&I or some other institution of higher education, the number of teaching staff (permanent staff, temporary or part-time staff, staff engaged solely in teaching translation) and number of students. The translator training programmes analysed all purported to have a vocational/professional component. Those who filled in the questionnaire gave exhaustive answers, which seemed to reflect their interest in providing an accurate representation of the situation. Full use was made of the "comments" sections of the questionnaire, particularly when the respondents thought the questionnaire was too rigid to reflect local reality. These comments were invaluable in elaborating the data since the socio-cultural constraints of the various national education systems naturally condition a given institution's curriculum and syllabus. Other responding institutions stated that the questionnaire was not sufficiently T&I oriented and that it posed questions they felt could be taken as a matter of course. These views were mainly expressed by those institutions which have a fully-comprehensive translation training programme.

Responses of this kind did not come as a surprise given that the questionnaire was designed to probe into the way centres other than strictly T&I institutions went about teaching translation and training translators. The questions were aimed at gauging just how translation-specific the courses offered by the various institutions actually were. It was therefore necessary to pose explicit questions on the basic discriminating components of an academic course for translator training as regards both course content and structure, on the one hand, and classroom management and dynamics, on the other. Importance was given to the level of the degree offered (undergraduate vs postgraduate) and the profile of the translator envisaged, which was strictly related to the questions that concerned the integration of professional criteria (e.g. attitudes to translation-related activities, general/specialised translation, literary/sci-tech translation, theoretical components, authentic assignments and technological aids).

The level of translation and interpreting degrees offered is closely linked to the issue of how best to train translators for their future careers in the professional environment. Some institutions provide undergraduate programmes specifically designed to train translators, others envisage such training within their postgraduate programmes. Of the institutions which responded to the survey 79% offer undergraduate programmes and 89% postgraduate programmes of which 74% at MSc/MA corresponding level lasting one or two years and 29% at PhD level lasting two to three years; 48% have both. Those that have both undergraduate and postgraduate programmes provide a general degree, leading to specialist training at a higher degree level. The degrees available were as follows: 38% translation only and 28% interpreting only (both mainly at postgraduate level); 71% translation and interpreting (mainly at undergraduate level).

Differences also emerged in relation to the number of years spent in completing the degree course and these were often conditioned by the various national education systems. Most (82%) reported that their undergraduate programme lasted four years while others (16%) stated that their first degree consisted in a three-year course. A small minority offered a two-year diploma course. The length of postgraduate courses ranged from one to two years in the case of an MA compatible programme and two to three years for a PhD, although some universities, notably in Scandinavian countries, pose no limits to the time spent in obtaining a degree.

It should, however, be pointed out that this is a time of flux as regards higher education as a consequence of the intention of governments throughout Europe to develop of a coherent and cohesive European Higher Education Area by 2010. What has now come to be known as the "Bologna Process" concerning Higher Education began on 25th May 1998 with the "Joint declaration on harmonisation of the architecture of the European higher education system" undersigned at the Sorbonne, Paris, by the Education Ministers of France, Germany, Italy and the United Kingdom. The signatories undertook to adhere to a set of uniform requirements governing university degrees in Europe, based on a European Credit Transfer System (ECTS), and to include them within their national systems. A year later, on 19th June 1999, 30 European Ministers of Education convened in Bologna and undersigned the "Joint declaration on the European space for higher education". The decision was also taken to hold conferences every two years in order to continue European cooperation within the area of higher education. In the light of the enlargement of the EU and as a symbol of the will to involve the whole of Europe, the venue chosen for the 2001 Conference was Prague. This was followed on 19th September 2003 by the Conference in Berlin where 33 European countries undertook to review the progress achieved and to accelerate the process of "Realising the European Higher Education Area". The next Conference is scheduled for May 2005 in Bergen, Norway.

Some of the institutions of higher education in these countries are currently in the throes of implementing the recommendations of the Bologna Process while others openly resist them. The main upheaval for T&I programmes will arise as a result of the full implementation of the so-called three plus two plus two course structure (i.e. three years for a first degree, two years for a specialised degree and a further two years for a PhD), as can be seen in relation to the results of the survey which indicate that four years is the norm for a first degree. One way or another, traditional departments are being reshuffled, new degrees are being established and curricula are undergoing profound changes. Nevertheless, the questionnaire provides interesting and thought-provoking data and insights into the underlying rationale of translator training programmes, a rationale which is destined to survive structural changes and even to provide the conceptual framework for the new curricula.

Questions were also included regarding admission criteria to see what institutions felt were the minimum requirements for eligibility to a degree course in translation. Knowing whether an institution had an entrance exam and/or *numerus clausus* was also important background information for assessing course structure and content since much teaching methodology and class management depends on the numbers of students attending. Again national education policies condition choice. In some countries anyone with a final school-leaving certificate is eligible to go on to higher education and universities have no legal right to select students. Most T&I schools, on the other hand, do have the legal right to select the candidates they consider as qualifying for their training programme, although selection is not always based on an entrance exam as the following results show.

Institutions with an entrance exam	32%
Institutions without an entrance exam	50%
Not stated	18%
Institutions with *numerus clausus*	28%
Institutions without *numerus clausus*	54%
Not stated	18%
Requiring proficiency in 1 foreign language	57%
Requiring proficiency in 2 foreign languages	39%
Requiring proficiency in 3 foreign languages	0%
No knowledge of a foreign language required	4%

Following these preliminary questions, aimed at contextualising the various institutions, was a section on course structure and content, which intended to delve into issues such as the kind of translation and translation-related courses offered, at what level, for how long, and in what sequence. The aim was essentially to gauge the range of the different curricula and to understand the different training approaches and underlying rationale. Again the survey highlighted the heterogeneity of translation courses as regards both structure and content. What seemed a straightforward question on the length of courses, for instance, revealed profound cultural differences in the way higher education is perceived and realised in various countries. The Danish and Finnish systems, for instance, are highly flexible, as emerged from the comments from Savonlinnia University regarding the length of courses ("There are all kinds of courses from 2 days to 27 weeks") and those from the University of Turku in answer to questions regarding course structure

("We do not work per year/per compulsory classes. It is up to the student to design his/her own curriculum"). This is actually fully in line with the concept of continuing education and life-long learning embodied in the Sorbonne declaration mentioned above. However, on average the length of courses ranged from 25 to 35 weeks per academic year or 12 to 16 weeks per semester.

Just as revealing were the answers to the question on the distribution of teacher-student contact hours and hours devoted to private study in terms of overall student effort hours. Student effort hours is the terminology used within the framework of the ECTS to refer to the overall time a student devotes to gaining a credit, divided into contact hours and student study time. Not all the institutions seemed to be familiar with this system, however. An additional problem, which was unfortunately overlooked when the questionnaire was devised, was the fact that student effort hours change according to the year of study at some institutions. Most responding institutions stated that the answers they gave were a yearly average of the overall course. Results ranged from eight to twenty student effort hours per week for translation activities and eight to twelve per week for translation-related activities. There were notable differences between the number of contact hours and number of student study hours. At some institutions contact hours predominate to a very large extent over the time allotted for private study, particularly so in Spain. The overall average distribution was, however, 50% for each.[3]

An important component of this section of the questionnaire was the balance between translation activities and translation-related activities in the course content insofar as it provided insights into how real-life criteria oriented towards market needs were integrated into the curriculum. The questions presented were based on the views expressed in the literature regarding what may be (or should be) considered a translation activity in terms of professional goals and thus including closely-related activities such as editing and technical writing. Editing, in particular, is an important component of the translation process as the final target language version is not achieved at the first attempt; re-encoding the message of the source text in the target text involves various stages of writing and rewriting. Professional translators edit not only their own texts but also texts written by non-native speakers, as well as machine translations drafted with the aid of CAT (computer-assisted translation) or translation memory systems. From a professional perspective, activities such as written composition into L1 and into L2, summary writing, reading comprehension and text analysis are all an integral part of the act of translation. It would therefore seem reasonable, as Mossop (2001: xvii) effectively argues in his book *Re-*

vising and Editing for Translators, to expect institutions to "incorporate editing components into translation courses".

The questions on translation activities were cross-referenced with a question which specifically asked whether the institutions integrated academic and professional criteria within their course content. If the answer was yes, they were asked whether the professional criteria determined the type of text chosen as a translation assignment and whether information regarding the circumstances that initiated the translation process and all the relevant socio-cultural parameters was given as an integral part of the assignment. The aim of all these questions was again to gauge how far real-life factors were accounted for. A translation activity should reflect "the realities of future professional needs" (Snell-Hornby 1992: 19), even within the setting of a training programme if it is to be viewed as an authentic task. Thus, given that translators in real life "work with genuine events at the level of discourse, rather than with neat abstractions" (Baker & Kaplan 1994: 3), the reason why an assigned text requires translation needs to be made clear and the full context of the source text given. Translation students who are assigned a translation with no idea either of its original context or why they have been asked to translate it cannot produce a version that is acceptable for anything but academic purposes. The results of the survey were as follows:

Integration of academic and professional criteria	96%
If yes, professional criteria include:	
– choice of text to translate	85%
– criteria for translating text	85%
– type of activity:	
– technical writing	57%
– editing	66%
– localisation	28%
– use of translation aids	76%

The way source texts are presented also contributes to the authenticity of the translation activity, apart from providing the necessary clues for identifying the genre (an information leaflet, a brochure, a contract and so on). The question on textual/contextual information also asked whether students were presented with a typed text or a text with its original layout, albeit as a xerox copy. An assignment that fulfils professional criteria would in particular present a text in its entirety, even if the assignment only envisages translating part of it. The results of the survey showed the following tendencies:

Textual/contextual information made available
  - source given   84%
  - purpose of exercise stated   68%
  - intended client stated   63%
  - typed text given   63%
  - text with original layout/format given   63%

Responses concerning the process of translating and the presentation of the translated text seemed encouraging from the point of view of realistic translator training. Although translation assignments were reported as being done in class (57%) and/or at home (76%), the overwhelming majority of institutions (90%) insist on the final end-product being written up by the individual students in a typed or word-processed form. Some institutions (23%) allow both typed and handwritten forms. Only a small minority of institutions (10%) stated that they accept handwritten student translations to the exclusion of typed texts. Producing an appropriate text for the task assigned, including the typographical layout, not only simulates professional conditions but also fosters a sense of responsibility and satisfaction for the finished product.

The results of the survey provided interesting insights not only into how the various respondents amalgamated professional goals within their course content but also into what they conceived of as constituting translation activities. The two aspects are very closely linked, of course, since professionally-oriented translation courses include a far broader range of activities than language-based translation courses. While there was general agreement on what were considered to be actual translation activities (90% translation into L1 and 76% translation into L2),[4] most responding institutions stated that the other activities listed fell within the territory of language classes. Nevertheless, 33% included written composition in L1 as a translation-related activity, 38% written composition in L2, 38% reading comprehension/text analysis, 33% summary writing, 42% multiple choice and 19% cloze test.

The results also indicated that T&I institutions are not necessarily more innovative and forward looking than other academic institutions, which is in keeping with reports in the literature. According to Gile (1995: 12):

> Most professional interpreter and translator training programs worldwide consist essentially of practical interpretation and translation exercises: a source-language text or speech is selected, students are invited to interpret or translate it, and the result is commented on and corrected by or under the guidance of the instructor. Judging by the literature, there does not seem to be any disagreement between teachers, practitioners, or students as to the princi-

ple that training should consist essentially of such exercises, although there are differing opinions as to implementation with respect to duration, progression, types of materials used, admission standards, graduation standards, etc.

Yet, if translation is to be envisaged in a professional perspective, the activities mentioned above and quoted as coming under the realm of language-enhancement classes take on a highly relevant and translation-specific guise. This is in agreement with large sectors of the literature on translation and translator training, which point out the necessity of broadening the concept of translation and thus of what constitutes a "translation exercise". According to Maier and Massardier-Kenney (1993: 156), "rewriting information to fit a different audience is a skill most translators must now possess". The function of the translation is often different from that of the source text, which makes it essential for the task assigned to include instructions as to the purpose of the translation activity. Students may, for instance, be asked to summarise the content for a target language audience, or reformulate it in a spoken medium from a written source, given that both these activities reflect what goes on in the real world of translation. Sager (1994) and Reiss (2000), point out that the functional category is the guiding principle for rendering target texts which are "intended to fulfil a specific function that is not addressed in the original" (Reiss 2000: 92–93). Besides, "translators are not infrequently confronted with defective texts, and they need to be able to summarize, explain or adapt according to the needs of the employer or reader concerned" (Snell-Hornby 1992: 20). Nida (2001: 8–9) suggests that intralingual translating, in the sense of "rewriting bad texts into a more understandable form [...] should be a regular part of a course in translating", since "many texts submitted for translation are extremely difficult to understand [...] because they are so badly written".

An even clearer picture of the various institutions' position in relation to academic and professional goals emerged from the questions on examinations. Apart from the actual typology of the test administered, questions also concerned the duration of the exam, the type of textual and contextual information made available and the range of materials allowed in the exam room. Since it is a methodological precept that the exam should reflect the conditions underlying the activities students engage in during their course, answers to this section were expected to be compatible with the earlier responses on course content. Thus, if students used dictionaries as an integral part of their coursework, then it would be reasonable to assume that they would be permitted to do so at the exam session and vice versa. The importance of using dictionaries within a professionally-oriented translation course has been stressed by a number of authors and Kussmaul (1995: 124) goes as far as to state that: "In a translation training syllabus, there should be a special course on the use of dictionaries or at least some hours should be allotted to this topic within a course."

The results concerning the materials allowed in written examinations were as follows:

– no materials allowed	21%
– monolingual dictionary	84%
– bilingual dictionary	73%
– thesaurus	63%
– grammar	36%
– translations done during course	36%
– model texts	31%

Comments to this section revealed that decisions as to what kind of materials could be used were largely left to course tutors and instructors and differences often correlated with the languages involved.

Another important component of the questionnaire was whether institutions offered both generalist and specialised courses and whether the former were prerequisite to the latter. Respondents were also asked whether specialised courses were elective or compulsory. Closely linked to this issue was the question of how much scope was allotted to literary and/or scientific-technical translation and whether these areas were considered as parts of a continuum of text typologies (Snell-Hornby 1988) or as distinct and even opposing or mutually-exclusive curricula. This particular point was evaluated by means of two questions which may have seemed contradictory at first glance but which were in fact complementary; the results were highly indicative of prevailing attitudes. One question listed "literary" among the specialised courses while the second distinguished between literary and sci-tech.

> 97% of institutions provided generalist courses
> 93% of institutions provided specialised courses

Of the institutions that provided both types of courses, generalist courses were prerequisite to specialised courses in 51% of cases.

> all specialised courses were compulsory in 25% of cases
> some specialised courses were compulsory in 57% of cases
> none of the specialised courses were compulsory in 18% of cases

A broad spectrum of specialist discourse areas was covered. High on the list, in (ranking) order were:

Technical	68%
Economic	68%
Legal	68%
Scientific	50%
Medical	50%
Literary	46%
Multimedia	46%
Social sciences	29%
Tourism	7%
Advertising	3%
Software localisation	3%
Computer science	3%

Most institutions that provided both literary and sci-tech courses (53%) had different curricula (14% specified they did not). This supported the widely-held view that literary translation and sci-tech translation cover distinct fields of study and practice. The new national specialised degree in translation in Italy, for instance, envisages two separate curricula for sci-tech and literary translation. The comments to this section of the questionnaire, read in combination with the answers regarding the theoretical approach adopted, indicated that literary translation tends to fall under the realm of comparative literature programmes while sci-tech translation combines with a predominantly linguistic and terminological approach.

3.   Methodological issues

This section of the chapter examines the translation teaching methodology adopted by the various institutions and discusses the rationale underlying features of course content and structuring not addressed in the previous section. Issues such as classroom management and dynamics, attitudes towards translation and translation-related activities, the use of translation aids, and the availability of generalist and specialist courses all presuppose certain conceptions of translations and translating. More importantly, they are indicative of whether translation is envisaged as the main learning goal and what constitutes translation competence. The issue of translation activities in a professional perspective has been discussed in the previous section. Here, we shall focus on the methodological details of classroom dynamics, the use of translation aids within a professional framework, the inclusion of theoretical and practical components in translation courses, and the way these aspects of translation teaching connect with translation competence. In the final section of this chapter the current situation, as it emerges from the findings of the survey, will be discussed in relation to present market needs and the future prospects of the translating profession.

The questions on classroom management and dynamics required the responding institutions to state whether they *always, often, sometimes* or *never* engaged in the activities specified. This was done in order to cater for possible variations within the same course, necessitating a broader range of responses than a straightforward yes/no answer. These expectations were borne out by the results, which showed an interesting mix of classroom behaviour:

Translations are done at home and discussed in class
29% always   66% often   0% sometimes   0% never

Discussions/corrections are carried out
– as teacher/student interaction
   33% always 52% often 9% sometimes   0% never
– by students in groups
   0% always   33% often 61% sometimes 0% never
– by students in pairs
   0% always   19% often 66% sometimes 9% never

The way translation is taught has important implications for students' future professions as translating is no longer an activity that is carried out in isolation. Professional translators generally contact their fellow translators and subject experts on-line and those working in or for translation agencies exchange views and information not only with their peers but also with project supervisors and coordinators. A further component of professional translation is the development of client-related skills since a significant part of translators' lives, whether they be in-house or freelance translators, is spent in establishing sound interpersonal relations with authors, publishers and requesters. It was therefore encouraging to see that teacher/student and student/student interaction featured prominently in the translation classroom. However, if evaluated in relation to the following two questions, the positive attitude to professional needs is somewhat diminished.

– students arrive at a consensus translation
4% always   47% often   19% sometimes   28% never

– students are required to write up their final corrected version for future reference
28% always   23% often   23% sometimes   14% never

Whereas the previous questions envisage the kind of classroom dynamics that is applicable to a foreign language-learning environment, the latter two reflect a translation-specific pedagogical approach and regard the status and re-usability of the translations produced by the students. Arriving at a consensus translation and storing it for future reference reflects real-life circumstances where each translation is not considered as an isolated occurrence but rather as part of a continuum of texts. The comments to this section showed that the term "consensus" translation elicited contrasting interpretations. For some it evoked the classic situation whereby a final version (usually teacher-guided) is presented as the "best" version – highly reminiscent of language-based translation exercises. Others interpreted the question in professional terms and saw consensus translation as the result of peer group work and consultancy, with a view to producing a text that would be appropriate for the brief received. A relatively larger percentage considered writing up a personal final version as an integral part of the translation course. This is in keeping with recent developments in translation pedagogy, which encourage students to build up their own files of source and target texts in order to combine their own data banks of personalised glossaries and texts with the computer-based systems at their disposal (Ulrych 2002).

Significant from a methodological perspective were the answers to the questions on the use made of translation aids. The questionnaire listed a variety of aids from the most traditional paper-based reference works to the most innovative developments in computer technology, covering, that is, not only the use of monolingual and bilingual dictionaries but also familiarity with modern technology systems such as hands-on practice with translation memory tools, on-line glossaries and terminological data-banks, and parallel/comparable computerised corpora. Computer skills are a basic requirement of professional translating today since they provide powerful tools for translators to work competently and reliably in various domains. They also contribute to raising translators' status and self-image, as Bowker (2002: 130) notes:

> Mastering sophisticated technology can significantly improve the way that translators see themselves and clients in turn pick up this positive image. Being able to use new technology represents an added professional skill for

translators, and it is a skill that is becoming increasingly appreciated in the marketplace.

Specific training is therefore needed if translators are to benefit from the opportunities offered by the rapidly evolving field of information technology, even if it poses a significant pedagogical challenge. The integration of technological tools in a translation programme inevitably has "an impact on the way translation itself is taught" (Bowker 2002: 15). Apart from the purely organisational aspects of getting students to work with computers as a class or course activity, it also entails selecting texts for translation with a certain degree of homogeneity and sequencing: texts will, for instance, need to be comparable as regards discourse and text type, language features, terminology and so on, especially if they are to be stored in a translation memory data bank. The results of the questions on the types of technological/machine aids available were as follows: computers/word processors 100%, Internet 100%, e-mail 100%, MT (Machine Translation) tools 47%, CAT (Computer-assisted translation) tools 47% (of these: on-line glossaries/dictionaries 85%, terminological data banks 90%, corpora 47%, translation memory tools 52%, translators workbench 52%). The most surprising answers concerned the use of monolingual and bilingual dictionaries, however, as we saw above in relation to examination procedure. A large number of institutions (or rather, individual teachers) still expect their students to translate without resort to what may legitimately be called a translator's basic resource, independently of whether or not more sophisticated technological tools are available (Kussmaul 1995).

The findings on translation aids are to be read in relation to the questions on the authenticity of the task presented. In the previous section we saw that 96% of the responding institutions stated that they integrated a mix of academic and professional criteria in their course content, although the percentages tended to drop in answer to specific questions regarding the actual textual and contextual information provided. Yet, for a translation assignment to be judged authentic, it should take account of all the variables that characterise professional translating. The reasons for this apparent discrepancy in the results are to be traced to the different ways the term "translation" is interpreted by the various respondents. The very notion of translation as Round (1996: 3) has pointed out "can mean tangibly different things to its practitioners and users" and to those involved in teaching it. This emerged quite clearly in the questions that touched on the issue of translation competence. There is no consensus as yet within translation training circles regarding the kind of competence that translators need to possess in order to practise their profession at their best and consequently regarding the type of knowledge and skills that should be included within an educational programme that is geared towards the demands of the profession and market needs. In particular, discussions revolve around the way translation competence is to be defined and how it is to be distinguished from language competence. The majority of reports in the literature uphold the view that translation competence is multifaceted and includes various components. Delisle (1992:42), citing Roberts (1984), for instance, lists five components: linguistic competence, translation competence, methodological competence, disciplinary competence and technical competence. Linguistic competence entails being able to understand the source language and to produce acceptable target language utterances; translation competence is the ability to express the meaning of the source text appropriately in the target text without unwarranted changes in form; methodological competence refers to the ability to research and select the right terminology; disciplinary competence means being able to translate texts in given discourse areas, such as medicine, law and so on; technical competence involves knowing how to use translation aids like word processors and data bases. According to Gile (1995:4–5) translation competence can be defined in terms of the type of knowledge professional translators are required to have and subsumes language-related, domain-specific and job-related components. Kiraly (1995:6), too, sees translation competence in complex and comprehensive terms, comprising a series of skills and types of knowledge: "A real act of translation presupposes that the translator has cognitive, social, and textual skills and access to appropriate stores of linguistic, cultural, and real-world knowledge."

The term competence, therefore, encompasses other elements such as skills and expertise,[5] and all are based on types of knowledge. Translation scholars seem to agree that translators need to possess two basic kinds of theoretical knowledge (Bell 1991; Round 1998; Schäffner & Adab 2000): an operative or procedural kind of knowledge by which they know how to translate and declarative or factual knowledge which shapes and models their procedural activity and sets their skills and expertise within a systematic framework. Together, declarative and procedural knowledge enable translators to tackle the multifarious fields of discourse that come their way without necessarily having specific content-based knowledge and to undertake the problem-predicting and problem-solving processes that constitute their day-to-day practice with greater self-knowledge and responsibility. Thus, a theoretical grounding in both these knowledge areas should constitute the mainstay of any translation training course. Procedural knowledge or, in other words, a theory of translating, is not in itself sufficient. Although heuristic "rules of thumb" obviously have their place in a translator's overall knowledge, they cannot be taken as entirely reliable and need to be rationalised and standardised within a wider body of declarative knowledge, within, that is, a theory of translation.

Besides a theory of translating and a theory of translation, there is a third theoretical component – that of Translation Theory, in the sense of Translation Studies as an academic discipline. The issue of whether Translation Theory should be an integral part of translator training is still debated today, however. Despite Neubert's conviction that "practice without theory is blind" in just the same way as "theory without practice is empty" (1989:11), the general feeling among translation professionals is that theory has no bearing on their day-to-day practice.[6] Theory is synonymous with abstract notions whereas a heuristic approach, acquired during their training or formulated on the basis of personal experience, is a much more viable option. In translation education circles, however, a more systematic approach is increasingly being advocated in support of the status of the translating profession. The relevance of this third theoretical component within a curriculum that purports to teach translation in a professional perspective has been pointed out most effectively by Baker (1996:42):

> What many of us think of as a "profession" is unlikely to achieve genuine professional status without some interaction with a discipline that provides it with a coherent framework, a sense of continuity and some insight into where it's going. We do not expect lawyers, for instance, to shun academia and theory and follow their innate sense of what is right and wrong. We accept law as a profession precisely because it is not (or not just) an intuitive practice, because it requires solid training in theoretical and practical matters, and because it is indisputably linked to a healthy and stable academic discipline.

Some sort of grounding in translation theory would therefore seem indispensable since it is only against a theoretical background of translation that effective decision-making and production can take place and the information and strategies acquired by working on particular texts be generalised. The results of the survey showed that, on the whole, there is recognition that some kind of theoretical premise is essential in order to foster the awareness that is at the basis of modern-day translating. There is, in other words, a tendency in all areas of translation studies to accept the inevitable fact that there cannot be practice without some kind of "guiding principles" and that any theory that is in any way applicable to translation must be constructed on empirical grounds. Thus, as far as a "theory of translating" and a "theory of translation" are concerned, the various institutions are in agreement that both are integral elements of a translation course.[7]

Integration of theoretical and applied aspects   92%
The theoretical component
  – is a separate course   76%
  – is part of the translation into L1 course   66%
  – is part of the translation into L2 course   47%
  – is language specific   23%
  – goes across languages   85%

What gave rise to some discrepancies, however, was the question regarding theories of translation. The aim was to identify attitudes towards the leading approaches. Respondents indicated that in their institutions theoretical aspects included the following:

  – a linguistic approach   95%
  – a functional approach   90%
  – a cultural studies approach   85%
  – a descriptive translation studies approach   85%
  – a comparative literary approach   57%
  – a gender studies approach   28%
  – a postcolonial approach   7%
  – a socio-historical approach   3%

Further investigations are needed to address the problem of how best to integrate a course on translation theory within the curriculum. A drawback of placing it within language-specific classes is that there will inevitably be a certain amount of repetition and overlapping as translation theory cannot be neatly categorised within national boundaries. The suggestions put forward by Mossop (1992:402–403) may provide a starting point for arriving at a workable model at various levels. Mossop gives an example of three possible types of "Translation theory courses". Type 1 course is based on the concept of theory as the systematising of practice and includes practical as well as theoretical components. Mossop (1992:403) insists on reflection being an integral part of such a course because students need to: "stand back and think about the *implications* of using a particular method, and about *conflicting* prescriptions for how to translate (italics in the original)". Type 2 is aimed at graduate students preparing to be translator trainers or researchers and provides an introduction to Translation Studies. The last, Type 3, is the most comprehensive and refers to translation methods and the main theories but, in Mossop's (1992:405) words: "its prime aim is to disturb received ideas about translation, communication and language, and confront students with the oddness of the translator's position".

Although the survey did not enquire into how theoretical components were actually included within the various translation curricula, it observed a correlation, as was pointed out above, between types of curricula and theoretical components. It was also clear that the majority of institutions envisaged some kind of translation theory course as constituting an integral part of translator education.

4. Future prospects

In recent years research into the nature of translating and translations has brought about an evolution in both depth and detail with the result that Translation Studies has broadened its horizons to encompass a multiplicity of approaches, schools and perspectives (Ulrych 2003). "Multiple" is perhaps the adjective that is most suited to describing the profound changes that have occurred within the field in recent years and the one that best characterises it. Apart from the multiple approaches that have emerged within the discipline itself, evidence from the working world indicates that professional translating entails multiple forms of communication, once considered as lying on the periphery of what was considered "translation proper": activities such as technical writing, editing, language consultancy and screen translation, for instance, are becoming core components of a translator's day-to-day practice. Translating has, moreover, become multimedial and multimodal as ever-greater use is made of computer-assisted tools such as hypertexts, translators' workbenches and Internet.

One of the most significant consequences of this changing scenario is that the profile of the translator is undergoing a profound transformation bringing the activity of translation closer to that of monolingual text production. The situation is such that some authors go so far as to state that what translators are asked to do can no longer be called translation but is rather "reader-oriented writing" or "multilingual technical communication" (Kingscott 1996:295, 297) since the term "translation" simply cannot transmit the range of skills that are, and will increasingly become, necessary. Other authors take a different view and see the new profile of modern-day translators and the enlargement of their activities simply as variants of "interlingual communication in which the traditional concept of translation is one option among many solutions

for overcoming a language barrier" (Sager 1994: 164). The picture of a translator's competence that emerges from the professional world is multifaceted
and agrees in spirit with Neubert's (1992: 420) integrated view of translation
competence which, he states, "corresponds very aptly with the disputed and
undisputed role of the translator as the great and only generalist in our age of
the unique and self-proclaimed specialist". The idea that professional translators work predominantly in one or two specialist fields is in fact swiftly
losing ground as the need for translation expands exponentially in volume and
variety. This shift away from monoprofessionalism "towards new models of
non-specialization, usually called 'flexibility'" reflects the phenomenon of job
mobilisation in general (Pym 1998: 161–162). It is becoming increasingly cus-
tomary (and necessary) for people to change their employment a number of
times in their careers. Continuing advances in technological progress and increasing globalisation will require people to adapt even more rapidly to these
changing circumstances. Translators and interpreters are no exception.

From the pedagogical perspective it is clear that only a fully comprehensive
formative approach to the teaching of translation and translator education will
enable translators of the future to survive the far-reaching transformations that
the profession is undergoing. The breadth of perspective in terms of skills and
knowledge areas required of translators (Coulthard & Odber de Baubeta 1996)
are such that translation courses need to be multidimensional if they are to
cater for realistic translational market requirements in tomorrow's world. First
and foremost, the importance of incorporating real world criteria within a
curriculum for translator training and education cannot be underestimated.
Trainee translators need to be prepared for the conditions they can expect to
find in their future working environment, bearing in mind that translation
is essentially a communicative activity that takes place within clear-cut socio-
cultural and historical contexts.

A training programme for translators will therefore ideally aim to develop,
within the framework of continuing education, a series of skills and competences that are relevant to both their professional status and their future work.
This entails not only an awareness of real professional conditions, but also de-
vising flexible and multidimensional translator training courses which can be
updated to keep abreast of changing requirements. Flexibility, the key word in
today's professional translation world, as we saw above, needs to be mirrored in
translator training. An important component of translators' competence is the
acquisition of the metacognitive skills that will enable them to go on developing
their competence and monitoring their performance throughout their professional careers.[8] In other words, the behaviourist principle according to which

one learns how to translate by translating needs to be bolstered by a sound theoretical and methodological foundation. Expertise, as Séguinot (2000:99) has
noted, "stems from the integration of experiential knowledge with the principles of the discipline". This broad educational process should begin at the
training stage in order to set trainee translators in good stead for what they will
encounter when they get out into the real world. The task of translator education is, in short, not to shape a finished product but rather to provide graduate
translators with the enabling (Fawcett 1987:37) and transferable skills that will
place them in a position to deal confidently with any text, on any subject, within
any situation at any time and to be able to discuss their performance with fellow
translators and clients.

Attitudes towards translation and translators are undergoing profound
transformations both in the professional world and that of scholarly research.
It is increasingly being acknowledged that translators play a pivotal role in
the dynamics of crosscultural communication and that it is thanks to their
mediation that frontiers can be transcended and contacts made. Thus, after
years of being relegated to a background position, translators are gradually
emerging as key figures in the world arena. There is, nevertheless, still a long
way to go before translators receive full recognition for their work and much
depends on how translator training is able to cope with the changes that the
internationalisation of economies and cultures will increasingly bring about
and to meet the challenges that the profession faces today. One of the main
aims of the present survey was to shed some light on how the teaching of
translation has adapted to the changing conditions of the professional world
and to the demands facing translators today. What emerged was a general
trend on the part of the majority of institutions to introduce a translation
training component into their curricula to satisfy not only market needs but
also the growing demands within higher education for professionally oriented
degrees. Much still needs to be done before the teaching of translation in higher
education can really be said to be in line with real-world criteria and before
all the institutions that have a translation component in their curricula accept
the fact that training translators constitutes a serious pedagogical challenge.
Teaching translation in a textual and contextual vacuum may still have a place
in preparing translators of the future if it is accepted for what it is: namely,
a formative academic exercise, used, for instance, to reinforce the acquisition
of certain structures and vocabulary. All-round translator education requires
greater sensitivity to broader communicative purposes. As Neubert (1989:5)
has pointed out: "the study of translation and, in particular, the academic
institutions where the practice of translation is taught do not exist in an

intellectual ivory tower. They serve social needs". Coming to terms with this basic concept is a crucial step towards adequately meeting the pedagogical challenges of training translators for the future and of ensuring more effective crosscultural communication.

Appendix

Questionnaire

TEACHING TRANSLATION AND TRAINING TRANSLATORS: CURRENT TRENDS AND PRACTICES

Questionnaire
Please put a cross (X) next to the relevant answer (N.B. more than one may be applicable) or fill in the pertinent information. If you are returning the questionnaire by e-mail, please use Rich Text Format (i.e. extension .rtf).

1. **Name of Institution** _____
2. **Address** _____
and contact   **e-mail address** _____
                 tel no. _____
                 fax no. _____
3. **Type of institution** (School, Faculty, Department etc.) _____

4. **Number of teaching staff**
4.1 permanent staff _____
4.2 temporary or part-time staff _____
4.3 staff engaged solely in teaching translation _____

5. **Number of students** _____

6. **Admission criteria**
entrance exam   yes☐   no☐
numerus clausus   yes☐   no☐
proficiency in
    1 foreign language ☐
    2 foreign languages ☐
    3 foreign languages ☐

7. **Type of degree/diploma**
undergraduate   yes☐   no☐
If yes, at what level?
    – diploma level   yes☐   no☐
    – first degree level   yes☐   no☐
postgraduate   yes☐   no☐

If yes, at what level?
  – MA/MSc   yes☐   no☐
  – PhD   yes☐   no☐

8. Duration of degree course
undergraduate: 2yrs☐   3yrs☐   4yrs☐
postgraduate: 1yr ☐   2yrs☐   3yrs☐

9. Curricula
9.1 Length of courses
9.1.1 Are the courses divided into:
  – academic years   yes☐   no☐
If yes, how many weeks per year?   _____
  – terms   yes☐   no☐
If yes, how many weeks per term?   _____
  – semesters   yes☐   no☐
If yes, how many weeks per semester?   _____
  – module   yes☐   no☐
If yes, how many weeks per module?   _____

9.1.2 Hours per week for translation activities
Overall student effort hours (SEH) 6hrs☐ 8hrs☐ 10hrs☐ 12hrs☐
of which:
        – contact hours 2hrs☐ 3hrs☐ 4hrs☐ 5hrs☐   6hrs☐   7hrs☐
        – private study 4hrs☐ 5hrs☐ 6hrs☐ 7hrs☐   8hrs☐   9hrs☐

9.1.3 Hours per week for translation-related activities
Overall student effort hours (SEH) 6hrs☐ 8hrs☐ 10hrs☐ 12hrs☐
of which:
        – contact hours 2hrs☐ 3hrs☐ 4hrs☐ 5hrs☐   6hrs☐   7hrs☐
        – private study 4hrs☐ 5hrs☐ 6hrs☐ 7hrs☐   8hrs☐   9hrs☐

9.2 Course structure
9.2.1 Studies abroad
  – compulsory   yes☐   no☐
  – duration per language   3–4mths☐   5–6mths☐   7–8mths☐   9–10mths☐   1yr☐
9.2.2 Choice of courses
  – compulsory   100%☐   90%☐   80%☐   70%☐   60%☐
  – elective   none ☐   10%☐   20%☐   30%☐   40%☐
9.2.3 Typology of translation courses
  – generalist   yes☐   no☐
  – specialised   yes☐   no☐
  – Are generalist courses prerequisite to specialised courses?   yes☐   no☐
  – Are specialised courses
        – compulsory   all☐   some☐   none☐
        – elective   all☐   some☐   none☐
9.2.4 Typology of specialised courses
  – scientific   yes☐   no☐
  – technical   yes☐   no☐

– medical	yes☐	no☐
– economic	yes☐	no☐
– legal	yes☐	no☐
– social sciences	yes☐	no☐
– literary	yes☐	no☐
– multimedia	yes☐	no☐
– other, please specify:		

9.2.5 Literary and/or sci-tech translation courses

– students can take *both* literary *and* sci-tech courses	yes☐	no☐
– students can take *neither* literary *nor* sci-tech courses	yes☐	no☐
– students select *either* literary *or* sci-tech courses	yes☐	no☐
– different curricula apply for literary and sci-tech courses	yes☐	no☐

If yes, please specify the most significant differences:

9.3 Course content

9.3.1 Integration of academic and professional criteria   yes☐   no☐

If yes, professional criteria include:

– choice of text to translate	yes☐	no☐
– criteria for translating text	yes☐	no☐
– type of activity:	yes☐	no☐
– technical writing	yes☐	no☐
– editing	yes☐	no☐
– localisation	yes☐	no☐
– use of translation aids	yes☐	no☐

9.3.2 Integration of theoretical and applied aspects   yes☐   no☐

If yes, the theoretical component

– is a separate course	yes☐	no☐
– is part of the translation into L1 course	yes☐	no☐
– is part of the translation into L2 course	yes☐	no☐
– is language specific	yes☐	no☐
– goes across languages	yes☐	no☐

Theoretical aspects include

– a linguistic approach	yes☐	no☐
– a comparative literary approach	yes☐	no☐
– a cultural studies approach	yes☐	no☐
– a gender studies approach	yes☐	no☐
– a descriptive translation studies approach	yes☐	no☐
– a functional approach	yes☐	no☐
– other, please specify		

9.3.3 Technological/machine aids available

– computers/word processors	yes☐	no☐
– Internet	yes☐	no☐
– e-mail	yes☐	no☐

     – MT tools   yes☐   no☐

     – CAT tools   yes☐   no☐

If yes, which?

     – on-line glossaries/dictionaries   yes☐   no☐

     – terminological data banks   yes☐   no☐

     – corpora   yes☐   no☐

     – translation memory tools   yes☐   no☐

     – translators workbench   yes☐   no☐

Other, please specify ――――――――――――――――――――――――

9.3.4 Classroom management/dynamics

     – translations are done at home and discussed in class

     always☐   often☐   sometimes☐   never☐

     – discussions/corrections are carried out

     – as teacher/student interaction

     always☐   often☐   sometimes☐   never☐

     – by students in groups

     always☐   often☐   sometimes☐   never☐

     – by students in pairs

     always☐   often☐   sometimes☐   never☐

     – students arrive at a consensus translation

     always☐   often☐   sometimes☐   never☐

     – students are required to write up their final corrected version for future reference

     always☐   often☐   sometimes☐   never☐

9.3.5 Continuous assessment assignments   yes☐   no☐

If yes, done

     – in class   yes☐   no☐

     – at home   yes☐   no☐

     – presented in handwritten form   yes☐   no☐

     – presented in typed/word processed form   yes☐   no☐

9.4. Examinations

9.4.1. Number of exam sessions per year   1☐   2☐   3☐   4☐   5☐   6 or more☐

9.4.2 Type of exam   oral☐   written☐   written+oral☐

If written, the exam includes:

     – translation into L1   yes☐   no☐

     – translation into L2   yes☐   no☐

     – written composition in L1   yes☐   no☐

     – written composition in L2   yes☐   no☐

     – reading comprehension / text analysis   yes☐   no☐

     – summary writing   yes☐   no☐

     – multiple choice   yes☐   no☐

     – cloze test   yes☐   no☐

9.4.3 Duration of exam   1hr☐   2hrs☐   3hrs☐   4hrs☐   over☐

9.4.4 Length of texts to be translated   No. words   100☐   200☐   300☐   400☐   500☐

other, please specify ――――――――――――――――――――――――

9.4.5 Number of texts to be translated   1☐   2☐   3☐   4☐

9.4.6 Textual/contextual information made available
  – source given   yes☐   no☐
  – purpose of exercise stated   yes☐   no☐
  – intended client stated   yes☐   no☐
  – typed text given   yes☐   no☐
  – text with original layout/format given   yes☐   no☐

9.4.7 Material allowed in written examination
  – no materials allowed   yes☐   no☐
  – monolingual dictionary   yes☐   no☐
  – bilingual dictionary   yes☐   no☐
  – thesaurus   yes☐   no☐
  – grammar   yes☐   no☐
  – translations done during course   yes☐   no☐
  – model texts   yes☐   no☐
  other reference texts, please specify   ⸺⸺⸺⸺⸺⸺⸺⸺⸺⸺

9.4.8 Assessment
  – assessment by examination only   yes☐   no☐
  – assessment by continuous assessment   yes☐   no☐
  – assessment by both   yes☐   no☐

9.4.9 Dissertations
  – a written dissertation is part of the degree/diploma course   yes☐   no☐
If yes,
  – length in words
    under 5,000 ☐   5,000–7,000 ☐   7,000–10,000 ☐   over 10,000 ☐
  – typology
  – research   yes☐   no☐
      – experimental   yes☐   no☐
      – translations   yes☐   no☐
      – glossaries   yes☐   no☐
    other, please specify   ⸺⸺⸺⸺⸺⸺⸺⸺⸺⸺

9.4.10 Degrees and certificates offered
      – translation only   yes☐   no☐
      – interpreting only   yes☐   no☐
      – translation and interpreting   yes☐   no☐

10. **Supplementary facilities**
  – training of translator trainers   yes☐   no☐
  – summer courses   yes☐   no☐
  – intensive courses   yes☐   no☐

11. **External contacts**
  – professional organisations   yes☐   no☐
If yes, which?   ⸺⸺⸺⸺⸺⸺⸺⸺⸺⸺
  – employers   yes☐   no☐
If yes:
  – EU organisations   yes☐   no☐

– international organisations	yes☐	no☐
– translation agencies	yes☐	no☐
– localisation agencies	yes☐	no☐
– dubbing/subtitling agencies	yes☐	no☐
– multinationals	yes☐	no☐
– local industry	yes☐	no☐
– local companies	yes☐	no☐
– public institutions	yes☐	no☐

12. **Comments**

Notes

1. Pym (2000:209) estimates that "there are now some 300 specialised university-level training programmes world-wide, plus countless courses given in private institutions and as components of modern language programmes" and comments that it is difficult "to find consensus on the fundamental questions of what should be taught, to whom, by whom and how". In view of such diverse scenarios the present survey aimed to present an overview of the state of the art in translation teaching in a cross-section of the leading and recognised higher education institutions rather than to offer an exhaustive picture of translation training world-wide. Reliability of results based on first-hand acquaintance with the institutions contacted was given priority over extent of coverage.

2. The following Institutions responded to the questionnaire:

Austria – Institut für Theoretische und Angewandte Translationswissenschaft, Karl-Franzens-Universität Graz, Graz; Institut für Übersetzer und Dolmetscherausbildung, Leopold-Franzens-Universität Innsbruck, Innsbruck; Institut für Übersetzer und Dolmetscherausbildung der Universität Wien, Wien.

Belgium – Hoger Instituut voor Vertalers en Tolken, Antwerpen; Lessius Hogeschool, Antwerpen; Ecole d'Interprètes Internationaux de l'Université de Mons Hainaut, Mons.

Brazil – University of Sao Paulo, Sao Paulo.

Canada – Département de linguistique et de traduction, Montréal (Québec); Ecole de traduction et d'interpretation / School of Translation and Interpretation, Ottawa (Ontario).

Denmark – The Aarhus School of Business, Faculty of Modern Languages, Aarhus.

Finland – Department of Romance Languages, University of Helsinki, Helsinki; Savonlinna School of Translation Studies, Savonlinna; Centre for Translation and Interpreting, University of Turku, Turku.

France – Ecole Supérieure d'Interprètes et de Traducteurs, Centre Universitaire Dauphine, Paris; Institut Supérieur d'Interprétation et de Traduction, Paris.

Germany – Fachbereich Angewandte Sprach- und Kulturwissenschaft (F.A.S.K.), der Johannes Gutenberg-Universität Mainz in Germersheim, Germesheim; Institut für Übersetzen und Dolmetschen der Universität Heidelberg, Heidelberg; Philosophische Fakultät II, Fachrichtung 4.6 – Übersetzen und Dolmetschen, Saarbrucken.

Hungary – ELTE, University of Budapest, Faculty of Humanities, Interpreter and Translator Training Centre, Budapest.

Israel – Bar Ilan University, Israel.

Italy – Scuola Superiore di Lingue Moderne per Interpreti e Traduttori, Università degli Studi di Bologna, Forlì; Università degli Studi di Genova, Facoltà di Lingue e Letterature Straniere, Genova; Università Cattolica del Sacro Cuore, Facoltà di Lingue e Letterature Straniere, Milano; Scuola Superiore di Lingue Moderne per Interpreti e Traduttori, Università degli Studi di Trieste, Trieste; Scuola Superiore Interpreti Traduttori di Vicenza, Vicenza.

Poland – Postgraduate School for Translators and Interpreters, Jagiellonian University of Kraków, Kraków; Institute of English Studies, University of Lòdz, Lòdz.

Portugal – Faculdade de Letras, Universidade do Porto, Porto.

Spain – Facultad de Filosofía y Letras, Universidad Pontificia Comillas, Madrid; Facultat de Ciències Humanes, Traducció i Documentació, Universitat de Vic, Vic (Barcelona).

Switzerland – ETI, Université de Genève, Genève.

United Kingdom – Department of Modern Languages, University of Bradford; School of Languages, Heriot-Watt University, Edinburgh; Centre for Translation Studies, UMIST, Manchester; University of Sheffield, MLTC, Sheffield; Centre for Translation Studies, Department of Linguistics and International Studies, University of Surrey, Guildford; Centre for British and Comparative Cultural Studies, University of Warwick, Coventry.

United States – Division of Interpretation and Translation, Georgetown University, Washington DC; Department of Modern and Classical Language Studies, Kent State University, Kent, Ohio; Department of Romance Languages and Literatures, University of Florida, Gainesville, Florida; Translation Center / Comparative Literature Department, University of Massachusetts, Amherst, Massachusetts; The Graduate School of Translation and Interpretation, Monterey Institute of International Studies, Monterey, California.

3. An interesting corollary of the survey was that the ECTS is not homogeneous across Europe as regards either the number of student effort hours envisaged per credit or the ratio between contact hours and student study time.

4. The questionnaire revealed that some (mainly T&I) institutions attribute a different meaning to L1 and L2. While in the general field of foreign language learning it is now standard practice to refer to the native language as L1 and to the foreign or second language as L2, in some translation training circles L1 is used to indicate the first foreign language and L2 the second foreign language.

5. For in-depth investigations of translation expertise, see Séguinot (2000), Jarvella et al. (2002) and Shreve (2002).

6. Chesterman and Wagner (2002) offer an interesting exchange of views between a translation scholar and a practising translator on the relations between translation theory and translation practice.

7. The results regarding the distribution of theoretical components may also have been influenced by the different meanings attributed to L1 and L2 pointed out in Note 4 above. Nevertheless, the large percentage of replies which stated that teaching "goes across languages" is an indication that theoretical courses are not language specific.

8. For an up-to-date and comprehensive discussion of translation evaluation, see House (2001).

References

Baker, M. (1996). "Professing Translation". *ESSE, V*(1), 42–44.

Baker, M. & Kaplan, R. (1994). "Translated! A new breed of bilingual dictionaries". *Babel, 40*(1), 1–11.

Bell, R. (1991). *Translation and Translating.* London: Longman.

Bowker, L. (2002). *Computer-Aided Translation Technology: A Practical Introduction.* Ottawa: Ottawa University Press.

Chesterman, A. & Wagner, E. (2002). *Can Theory Help Translators? A Dialogue between the Ivory Tower and the Wordface.* Manchester: St. Jerome.

Coulthard, M. & Odber de Baubeta, P. A. (1996). *The Knowledges of the Translator: From Literary Interpretation to Machine Classification.* Lewiston/Queenston/Lampeter: Edwin Mellor Press.

Delisle, J. (1992). "Les manuels de traduction: Essai de classification". *TTR, 1*, 17–47.

Dollerup, C. (1994). "Systematic feedback in teaching translation". In C. Dollerup & A. Lindegaard (Eds.), *Teaching Translation and Interpreting 2. Insights, Aims, Visions* (pp. 121–132). Amsterdam and Philadelphia: John Benjamins.

Fawcett, P. (1987). "Putting translation theory to use". In H. Keith & I. Mason (Eds.), *Translation in the Modern Languages Degree* (pp. 31–38). London: CILT.

Gile, D. (1995). *Basic Concepts and Models for Interpreter and Translator Training.* Amsterdam and Philadelphia: John Benjamins.

House, J. (2001). "How do we know when a translation is good?". In E. Steiner & C. Yallop (Eds.), *Exploring Translation and Multilingual Text Production: Beyond Content* (pp. 127–160). Berlin and New York: Mouton de Gruyter.

Jarvella, R. J., Jensen, A., Jensen, E. H., & Anderson, M. S. (2002). "Towards characterizing translator expertise, knowledge and know-how: some findings using TAPs and experimental methods". In A. Riccardi (Ed.), *Translation Studies: Perspectives on an Emerging Discipline* (pp. 172–197). Cambridge: Cambridge University Press.

Kingscott, G. (1996). "The impact of technology and the implications for teaching". In C. Dollerup & V. Appel (Eds.), *Teaching Translation and Interpreting 3. New Horizons* (pp. 295–300). Amsterdam and Philadelphia: John Benjamins.

Kiraly, D. C. (1995). *Pathways to Translation: Pedagogy and Progress.* Kent, Ohio: Kent University Press.

Klein-Braley, C. (1996). "Teaching translation, a brief for the future". In P. Sewell & J. Higgins (Eds.), *Teaching Translation in Universities: Present and Future Perspectives* (pp. 15–29). London: AFLS-CILT.

Klein-Braley, C. & Franklin, P. (1998). "'The foreigner in the refrigerator'. Remarks about teaching translation to university students of foreign languages". In K. Malmkjær (Ed.), *Translation and Language Teaching. Language Teaching and Translation* (pp. 53–61). Manchester: St. Jerome.

Kussmaul, P. (1995). *Training the Translator.* Amsterdam and Philadelphia: John Benjamins.

Maier, C. & Massardier-Kenney, F. (1993). "Toward an expanded pedagogy of specialized translation". *Scientific and Technical Translation. ATA Scholarly Monograph Series, 6*, 151–160. Amsterdam and Philadelphia: John Benjamins.

Mossop, B. (1992). "Goals and methods for a course in translation theory". In M. Snell-Hornby, F. Pöchhacker, & K. Kaindl (Eds.), *Translation Studies. An Interdiscipline* (pp. 401–409). Amsterdam and Philadelphia: John Benjamins.

Mossop, B. (2001). *Revising and Editing for Translators.* Manchester: St. Jerome.

Neubert, A. (1989). "Translation as mediation". In R. Kolmel & J. Payne (Eds.), *Babel. The Cultural and Linguistic Barriers Between Nations* (pp. 5–12). Aberdeen: Aberdeen University Press.

Neubert, A. (1992). "Competence in translation: A complex skill, how to study and how to teach it". In M. Snell-Hornby, F. Pöchhacker, & K. Kaindl (Eds.), *Translation Studies. An Interdiscipline* (pp. 411–420). Amsterdam and Philadelphia: John Benjamins.

Nida, E. A. (2001). *Contexts in Translating.* Amsterdam and Philadelphia: John Benjamins.

Nord, C. (1991). "Scopos, loyalty, and translational conventions". *Target, 3*(1), 91–109.

Nord, C. (1997). *Translating as a Purposeful Activity.* Manchester: St Jerome.

Pym, A. (1998). *Method in Translation History.* Manchester: St. Jerome.

Pym, A. (2000). "Innovation in translator and interpreting training. Report on an online symposium". *Across Languages and Cultures, 1*(2), 209–211.

Reiss, K. (2000). *Translation Criticism – The Potentials and Limitations. Categories and Criteria for Translation Quality Assessment.* Manchester: St Jerome.

Roberts, R. P. (1984). "Traduction et qualité de la langue". *Actes du colloque, Société des traducteurs du Québec/Conseil de la langue française,* 172–184. Québec. Editeur official du Québec.

Round, N. G. (1996). "'Interlocking the voids': Knowledges of the translator". In M. Coulthard & P. A. Odber de Baubeta (Eds.), *The Knowledges of the Translator: From Literary Interpretation to Machine Classification* (pp. 1–30). Lewiston/Queenston/Lampeter: Edwin Mellor Press.

Round, N. G. (1998). "Monuments, markars and modules: A British experience". In P. Bush & K. Malmkjær (Eds.), *Rimbaud's Rainbow. Literary Translation in Higher Education* (pp. 11–20). Amsterdam and Philadelphia: John Benjamins.

Sager, J. C. (1994). *Language Engineering and Translation: Consequences of Automation.* Amsterdam and Philadelphia: John Benjamins.

Schäffner, C. (1998). "Qualification for professional translators. Translation in language teaching versus teaching translation". In K. Malmkjær (Ed.), *Translation and Language Teaching. Language Teaching and Translation* (pp. 135–159). Manchester: St. Jerome.

Schäffner, C. & Adab, B. (Eds.). (2000). *Developing Translation Competence.* Amsterdam and Philadelphia: John Benjamins.

Séguinot, C. (2000). "Knowledge, expertise and theory in translation". In A. Chesterman, N. Gallardo San Salvador, & Y. Gambier (Eds.), *Translation in Context* (pp. 87–104). Amsterdam and Philadelphia: John Benjamins.

Sewell, P. (1996). "Translation in the curriculum". In P. Sewell & I. Higgins (Eds.), *Teaching Translation in Universities: Present and Future Perspectives* (pp. 135–159). London: AFLS and CILT.

Shreve, G. M. (2002). "Knowing translation: Cognitive and experiential aspects of translation expertise from the perspective of expertise studies". In A. Riccardi (Ed.), *Translation Studies. Perspectives on an Emerging Discipline* (pp. 150–171). Cambridge: Cambridge University Press.

Snell-Hornby, M. (1988). *Translation Studies. An Integrated Approach.* Amsterdam and Philadelphia: John Benjamins.

Snell-Hornby, M. (1992). "The professional translator of tomorrow: Language specialist or all-round expert". In C. Dollerup & A. Loddegaard (Eds.), *Teaching Translation and Interpreting. Training, Talent, Experience* (pp. 9–22). Amsterdam and Philadelphia: John Benjamins.

Ulrych, M. (2002). "An evidence-based approach to applied translation studies". In A. Riccardi (Ed.), *Translation Studies: Perspectives on an Emerging Discipline* (pp. 198–213). Cambridge: Cambridge University Press.

Ulrych, M. (2003). "Diversity, uniformity and creativity in translation". In S. Petrilli (Ed.), *Translation Translation (Approaches to Translation Studies 21)* (pp. 133–151). Amsterdam and New York: Rodopi.

Vermeer, H. J. (1996). *A Skopos Theory of Translation. Some Arguments For and Against.* Heidelberg: TextconText.

Viaggio, S. (1994). "Theory and professional development: Or admonishing translators to be good". In C. Dollerup & A. Lindegaard (Eds.), *Teaching Translation and Interpreting 2. Insights, Aims, Visions* (pp. 97–105). Amsterdam and Philadelphia: John Benjamins.

Vienne, J. (1998). "Teaching what they didn't learn as language students". In K. Malmkjær (Ed.), *Translation and Language Teaching. Language Teaching and Translation* (pp. 111–116). Manchester: St. Jerome.

Chapter 2

Training interpreters

Programmes, curricula, practices

Helge Niska

1. Current training practices

1.1 Professional interpreting

Interpreting is an activity which is normal in the daily lives of most of the world's population and a perfectly trivial affair in everyday communication in bilingual or multilingual societies, i.e. the greatest part of the world. Professional interpreters have played a major role as guides and spies in every imperialistic endeavour to take control over foreign peoples' lands, long before Hernando Cortez. In more peaceful circumstances, business trips like Marco Polo's would not have been so successful without the help of skilled interpreters. From modern times there are documents describing the importance of interpreters, for example path-finders and guides in the conquest of the American Wild West (Horn & Krakel 1979) and spies in Her Majesty's Service (Harris 2002). After World War II a number of books appeared, containing the memoirs of interpreters of internationally known politicians like Stalin (Berezhkov 1994) and Gorbatchev (Palazchenko 1997).

While the above kind of liaison interpreting is still conducted, the concern of this chapter will mainly be to deal with the types of professional interpreting which have emerged at the end of the twentieth century: professional conference interpreting and professional community interpreting. The emphasis will be on the training and education of professional interpreters between spoken languages. This does not exclude the great number of interpreters who are not full-time interpreters and those who only do occasional assignments – the emphasis is on the word professional, meaning according to professional qualifications.

The boom in conference interpreting started in the aftermath of World War II at the Nuremberg trials (Bowen & Bowen 1985). It was then that the technical equipment needed for simultaneous interpreting was tested on a large scale and proven to be efficient. In fact, it is difficult to imagine the large growth in international conferencing without the advent of simultaneous interpreting technology.

The growing need for interpreters gave rise to a great number of training institutions. Most of the academic interpreting schools[1] are in Europe, but there are a number of universities and colleges offering interpreter training in all continents. By the end of the twentieth century there were some 230 academic institutions world-wide offering interpreter training in more than sixty countries. Table 1 is based on information available at the end of 1999; the exact number of schools is continuously changing, so the figures must be seen as tentative. Sources for information have been Brian Harris' *Translation and Interpreting Schools* (Harris 1997), *Translator-Training Institutions World-Wide* by Caminade and Pym (Pym 1999) and other compilations on the Internet.

1.2 In-house training: European Commission and Parliament

The European Union claims to be the world's largest user of interpreter services, and both the Commission and Parliament used to train their own interpreters by means of in-house practice. Until recently the European Commission's Joint Interpreter and Conference Service (SCIC) organised its own six-month training course. Prerequisites for admission included holding an academic degree and passing an entrance examination. To cater for the increased need of interpreters in new member countries, interpreting courses were often modelled on this course. Such examples are the Copenhagen Business School (Denmark) and Stockholm University (Sweden).

SCIC has now abandoned its in-house training activities in favour of co-operation with a few academic institutions. In 1998 it provided "experienced interpreter trainers" to some 27 university programmes and granted subsidies to some 14 universities so that an "EU dimension" could be added to existing courses (Pym 2000). The EU has also initiated the European Masters' programme in Conference Interpreting, which will be described later in this chapter.

Table 1. Regional distribution of interpreting schools

Region	Number of schools. c. year 2000	Countries	
Europe including all of Russia and Turkey Austria (3), Belarus (1), Belgium (12), Czech Republic (1), Denmark (2), Estonia (1), Finland (5), France (10+3), Germany (11), Greece (1), Hungary (2), Ireland (1), Italy (25), Latvia (1), Netherlands (1), Norway (1), Poland (4), Portugal (2+1), Romania (1), Russia (3), Slovakia (1), Slovenia (1), Spain (18), Sweden (1), Switzerland (2), Turkey (3), Ukraine (1), United Kingdom (6+4)	121	28	3–5 yrs undergraduate: 100 schools 1–2 yrs postgrad.: 23 Community interpreting c. 10 (+ : only "liaison" interpreting, i.e. for business negotiations and the like)
Middle East and North Africa Algeria (2), Egypt (2), Iraq (1), Israel (2), Jordan (1), Kuwait (1), Lebanon (3), Morocco (1), Palestine (1), Sudan (1), Syria (1)	16	11	4 yrs undergraduate: 5 1–3 yrs postgraduate: 11
Africa except North Africa Cameroon (1), South Africa (5+1)	6	2	1 yrs postgraduate: 2 schools +1 : only liaison (business negotiations)
Asia except Middle East China (6), Hong Kong (5), Japan (7), Kazachstan (1), Macao (1), Malaysia (2), North Korea (1), South Korea (1), Taiwan (2), Thailand (1)	27	10	3–5 yrs undergraduate: 10 1–3 yrs postgraduate: 15
Australia, New Zealand	12	2	1–3 yrs. Cf. NAATI table below 1 yr postgraduate
North America Canada (13 incl. 8 colleges), USA (17)	30	2	1–4 yrs undergraduate 1 yr postgraduate
South & Central America Argentina (2), Brazil (3), Chile (2), Colombia (2), Costa Rica (1), Guatemala (2), Mexico (3), Nicaragua (1), Venezuela (1)	17	9	4–5 yrs undergrad. 9 1–2 yrs postgrad. 7

1.3   Fields of training

Most interpreting schools have until now been training conference interpreters and some have also offered special courses for court interpreters. In a number of schools "liaison interpreting" has been taught for business needs; but for the most part, the kind of liaison interpreting which is usually called "community interpreting", i.e. interpreting for immigrants in public service institutions, has been absent from the interpreter training programmes. Notable exceptions are those universities in Scandinavia and Australia which have offered courses for community interpreters since the 1970s.[2]

In Australia, 12 institutions organise interpreter training courses, the majority of which are community interpreting courses on the "paraprofessional level", see Table 1. The length of courses varies from one to three years, depending on the level.

In Sweden, community interpreter training at the university consists of a one year basic course plus 1 + 1 semester specialisation (medical and/or legal interpreting), leading to a degree and government authorisation (certification). Outside the university, community interpreter training at adult education centres consists of a series of short courses of 80 hours; trainees normally take four 80-hour courses. There is no final examination, but students can take the special authorisation/certification examination organised by the government.

Recent developments such as the growing number of refugees and increased mobility of labour have meant that established schools in other countries are becoming increasingly interested in the training of community interpreters. Trends and future prospects will be discussed in the last section of this chapter.

1.4   Organisation and content of courses

Given the great diversity of approaches, aims and organisational models of training programmes world-wide, it is not possible to give a full description of the training scene. What follows is an attempt at sifting out, from amongst the large number of programmes, a couple of "models" or approaches, and giving a few typical examples from different countries.

1.4.1   The Continental model
Interpreter training is mainly carried out as academic courses in universities. In many countries, for example in Continental Europe, training has been organised in the form of complete undergraduate programmes, leading to a

degree in interpreting or "translation and interpreting". A common model is a two year "introductory" or "general" part, consisting mainly of translator training, followed by a "specialisation" phase with two years of interpreter training. In this way, most students from these institutions receive a relatively thorough training in both translation and interpreting. After a basic degree, students can continue to postgraduate courses.

In this model, language instruction in the working languages (usually at least three) is part of the curriculum. Formal entrance tests are usually not allowed.

1.4.2   *The British/liberal approach*

The rather fixed continental traditions in the field of interpreter training are in stark contrast with the liberal educational culture in the United Kingdom. A number of universities offer interpreter training, but the organisation and emphasis of training varies so much between different universities that it is difficult to schematise the British system. This liberal attitude also prevails to a large extent in the organisation of interpreter training in the United States and non-Francophone parts of Canada. The Commonwealth countries of Australia and New Zealand, on the other hand, have centralised systems with a high degree of homogeneity with regard to length and content of interpreter training courses.

As the courses are mostly short (one to two years) training programmes, students must possess the necessary language skills before entering the programme.

1.4.3   *The market-oriented approach*

A third trend, not tied to academic traditions, is the strictly labour-market oriented education given by academic and non-academic institutions around the world, where emphasis lies on the training of interpreting skills. These skills have been predefined by the professional organisations, most notably AIIC, the international organisation of conference interpreters. Teaching and examination is carried out by professional interpreters, and schools are assessed according to quality criteria set by the professional organisations. Students are admitted on the basis of formal qualifications, i.e. educational background and the results of an entrance test.

1.4.4   *The Scandinavian/flexible approach*

A special model for interpreter training is the organisation of community interpreter training in some Scandinavian countries, most notably Sweden.

In this very flexible system, interpreters attend vocational training classes which are not academic courses but are organised by so-called "liberal adult education organisations", a form of adult education centres. There are no fixed curricula, but the Institute for Interpretation and Translation Studies at Stockholm University issues recommendations for course profiles, supervises the training and distributes the government funding for the courses. Formal examinations are not allowed, but the goal of the course is that students pass the government accreditation test after finishing the programme.

1.5 Organisation of interpreter training in some European countries

To illustrate the above, here are short descriptions of the organisation of interpreter training in some European countries. The information is drawn from the country reports published by the European Language Council's Thematic Network Project (TNP) on translation and interpreting (ELC 1999).

AUSTRIA

Interpreter training is conducted at the universities of Graz (http://www.kfunigraz.ac.at), Innsbruck (http://www.uibk.ac.at) and Vienna (http://www.univie.ac.at). The course is divided into two sections. Each Studienabschnitt comprises at least four semesters. At the end of each, students take a Diplom-prüfung.

BELGIUM

Basic four-year training in translation offered immediately after completing secondary school is available at nine institutions. All of them have an option in interpreting in the third and fourth years. There are also a number of schools offering three-year programmes. In all institutions offering a four-year degree the first two years establish a broad general basis on which specialisation can be developed. In the third and fourth years students have to choose between translation and interpreting.

Dutch-speaking community
Erasmushogeschool: http://www.erasmushogeschool.be

Hogeschool Antwerpen – Vlaamse Autonome Hogeschool (formerly Hoger Instituut voor Vertalers en Tolken, HIVT), http://www.ha.be/hivt/

Hogeschool voor Wetenschap en Kunst, Vlekho, http://www.vlekho.be/

Lessius Hogeschool, Departement Vertaler-Tolk, http://www.lessius-ho.be/

Bedrijfskunde Mercator (BMER) – Hogeschool Gent, http://bmer.hogent.be/

French-speaking community
Ecole d'Interprètes Internationaux (EII), part of the Université de Mons-Hainaut, http://www.umh.ac.be/~eii

Institut Libre Marie Haps (ILMH), part of the Haute Ecole Léonard de Vinci, http://www.ilmh.be

Institut Supérieur de Traducteurs et Interprètes de la Communauté Française de Belgique (ISTI) – part of Haute Ecole de Bruxelles, http://www.heb.be/isti/

Haute Ecole Francisco Ferrer – Catégorie de traduction et interprétation – Cooremans, http://www.brunette.brucity.be/ferrer/

A handful of schools offer at least one-year postgraduate training courses for interpreters. Postgraduate training in translation is available at most of the above-mentioned institutions.

DENMARK
The degree in translation and interpreting (cand.ling.merc.) is awarded by the Copenhagen Business School – Handelshøjskolen i København (http://www.cbs. dk) and the Aarhus School of Business – Handelshøjskolen i Århus (http:// www.hha.dk).

The two-year translation and interpreting programme leading to the degree builds on a three-year BA degree in two foreign languages (languages for special purposes).

FINLAND
Five universities offer interpreter training as a specialisation within translator training, leading to a Master's degree in translation:

University of Helsinki (institute located in the city of Kouvola), http://www.helsinki.fi

University of Joensuu (institute located in the city of Savonlinna), http://www.joensuu.fi

University of Tampere, http://www.uta.fi

University of Turku, http://www.utu.fi

University of Vaasa, http://www.uwasa.fi

The University of Turku also offers a national eight-month postgraduate course in conference interpreting (40 credits) specially geared towards the European Union.

FRANCE

Professional interpreting is taught in only a handful of institutions in France. Postgraduate courses in conference interpreting (two or three years after the Licence) can be found in the following institutions:

ESIT, École Supérieure d'Interprètes et de Traducteurs (Paris), http://www.univ-paris3.fr/esit/

ISIT, Institut Supérieur d'Interprétation et de Traduction (Paris), http://www.isit.icp.fr/

ITI-RI, Institut de Traducteurs, d'Interprètes et de Relations Internationales (Strasbourg), http://u2.u-strasbg.fr/itiri/

IPLV, Institut de Langues Vivantes, Université Catholique de l'Ouest (Angers), http://www.uco.fr/refonte2002/instituts/iplv/

Conference interpreting is a two-year specialisation, beginning in year four at ESIT and year five at ISIT. Conference interpreting is offered as a specialisation by ESIT and Strasbourg.

GERMANY

Over the past 10 years there has been a rapid expansion in the number of institutions offering translation and/or interpreting courses, mostly at "Fachhochschule" level.

C.I.U.T.I. member universities[3]

Fachbereich Angewandte Sprach- und Kulturwissenschaft (GER), Studiengänge Diplom-Übersetzer und Diplom-Dolmetscher, Johannes-Gutenberg-Universität (Mainz), http://www.uni-mainz.de

Institut für Übersetzen und Dolmetschen (HD), Studiengänge Diplom-Übersetzer und Diplom-Dolmetscher, Universität Heidelberg, http://www.uni-heidelberg.de

Fachrichtung 8.6 "Angewandte Sprachwissenschaft (SB), sowie Übersetzen und Dolmetschen", Studiengänge Diplom-Übersetzer und Diplom-Dolmetscher, Universität des Saarlandes, http://www.uni-saarland.de

Institut für Angewandte Linguistik und Translatologie, Universität Leipzig, http://www.uni-leipzig.de

Other universities
Bachelor of Arts in International Communication and Translation, Universität Hildesheim, http://www.rz.uni-hildesheim.de

Humboldt-Universität Berlin, Philosophische Fakultät II, Kommission Lehre und Studium, Interkulturelle Fachkommunikation/Dolmetschen/Übersetzen, http://www.hu-berlin.de

Fachhochschulen
Fachhochschule Köln (K), Institut für Translation und Mehrsprachige Kommunikation, http://www.spr.fh-koeln.de/

Fachhochschule Magdeburg (MBG), Fachbereich Fachkommunikation, Studiengänge Diplom-Fachübersetzer (FH) und Diplom-Fachdolmetscher (FH), http://www.fachkommunikation.hs-magdeburg.de/

Fachhochschule München (FHM), Studiengang Übersetzen und Dolmetschen, http://www.fh-muenchen.de

The professional training programmes of interpreters at CIUTI member universities Heidelberg, Mainz-Germersheim and Leipzig have a largely identical structure with a basis of a four-semester training in translation and interpreting and a main course study of a further four semesters separating translation from interpreting. Graduation is through a diploma for translation and interpreting on a university level.

GREECE
For many years translator and interpreter training was provided by European Institutes specialising in this field. One of them (The Centre of Training for Translators and Interpreters) was transformed into the Department of Languages, Translation and Interpreting of the Ionian University (Corfu), http://www.uion.edu.gr.

This Department is the only university department which is in charge of interpreting. It is an autonomous department receiving 30 students every year.

ITALY
Full-degree courses in translation and interpreting are organised by the School of Modern Languages for Translators and Interpreters of the Universities of Trieste (http://www.sslmit.univ.trieste.it) and Bologna (the latter in Forlì, http://sslmit.unibo.it). Other universities have in the recent past organised one-year courses or have integrated other courses, for example the course in Diplo-

matic Studies of the University of Udine (in Gorizia, http://web.uniud.it/fali/), with courses in translation and even conference interpreting.

A number of private schools and municipally-founded schools offer three-year diploma courses, for example Scuola Superiore per Interpreti e Traduttori del Comune di Milano (http://www.ssit.it).

Forlì also holds courses in interpreting for the media.

THE NETHERLANDS

In the Netherlands there is only one typical School of Translation and Interpreting, the Vertaalacademie Maastricht of the Hogeschool Zuyd (http://www.hszuyd.nl) (formerly Faculteit Tolk-Vertaler of the Hogeschool Maastricht). The four-year course is divided into a foundation year (propedeuse) and a main phase of three years, as is normally the case in Dutch higher education. In the fourth year, students specialise in technical translation or technical writing or interpreting.

Recently the Ministry of Education has accredited certain non-subsidised private organisations that offer part-time higher education programmes (meeting certain requirements). Some of these schools have T&I training courses. One private institution (SIGV, Stichting Instituut van Gerechtstolken en -Vertalers, Utrecht) specialises in the training of legal translators and court interpreters, also on a part-time basis.

PORTUGAL

Six schools offer various degrees with interpreting in its title, usually combined with translation studies:

Universidade do Minho, http://www.uminho.pt

Universidade Autónoma de Lisboa, http://www.universidade-autonoma.pt

Instituto Superior de Assistentes e Intérpretes, http://www.isai.pt

Instituto Superior de Línguas e Administração, http://www.isla.pt

Instituto Politécnico de Leiria, http://www.implei.pt

Escola Poliglota (Lisboa)

However, only the one at the Universidade do Minho has received any recognition both from the professional bodies and from the large international institutional employers.

The contents of the interpreter training programmes are usually quite standard: consecutive and simultaneous interpretation. However, most courses do not make the distinction between conference, courtroom and community interpreting. There is no training whatsoever for sign language interpreting.

SPAIN

The Licenciatura en Traducción e Interpretación (a four-year degree in Translation and Interpreting) is offered at the present time in 18 different public and private universities in Spain. These 18 centres have created the Conferencia de Centros y Departamentos Universitarios de Traducción e Interpretación, an association which meets annually to discuss matters of interest to the field in Spain.

Alicante	Universidad de Alicante, www.ua.es
Castellón de la Plana	Universidad Jaume I, www.uji.es
Catalonia	Universitat Autònoma de Barcelona, www.uab.es
	Universitat Pompeu Fabra, www.upf.es
	Universitat de Vic, www.uvic.es
Granada	Universidad de Granada, www.ugr.es
Las Palmas	Universidad de Las Palmas de Gran Canaria, www.ulpgc.es
Madrid	Universidad Pontificia Comillas, www.upco.es
	Universidad Alfonso X el Sabio, www.uax.es
	Universidad Europea de Madrid, www.uem.es
Málaga	Universidad de Málaga, www.uma.es
Salamanca	Universidad de Salamanca, www.usal.es
Soria	Universidad de Valladolid, www.uva.es
Vigo	Universidade de Vigo, www.uvigo.es

Translation and Interpreting is a four-year degree, which is divided into two cycles of two years. Interpreting is studied in years three and/or four. Whereas a lot of universities limit the training in Interpreting to the 16 core credits required by the Ministry of Education, others offer additional optional credits in this field (in one case, Vic, 57) in an attempt to prepare students with the necessary skills for conference interpreting.

SWEDEN

Tolk- och översättarinstitutet (TÖI) at Stockholm University (http://www.tolk.su.se) has an overall responsibility for the training of translators and interpreters in Sweden. Most studies, both at university level and in vocational training courses, are under the supervision of TÖI, which also distributes the funding. Training courses are given at various language departments and other institutions all over Sweden. So far, most of them have been community interpreting courses. A one-year conference interpreting course is given at post-graduate level.

Vocational training of interpreters, mainly community interpreters, has been given at about 30 adult education centres and study organisations throughout the country.

UNITED KINGDOM
There are a few universities in the United Kingdom which offer undergraduate degrees in translating and/or interpreting and quite a number which offer a postgraduate qualification in this area. Each programme is very different in course content, approach, aims and range of languages offered.

Anyone wishing to be absolutely up-to-date with the courses offered at all British Universities and Colleges should consult UCAS (the Universities and Colleges Admissions Services for the UK) which provides a comprehensive guide on all undergraduate courses offered at British Higher Education institutions. UCAS is a central body which organises and administers the selection procedure for undergraduate entry to British Universities and Colleges and can be found at: http://www.ucas.ac.uk

Undergraduate courses in Interpreting and Translating
Heriot-Watt University (a CIUTI member institute): Degree of MA in Languages (Interpreting and Translating). This is a four-year course (includes one academic year abroad divided between two partner institutions which cover the two languages being studied by the student). This course includes Conference Interpreting (Simultaneous and Consecutive) as well as Liaison Interpreting. http://www.hw.ac.uk/prosp/ug/courses/lint.php

University of East Anglia: BA French and German Language with Interpreting and Translation. This is a four-year course (includes one year abroad). http://www.llt.uea.ac.uk

Postgraduate courses in Interpreting / Interpreting and Translating
Bath University (a CIUTI member institute): MA/Diploma in Interpreting and Translating. http://www.bath.ac.uk

Bradford University (a CIUTI member institute): MA/PgDip in Interpreting and Translating for International Business. MA/PgDip in Interpreting and Translating. http://www.brad.ac.uk

Heriot-Watt University (a CIUTI member institute): MSc/Diploma in Interpreting and Translating. MSc/Diploma in Arabic/English Translation and Interpreting. http://www.hw.ac.uk

Salford University: MA/Diploma for Advanced Studies in Translating and Interpreting. http://www.salford.ac.uk

Westminster University: Postgraduate Diploma in Conference Interpreting Techniques. Two terms full-time (intensive). Usually three or four active languages will be offered in any given year and up to eight passive languages. The languages offered vary according to demand. http://www.wmin.ac.uk

Leeds University: MA/PgDip in English-Arabic: Translation or Interpreting. http://www.leeds.ac.uk

1.6 Academic profile

The need for an academic profile of interpreter training is emphasised by a policy document issued in 1999 by the European Language Council's Thematic Network Project (TNP) on translation and interpreting, where it is recommended that "T&I training be recognised only as a university degree course with the academic underpinnings and research activities traditionally connected to such courses." The same TNP has also issued recommendations for a course profile for conference interpreting which apply to degrees in conference interpreting whose fundamental characteristics are Interpreting studies – one or two T/I modules incorporated into the curriculum of language courses are not considered – and the degrees are typically conferred after four or five years of university level study.

1.7 Translation as prerequisite

The rationale behind a model where the training of translators is seen as a prerequisite for interpreter training is expressed in the following statement by the TNP:

> Though both require the ability to transfer a text expressed in one language into another, in performance the two processes of translation and interpreting respectively draw upon fundamentally different aptitudes and skills. The execution of a written translation permits (long) reflection and the consultation of documents and auxiliary material, whereas all forms of interpreting presuppose that this has already taken place and exploit the interpreter's rapidity and spontaneity in conveying an immediately comprehensible text. A course

profile for interpreting would therefore include or presuppose a certain level of translation skills, and (…) part of the course profile for translation will be considered a prerequisite for a course in conference interpreting in undergraduate courses irrespective of whether the final degree is one of translation and/or interpreting.   (ELC 1999)

2.   Pedagogy and methodology of interpreter training

2.1 Organisation of classes

It is usually agreed that the number of students in interpreting classes should not be too high; eight to twelve students is often mentioned as optimal in order to give every student ample training time. It is also agreed that the number of teachers per class has to be higher than in traditional "lecture-based" education: ideally, in both conference and community interpreter training classes, two teachers per language pair should be present to ensure the highest quality possible. For financial reasons, this ideal cannot usually be upheld. Instead, many schools provide the students access to language labs where interpreting can be trained individually, or they expect the students to train in groups without the supervision of a teacher.

2.2 Subjects taught: Interpreting skills

In conference interpreting courses, it is considered important to start with consecutive interpreting. Simultaneous interpreting is introduced only when the students master consecutive interpreting. The rationale is that students must learn to listen to the meaning of the utterance, and not translate the words, as it were, that the speaker is using. The theoretical foundation for this is obviously the interpretation theory of the "Paris school", whose main proponents are Danica Seleskovitch and Marianne Lederer, ESIT (École Supérieure d'Interprètes et de Traducteurs). The main idea behind this theory is that interpreting is based on meaning (Fr. "*sens*"), not on words or linguistic structures, and it has therefore become known as the "*théorie du sens*".[4]

2.3 Example: European Master's in Conference Interpreting

The European Master's in Conference Interpreting is a Master's-type university programme launched by the European Commission, first as a pilot project in 1997 and subsequently as a regular training programme. The main motivation for the initiative was the shortage of highly qualified conference interpreters and the realisation that neither the European Commission's Joint Interpreter and Conference Service (JICS) nor the university-level institutions in the member states had the potential to meet existing and future demand, particularly for language combinations which include less widely used and less-taught languages. Eight universities took part in the pilot project, setting up aims and a core curriculum for the training programme. European Master's programmes are now being set up at an increasing number of universities in several countries.

The *core curriculum* covers the following essential elements:

> *Theory of interpretation:* Introduction to theoretical aspects of interpretation and research findings which have a bearing on interpretation.

> *Practice of interpretation:* Communication skills, voice coaching, public speaking, conference preparation techniques, professional ethics, conference procedures, work practices and conditions.

> *Consecutive interpretation:* Training in consecutive interpreting skills includes a variety of exercises, such as content analysis and memory exercises, consecutive interpretation without notes, summarisation, sight translation and note-taking techniques, and cover texts from a diverse range of subject areas, written in a variety of styles and registers.

> *Simultaneous interpretation:* Training in simultaneous interpreting will essentially build on the skills used to practise consecutive interpretation. Additional components include booth techniques and team interaction.

> *European Union and international organisations:* The aim of this course is to introduce students to these institutions, their institutional processes and procedures.

2.4 Course structure and workload

The course is designed as a full-time study programme and corresponds to 60 credits (i.e. the equivalent of one year of full-time study) under the European Credit Transfer System (ECTS).

2.4.1 *Prerequisites for admission*
Applicants must:

- hold a recognised University degree or equivalent (in any subject)

- have an excellent command of their mother tongue (A language) over a wide range of topics and registers
- have an in-depth knowledge of their working languages (B and C)
- have a good overall knowledge of international affairs and be well-informed of the economic, social and cultural background of the countries in which their working languages are used.

In addition, candidates will be expected to have

- a good capacity for analysis and synthesis
- good communication skills
- flexibility, good powers of concentration and the ability to work under pressure.

2.4.1.1 *Admission.* Applicants who fulfil the formal requirements will be given an aptitude test. The aim of this test is to verify competence in the aforementioned areas and to assess the applicants' suitability for the programme.
The test includes:

- the oral reproduction of short, structured speeches from the candidate's B and/or C languages into A, and, where appropriate, from A into B
- a general knowledge test
- an interview with the candidate.

Additionally, the test may include:

- sight translation
- a brief oral presentation by the candidates on a subject chosen by the panel of examiners
- written tests.

2.4.1.2 *Assessment.* At the final examinations the students will be assessed in both consecutive and simultaneous modes of interpreting. The examinations are assessed by a panel of examiners which is composed of a majority of experienced interpreters. The panel normally includes representatives of the European Institutions (European Commission, European Parliament), other international organisations and other member institutions of the consortium.
Some participating universities also organise intermediate examinations at the end of the first term.

2.5 Evaluation of training programmes

The training programmes for conference interpreters are continuously assessed by AIIC, the international organisation of conference interpreters. AIIC uses a system of stars to mark the compliance of training programmes with the quality criteria set by AIIC. The lowest mark is one star and the highest three stars.

The AIIC Training Committee has drawn up a list of ten points which set out its basic training criteria:

1. Applicants to courses in Conference Interpretation should have a university degree (three years of higher education) or equivalent training.
2. An oral selection process is essential for proper assessment of the general knowledge and aptitude for interpretation of prospective candidates.
   a. In the case of a course lasting for one academic year, the selection process should take place before the beginning of the course.
   b. In the case of those courses lasting for more than one academic year, the selection process should take place preferably before the beginning of the course, or else before the course is one-third complete.
3. The course syllabus and curriculum, as well as language combinations offered, should reflect market requirements.
4. Training in both consecutive and simultaneous interpretation should be included in the programme.
5. The syllabus shall include professional ethics and practice.
6. The syllabus for consecutive and simultaneous interpretation should be designed, directed and taught by practising conference interpreters, preferably AIIC members.
7. The target language of any given course on the syllabus should be the corresponding tutor's A language.
8. At the final examination, failure to pass any one of the simultaneous or consecutive interpretation tests should be eliminatory. In the event of a resit, all parts of the final examination should be attempted.
9. The Diploma Examining Board should be made up of tutors having taught on the course and external examiners who are practising conference interpreters, preferably AIIC members. They should have the right to vote.
10. The Conference Interpreter's Diploma must clearly state the language combination of the diplomate: i.e. which are the active and which are the passive languages for which the Diploma has been awarded (AIIC 2000).

2.5.1 Conference interpreting training courses by country in order of compliance with the AIIC criteria

The list in Table 2 only shows courses which meet some (*), most (**), all or almost all (***) of the training criteria set out by AIIC.

The list is updated on the basis of information received by the Training Committee of AIIC in the form, *inter alia*, of replies to a questionnaire, course prospectuses, as well as any information students, graduates, colleagues, teachers and employers of interpreters may communicate to AIIC (AIIC 2000).

2.6 Accreditation and testing of interpreters

Accreditation or certification of interpreters is conducted in some countries in Europe, in Australia and in North America. The most sophisticated system is probably the one in Australia, where the National Accreditation Authority for Translators and Interpreters (NAATI) approves training programmes if they comply with NAATI standards. NAATI has the following levels of interpreter standards: Paraprofessional Interpreter, Interpreter, Conference Interpreter and Advanced Conference Interpreter (Senior).

2.6.1 Paraprofessional Interpreter

This is a paraprofessional level and represents a level of competence in interpreting and translation for the purpose of general conversations. Paraprofessional Interpreters generally undertake the interpretation of non-specialist dialogues. Practitioners at this level are expected to proceed to the professional levels of accreditation.

2.6.2 Interpreter

This is the first professional level and represents the minimum level of competence for professional interpreting. Interpreters at this level are capable of interpreting across a wide range of subjects involving dialogues at specialist consultations. They are capable of interpreting presentations in the consecutive mode. Their specialisations may include banking, the law, health, and social and community services.

2.6.3 Conference Interpreter

This is the advanced professional level and represents the competence to handle complex/technical/sophisticated interpreting. Conference Interpreters practise both consecutive and simultaneous interpreting in diverse situations, including at conferences, high level negotiations, and court proceedings. Conference In-

Table 2.

Country	Meeting criteria	Institution	Compliance with AIIC criteria
Australia	**	Department of Asian Languages and Studies, University of Queensland, Brisbane. http://www.uq.edu.au/ALS	English-Japanese both ways only. MA degree plus NAATI accreditation recognised as being equivalent to professional qualifications.
Austria	*	Institut für Übersetzen und Dolmetschen, Universität Wien. http://www.univie.ac.at/transvienna	Regulations make it impossible to comply with some of the criteria. Primarily for German mother tongue. Classification valid for English-French-German.
	*	Institut für Theoretische und Angewandte Translationswissenschaft, Karl-Franzens-Universität Graz. http://www-gewi.kfunigraz.ac.at/uedo	Regulations make it impossible to comply with some of the criteria. Primarily for German mother tongue.
Belgium	*	Hoger Instituut voor Vertalers en Tolken, Antwerpen. http://www.ha.be/tolken/tolken.html	Regulations make it impossible to comply with some of the criteria. Solely for Dutch mother tongue.
	*	Institut Supérieur de Traducteurs et d'Interprètes, Bruxelles. http://www.technopol.be/isti	Regulations make it impossible to comply with some of the criteria. Mainly for French mother tongue.
	*	Ecole d'interprètes internationaux, Université de Mons. http://www.umh.ac.be/~eii/	Regulations make it impossible to comply with some of the criteria. Mainly for French mother tongue.
Cameroon	**	Advanced School of Translators and Interpreters, Buea. http://uycdc.uninet.cm/ed_sup/External/universities/buea/frame.html	English-French both ways only.
Denmark	***	Center for Konferencetolkning, Frederiksberg (Copenhagen Business School). http://www.cbs.dk	Mainly for Danish mother tongue. Training focuses on the needs of the European Union.
Finland	**	Center for Translation and Interpreting, University of Turku. http://www.konftulk.utu.fi/	
France	***	ESIT, Université Paris III. http://www.univ-paris3.fr/esit	
	**	ISIT, Paris. http://www.icp.fr/html/c-en-re.htm#isi	

Table 2. (*continued*)

Country	Meeting criteria	Institution	Compliance with AIIC criteria
Germany	*	Johannes Gutenberg-Universität Mainz, Fachbereich für Angewandte Sprach- und Kulturwissenschaft Germersheim. http://www.fask.uni-mainz.de	Regulations make it impossible to comply with some of the criteria. Mainly for German mother tongue.
	*	Institut für Übersetzen und Dolmetschen der Universität Heidelberg. http://www.iued.uni-heidelberg.de	Regulations make it impossible to comply with some of the criteria. Mainly for German mother tongue.
	*	Sprachen- und Dolmetscher Institut München. http://www.sdi-muenchen.de	Non-graduate training. Mainly for German mother tongue.
Israel	**	Bar Ilan University Department of Translation and Interpretation, Ramat Gan. http://www.biu.ac.il/HU/tr	Mainly for Hebrew mother tongue.
Italy	*	Scuola Superiore de Lingue Moderne per Interpreti e Traduttori, Università di Trieste. http://www.sslmit.univ.trieste.it	Regulations make it impossible to comply with some of the criteria. Mainly for Italian mother tongue.
	*	Scuola Superiore per Interpreti e Traduttori del Comune di Milano. http://www.ssit.archivio.it	Mainly for Italian mother tongue.
Korea	*	Hankuk University of Foreign Studies, Seoul. http://eng.hufs.ac.kr	For Korean mother tongue.
Lebanon	***	Ecole de Traducteurs et d'Interprètes de Beyrouth, Université St. Joseph, Beirut. http://www.usj.edu.lb/form/lshu/flsh/iltr/etib/accueil.htm	Solely for students having Arabic mother tongue plus English and French (with requirement also to be able to interpret from Arabic into one of these two).
Portugal	***	Instituto de Letras e Ciências Humanas, Universidade do Minho, Braga. http://www.ilch.uminho.pt	Mainly for Portuguese mother tongue. Training focuses on the needs of the European Union.
Spain	**	Universidad de la Laguna, Tenerife. http://www.ull.es/master/mic	

Table 2. (*continued*)

Country	Meeting criteria	Institution	Compliance with AIIC criteria
Sweden	***	Tolk- och Översättarinstitutet, Stockholms Universitet. http://www.tolk.su.se	
Switzerland	***	Ecole de traduction et d'interprétation de l'Université de Genève. http://www.unige.ch/eti	
	*	Dolmetscherschule Zürich. http://www.doz.ch	Primarily for German mother tongue.
Taiwan	**	Graduate Institute of Translation and Interpretation Studies (GITIS), Fu Jen University, Taipei. http://www.fju.edu.tw/enghtm/fg/fg296.htm	English–Chinese (Mandarin) or Japanese-English both ways.
United Kingdom	**	Postgraduate Diploma in Conference Interpreting Techniques, University of Westminster, London. http://www.wmin.ac.uk/dal/prolang.htm	
United States	**	Monterey Institute of International Studies, Monterey CA. http://www.miis.edu	
	**	Division of Translation and Interpretation, Georgetown University, Washington, DC. http://georgetown.edu/departments/translation/	

(Source: AIIC 2000)

terpreters operate at levels compatible with recognised international standards and may choose to specialise in certain areas.

2.6.4   Conference Interpreter (Senior)

Practitioners at this senior level are Conference Interpreters with a level of excellence in their field, recognised through demonstrated extensive experience and leadership.

NAATI accreditation may be obtained in three ways:

- by passing a NAATI test;
- by completing successfully a course of studies at an Australian institution approved by NAATI;
- by providing evidence of specialised qualifications in interpreting/translating obtained from a recognised training institution overseas, or membership in a recognised international professional association.

Currently NAATI has approved interpreter training courses at 12 institutions, the majority on the paraprofessional level, leading to the National Diploma of Interpreting.

3.   Future prospects of interpreting

3.1   The impact of new technologies

3.1.1   Remote interpreting

Remote interpreting is often envisaged as a cost effective way of breaking the language barrier in international and intercultural communication. Telephone interpreting has been used in various settings for a long time, e.g. in health care and legal institutions, in many countries. Several telephone companies have set up telephone interpreting units to serve both public service and business interests, nationally as well as internationally. One example is the AT&T Language Line, whose interpreters were the target of a study by Oviatt and Cohen (1992).

Videophone interpreting for deaf and hard-of-hearing persons is used in some countries. A person who does not know sign language can communicate with a deaf person via an interpreter, who connects to the deaf person with the use of a special telephone with a video monitor.

Standard	Meaning	Related tasks
Paraprofessional Interpreter from 1.1.95, awarded in a very limited range of languages	This represents a level of competence in interpreting for the purpose of general conversations, generally in the form of non-specialist dialogues.	– interpreting in general conversations – interpreting in situations where specialised terminology or more sophisticated conceptual information is not required – interpreting in situations where a depth of linguistic ability is not required
Interpreter	This represents the minimum level of competence for professional interpreting or translating. It may be regarded as the Australian professional standard. Interpreters are capable of interpreting across a wide range of subjects involving dialogues at specialist consultations. They are also capable of interpreting presentations by the consecutive mode.	– interpreting in both language directions for a wide range of subject areas usually involving specialist consultations with other professionals, e.g. doctor/patient, solicitor/client, bank manager/client, court interpreting – interpreting in situations where some depth of linguistic ability in both languages is necessary
Conference Interpreter	This represents the advanced professional level and a level of competence sufficient to handle complex, technical and sophisticated interpreting and translation. Conference interpreters practise both consecutive and simultaneous interpreting in diverse situations including at conferences, high level negotiations, and court proceedings. Conference interpreters operate at levels compatible with recognised international standards.	– tasks involving international conferences, diplomatic missions, trade negotiations, and other high level negotiations – tasks involving complex court proceedings – interpreting in situations where a depth of linguistic ability in both languages is required
Conference Interpreter (Senior)	This is the highest level of NAATI accreditation and reflects both competence and experience. It represents an international standard together with demonstrated extensive experience and leadership.	– interpreting tasks, as for Conference Interpreters – tasks involving the organisation of international conferences – providing advice for interpreting services within and outside Australia

Figure 3. NAATI standards for interpreting

Mouzourakis (1996) has an elaborate classification of videoconferencing where interpreting may be conducted:

- *Teleconferencing* is any form of communication, comprising at least an audio stream, between spatially distant participants in a meeting.
- *Audioconferencing* refers to sound-only teleconferencing, as for instance in a conventional conference hall.
- *Videoconferencing* is a special case of teleconferencing involving a video stream. It is an example of a multimedia application, i.e. one involving at least two different media, sound and image, in digital form. The term videoconferencing includes different variants such as:
  - *Videophony*: transmission of a facial image in conjunction with a telephone call;[5]
  - *Whiteboarding*: the electronic exchange and/or common editing of documents on two or more computers;
  - *Desktop videoconferencing*: transmission of images captured by a camera attached to PCs, with or without whiteboarding.
- *Studio or room videoconferencing* takes place when two or more studios are linked together by video and audio.
- *Multilingual videoconferencing* is room videoconferencing in more than one language with interpretation.
- *Remote interpretation* is simultaneous interpretation where the interpreter is not in the same room as the speaker or his/her audience, or neither (Mouzourakis 1996: 22–23).

Videophone interpreting eliminates some of the problems with telephone interpreting, as all parties can see each other and can monitor also the "silent" communication, important for the interpreter. The technology must however be further refined to eliminate irritating delays, echoes, etc.

Remote interpreting puts higher demands on the interpreters, and because of that, only the best interpreters should be allowed to work remotely. Unfortunately, in these times of economic decline, a disastrous combination has emerged: to save money many service providers require both telephone interpreting and the least expensive service, i.e. the least competent interpreter (Niska 1999).

To conclude: remote interpreting can be a good solution in the future, provided that only the most competent interpreters are used for this type of interpreting. The training institutions should offer training in remote interpreting, as this is an area that is becoming more and more important.

3.1.2   *Remote-simultaneous interpreting*

A very interesting and seemingly viable way of rationalising interpreting services without causing quality loss has recently been tried in the United States (Hornberger et al. 1996; RSI 1998). A new language service was developed in which interpreters are trained in the skills of simultaneous interpreting commonly used at international conferences. The interpreters are linked, by means of standard communication wires, from a remote site to headsets worn by the clinician and patient. The service is called "remote-simultaneous interpretation" (RSI), to contrast it with the traditional method of an interpreter being physically present at the interview and interpreting consecutively, which the researchers call "proximate-consecutive interpretation."

According to Hornberger et al., mothers and physicians significantly preferred the remote-simultaneous service to the usual consecutive interpretation service. Interpreters stated that they thought mothers and physicians better understood each other using the remote-simultaneous service, although the interpreters preferred to work with the proximate-consecutive service.

In later follow-up studies, even the interpreters were enthusiastic about the new technology. One important reason for the interpreters' satisfaction with the new technology is probably that they were given extensive training in simultaneous interpreting. Thereby they increased their professional abilities, which broadened their potential marketable skills.

3.2   New talents for new situations: Immigration, increased international mobility

3.2.1   *Community interpreting*

Community interpreting, in the form of linguistic assistance in communication with people in ethnic communities, has been around for thousands of years. Mostly this work has been done without any remuneration or with only a very modest remuneration. This historical combination of trivial, everyday activity and giving humanitarian linguistic help to fellow community members has been an obstacle in the contemporary efforts of professionalising community interpreting. International migration of labour and refugees has increased the need for interpreting in public institutions in many countries where there is no tradition of organised interpreter services for immigrants.

There are high demands on the community interpreter's competence: not only linguistic and educational but also socio-cultural and psychological, concerning setting, status of participants, purpose of encounter, societal norms and rules regarding interpreter behaviour, professional ethics, etc. At the same time, the interpreters' labour market is highly influenced by the overall economic situation, fluctuation in migration, etc. The advent of new technology, e.g. remote interpreting, is challenging established "truths" about interpreting quality. There is a need to set up flexible training programmes that take into account all of these factors and are able to meet the training needs of today and tomorrow.

Migration in the form of going abroad to work has always existed, and the globalisation and internationalisation of our societies, not to mention the influx of refugees, will result in growing population groups which do not master the official language(s) of the host country. This means that the need for community interpreters will continue to grow. Not necessarily at once in all countries, all regions, or all immigrant languages, but one of the challenges for training institutions is to build up a flexible organisation for setting up courses once the need arises.

Taking into account the variations in language proficiency of the prospective community interpreting students, the training course should allow for extra language support if needed, flexible course lengths depending on the students' educational background, etc. Does the University have this flexibility or would it be better to choose another form of training? Adult education centres, open university ...? How long is the planning time for a new training course in a language which has not been given before? If it is more than six weeks, it may be too long!

Ideally, an interpreting course should consist of about 50% theory and 50% practice. Does the institution have its own teachers for a course in community interpreting? If not, do we know where to find those teachers? How do we educate our own staff so they can teach interpreting courses?

Community interpreter training is not a matter solely for language departments. A good and intensive co-operation with other departments, e.g. Law, Economics, Psychology, is very valuable, and so is the ability to find guest lecturers from relevant professions which the students will meet when they go out to interpret: doctors, policemen, labour union representatives, etc.

As an example, the following objectives of training have been adopted by the Institute for Interpretation and Translation Studies, Stockholm:

The objectives of interpreter training at adult education centres and voluntary educational associations are:

– to develop the community interpreters' language proficiency and knowledge of terminology in Swedish and in their other interpreted language,

based on both the language milieu from which the immigrants to Sweden come and the one in which they now live;
- to provide training in interpretation technique as well as knowledge of the ethical and psychological demands of interpreting;
- to provide factual information in relevant fields;
- to provide a good understanding of social, political, cultural and labour affairs in the immigrants' native country and in Sweden.

3.2.2   Public Service and Business Interpreting

In 1999 the European Language Council's TNP (Thematic Network Project) on translation (ELC 1999) and interpreting adopted recommendations concerning "Public Service and Business Interpreting" (PSBI). These are mainly recommendations for "traditional" community/public service interpreting courses. The rationale behind the recommended courses in Public Service and Business Interpreting is the hope that they will "contribute to giving all types of PSBI (business interpreting, court interpreting, etc.) equal status and attention, and that the level of PSBI as a whole will be raised, so that PSBI will obtain a higher level of professionalism and prestige."

Summary of recommendations for PSBI:

It is recommended that efforts be made to ensure the quality and professionalisation of PSBI activities either by setting up full degree courses or by offering separate modules within the framework of continuing education. The content of the courses and the modules should reflect the above-mentioned philosophy and principles and, in every respect, be of the highest possible quality. These quality standards also apply to teaching methods and staff.

In either case, entrance requirements and tests upon entry as well as final examinations or assessments followed by certification procedures are strongly recommended.

It is recommended that user groups (i.e. various institutions, hospitals, courts, etc.) and the interpreters themselves are informed of – and thus, hopefully, convinced of – the importance of being able to offer PSBI assistance of the highest possible quality.

It is recommended that national governments/authorities support the developments of the sufficient and necessary PSBI courses to secure high-quality interpreting services for everyone (native and non-native speakers) in these vital areas of community life.

In order for these recommendations to be put into practice throughout the European Union, it is recommended that the European Commission supports (financially and otherwise) the development of the sufficient and necessary courses in all EU Countries, e.g. by means of CDA initiatives and affirmative action through awareness-raising campaigns.

(TNP: Course Profile Recommendations; see ELC 1999)

3.2.3   Example: BA in community interpreting

The *Fachhochschule Magdeburg-Stendal*, Magdeburg, Germany, offers a BA in public service, court and medical interpreting (Fachdolmetschen bei Behörden, Gerichten und im Gesundheitswesen), http://www.fachkommunikation. hs-magdeburg.de/index/gkbdolm.htm. In addition, the School offers continuing education in court interpreting, leading to state certification.

The BA programme has a duration of seven semesters, and the students can choose between two specialisations: court or medical interpreting. Contrary to general practice in Germany, the applicants have to pass an entrance test (*Eignungsprüfung* = aptitude test) to be admitted to the course. The programme is open both to German and foreign students. Foreign students must have proof of satisfactory knowledge of German.

Students must master two languages in addition to their mother tongue. The following language combinations are possible: German–English–Russian, German–English–French, German–English–Spanish. Other languages can be added on demand.

The goal of the training programme is to give the students a scientifically based and principally practice-oriented education for working as interpreters in public service institutions, courts and health services. The programme leads to a Bachelor in interpreting with the chosen specialisation (court or medical).

The syllabus includes: Theoretical and practical problems of interpreting and translation, interpreting at local authorities, in court, in hospital, translation of general texts, translation of documents, terminology work, rhetoric, psychology, basics of medicine or law, cultural knowledge, introduction to informatics, data banks and information research. The students have two periods of study abroad, in the fifth and sixth semester, at some partner university.

During the course of the programme, students have several weeks of practice in various institutions, according to their choice of specialisation, for example: police, local government, civil and criminal courts, medical service providers (hospitals, physicians, etc.).

3.3   Conclusion

In the framework of this chapter it has only been possible to give a general and rather sketchy view of the international interpreter training scene, with an emphasis on Europe. It is interesting to note the difference in traditions, especially between the interpreting schools on the European continent and the training institutions in the UK and Scandinavia. What is striking, however, is how fast at present the universities are revising their courses and training programmes and developing new ones. The co-operation within the European Language Council and Socrates, Leonardo da Vinci and other EU programmes has been an important factor in this process. CIUTI and EST, the European Society for Translation Studies, and regional networks have also played an important role in promoting the birth and spreading of new ideas.

Training institutions must be prepared for changes in the labour market of interpreters. In public service settings, the education of interpreters – who often work in highly stressful situations and in languages where it is diffi-cult to find competent teachers, relevant course material and even qualified participants – puts high demands on the institutions. This calls for an open and unprejudiced approach, including the use of new and flexible organisa-tional models, requiring cooperation between academic and non-academic training institutions, as well as between training institutions and the users of interpreters' services.

Notes

1. I will be using the term "interpreting school" for any academic institution which offers interpreter training, regardless of the name or administrative status of the institution.

2. Other exceptions are universities giving courses for interpreters for the Deaf; in this chapter I will only deal with interpreting between spoken languages.

3. Conférence Internationale des Instituts Universitaires de Traducteurs et Interprètes.

4. It has nowadays been renamed "*La théorie interprétative de la traduction*", the interpreta-tive theory of translation.

5. The term *videotelephony* seems to be in use elsewhere.

References

AIIC (2000). *Conference interpreting training courses by country in order of compliance with the AIIC criteria.* http://www.aiic.net/en/tips/students/students9.htm
Berezhkov, V. M. (1994). *At Stalin's Side: His Interpreter's Memoirs from the October Revolution to the Fall of the Dictator's Empire.* New York: Birch Lane Press.
Bowen, D. & Bowen, M. (1985). "The Nuremberg Trials – Communication through Translation". *Meta, 30*(1), 74–77.

ELC (1999). *Thematic Network Project in the Area of Languages. Project Results and Outcomes. Studies and reports produced by the various Scientific Committees.*

Harris, B. (1997). *Translation and Interpreting Schools.* Language International World Directory, Vol. 2. Amsterdam and Philadelphia: John Benjamins.

Harris, B. (2002). "Ernest Satow's early career as Diplomatic Interpreter". *Diplomacy & Statecraft, 13*(2).

Horn, T. & Krakel, D. (Designer). (1979). *Life of Tom Horn, Government Scout and Interpreter.* Norman: University of Oklahoma Press.

Hornberger, J. C., Gibson Jr., C. D., Wood, W., Dequeldre, C., Corso, I., Palla, B., & Bloch, D. A. (1996). "Eliminating language barriers for non-English-speaking patients." *Medical Care,* August 1996, *34*(8), 845–856.

Mouzourakis, P. (1996). "Videoconferencing: Techniques and challenges." *Interpreting. International journal of research and practice in interpreting, 1*(1), 21–38.

Niska, H. (Coord.). (1999). "Quality issues in remote interpreting." In A. Á. Lugrís & A. F. Ocampo (Eds.), *Anovar/anosar: estudios de traducción e interpretacion* (pp. 109–121). Vigo: Servicio de Publicacións da Universidade de Vigo.

Oviatt, S. L. & Cohen, P. R. (1992). "Spoken language in interpreted telephone dialogues". *Computer Speech and Language, 6,* 277–302.

Palazchenko, P. (1997). *My Years With Gorbachev and Shevardnadze: The Memoir of a Soviet Interpreter.* Philadelphia: Pennsylvania State University Press.

Pym, A. (1999). *List of Translator-Training Institutions by Country.* Compilation by M. Caminade & A. Pym. http://www.ice.urv.es/trans/future/tti/tti.htm

Pym, A. (2000). *Training Translators and European Unification: A Model of the Market.* Version 2.1 (April 2000). http://europa.eu.int/comm/translation/theory/lectures/2000_tp_pym.pdf

RSI (1998). *Remote Simultaneous Interpretation Project at Santa Clara Valley Medical Center. Summary Administrative Report. January 15, 1998.* Stanford University School of Medicine, Department of Health Research and Policy. 3 pp + 4 appendixes.

PART II

Pedagogical strategies

Chapter 3

Minding the process, improving the product
Alternatives to traditional translator training

María González Davies

1. Introduction

> Setting a goal is one thing; finding concrete means of reaching it is another
> matter altogether.   (Delisle 1988:40)

Much has been written about the process and product of translation, but
little about class dynamics. The literature on translator training seems to lean
towards a description of what happens in translation but not of what happens
in the classroom. An approach which includes both issues is needed (González
Davies 2004).

Teaching techniques in second and foreign language teaching have changed
since the pedagogical debate which led to the Communicative Approach in the
70s and 80s (Candlin 1978; Brumfit & Johnson 1979). But has translator training changed? How many university courses are there to train translation teachers? Are all translation teachers familiar with the main existing pedagogical
approaches and basic principles?

Many questions are awaiting an answer both on what should be taught, the
syllabus, and on how this should be done, the teaching method. In a university environment, should we plan a professionally- or an academically-oriented
syllabus? Should training be similar for undergraduates and for postgraduates?
Who should train our students, a teacher who translates or a translator who
teaches? Should we evaluate from a pedagogical or a professional standpoint?
What is really important is the fact that we cannot fully answer these questions without more empirical research and reflection on what goes on in the
translation classroom.

This chapter presents a communicative and interactive approach to translator training and suggests that there is a need to explore new ways to train

effectively and to share teaching ideas, as well as a need for more experimental research. Present trends in both teaching and Translation Studies will be covered in this chapter, for "To build the competence we want in our students we have to design precise pedagogical tools – tools for particular purposes that will yield specific desired effects" (Shreve, in Kiraly 1995:xiv).

2. Can translation be taught?

The answer to the question "Can translation be taught?" will depend, to a great extent, on our beliefs about translation and about learning. Bearing in mind the practical purposes of pedagogy, I present translation to the students as *communication, an interdisciplinary process of linguistic mediation to which constant decision-making is inherent.* As to learning, here it is taken as *a global experience, that is, one that includes the participants' emotions and purposes as well as their mental activity.*

Unfortunately, there is some distance separating the three people who could most help students of translation: teacher, theorist and translator. It may not be possible to teach creativity and inspiration, but a systematisation of the translation experience and a reflection on theoretical readings can improve the global quality of students' translations. Positions vary from those who believe a translator is born and those who believe translators are made: students are either "innate" translators or "non-innate" translators.[1] I would subscribe to the following:

> Ideally, translators should combine their natural talent with acquired skill. The answer to anyone who is sceptical about the formal teaching of translation is twofold: students with a gift for translation invariably find it useful in building their native talent into a fully developed proficiency; students without a gift for translation invariably acquire some degree of proficiency.
>
> (Hervey et al. 1995:5)

I would like to explore alternatives to the traditional teacher- and writing-centred translation class, alternatives which attempt to reconcile the positions mentioned above. A real need for steps to be taken in this direction is repeatedly and clearly implied by the many Conference papers on translator training. There may not exist a single final methodology to train translators, but there are approaches to teaching which enable the students to become more involved in what they are doing and, thus, understand better the whole learning process. The following reflections point in this direction.

2.1   Should training be similar for undergraduates and postgraduates?

Books on translator training are mostly addressed to mature students, either in postgraduate courses or carrying out academic research, or to professional translators. Training at the undergraduate level has received little attention.[2] Postgraduate students usually have a more developed personal and professional background than undergraduate students. Pedagogical research, principles and material cannot, therefore, be presented in the same manner for both levels, vaguely hoping that the more inexperienced students will "catch on" to the intricacies of translation at some unclear stage of their training or, as is sometimes argued, when they go out into the "real world". When the focus is on the undergraduate student, pedagogical techniques should take into account several variables: age, maturity and world experience, the educational background of the new generations, their expectations, and the "myths" they hold about translation and Translation Studies. Two groups of translation practitioners have been described: on the one hand, students of translation and "amateur" translators, and, on the other, professionals and bilinguals (Lörscher 1992: 107; Delisle 1988: 19) with aptitudes for translation. This distinction is relevant to the establishment of a methodological basis for translator training because it will determine the students' capacity to mediate at each stage and, consequently, will shape the curriculum.

It follows that a number of the assigned activities should be pedagogic, enhancing skills aimed at preparing students for carrying out a more complex translation performance, whereas others should be professional or "real life", that is, tasks students could easily encounter in their future professional life (Nunan 1989: 40). Examples of the latter are peer editing, translating with the help of parallel texts which the students are required to hand in with their assignment, exchanging Internet addresses found to solve specific problems, glossary building from the texts used in the classroom to complement published material, assignments based on "real life" tasks such as asking students to work on a translation following the terms of a Literary Translation Prize, or giving their translations to a professional in the specialised field for assessment (see Section 2.3).

From this perspective, therefore, translation classes should adapt to the students and encompass a variety of pedagogical approaches, laying the emphasis on pedagogic or on professional activities depending on whether the sessions are aimed at undergraduates, postgraduates, or professional translators.

2.2 Pedagogy studies in translator training: Class dynamics and interaction

At its best, translation is taught according to views on the act of translating. However, the fact that translation is being *taught* is often forgotten; that is, class dynamics and pedagogical studies are considered only briefly in the literature – if at all. Because as teachers we move in a pedagogical as well as a translational environment, it seems logical that both disciplines and the research carried out in them should form the framework of our approach to translator training.

For many years so-called traditional translation classes[3] have usually been teacher- and text-centred as well as writing-based, with little or no connection between the different sessions, where the aim was to produce an ideal model translation sanctioned by the teacher. As Kiraly (1995: 11) says: "There has been little or no consideration of learning environment, student-teacher roles, scope and appropriateness of teaching techniques, co-ordination or goal-oriented curricula, or evaluation of curriculum and instructor." Traditional translation classes seem to lack both pedagogical guidelines and a motivating component. On the contrary, in an interactive context, the teacher will take the part of informer, guide, counsellor and evaluator instead of acting as the sole problem-solver or, as Kiraly puts it "the guardian of translatory truth – keeper of the correct translation" (1995: 99).

Moreover, student-centred classes will favour interaction and will provide a stimulus for learner autonomy. In this setting the passive and silent translation student becomes an active participant in classes where pair and group work are carried out. Establishing different grouping possibilities is essential in order to move towards interactive classes and the creation of a positive and co-operative working atmosphere where learning is experiential and negotiated. It is important, however, to emphasise that this does not mean that individual work and reflection are left aside. Discussion about the source language or the target language, or about the cultural components embedded in a text, and problem-solving tasks are at the basis of the activities. An example of the latter could be a "coinage activity" in which students are asked to make up a word for objects or concepts which do not exist (yet!). For "an object to scratch your toes", my students have suggested a "toescratcher" or a "happytoeser". They then make a list of the strategies they have used to invent the word, pool their lists with those of other students and use it when translating word play.

Non-verbal activities combined with verbal ones can also be included in classes to sensitise students towards the non-linguistic features in a text and to promote discussion about transference according to culture-specific con-ventions and the translator's approach (Nord 1997a). In the class this can be practised with a sequence such as reading or describing a text, visualising it, drawing it and then comparing the students' interpretations of it. A good example of this can be found in Alan Duff's book *The Third Language* (1981:10) where the same landscape painted by two artists, one British and the other Chinese, is reproduced. The resulting paintings are quite different in a way that can be clearly related to culture-specific interpretations of the world.

2.3 Experiential learning and negotiation: Respecting teacher and learner styles

Classrooms are sometimes considered by theorists and professionals as artificial settings, and most teachers would agree. However, as things stand at present, it is not so much a question of demanding a return to the apprenticeship system or to unplanned "in-house on-the-job training" (Gile 1995:8), comparable to asking medical students or future teachers to learn at a hospital or school with no parallel formal training, as a question of optimising the classroom setting. I would propose the following:

1. Adapt classroom organisation by transforming the classroom into a discussion forum and hands-on workshop.
2. Establish contact with the outside world by means of projects which involve professional translators, bilinguals with an aptitude for translation and professionals from the different fields of specialisation (corresponding to the texts to be translated).
3. Design syllabuses with specific aims that have been thought about beforehand and sequence the material accordingly.
4. Favour an adequate learning environment which will enhance students' potential and respect different learning styles as much as possible.
5. Include as many real life situations as possible so that the students have the chance "to live", however slightly, in the professional world.

Research in language teaching lends support to the notion that learning is best enhanced when it is negotiated and experiential, with the students taking an active role in the process (Chaudron 1988; Gardner & Lambert 1972; Holec 1979; Legutke & Thomas 1991; Nunan 1988). This was the principle underlying a pilot study carried out at the *Facultat de Ciències Humanes, Traducció i Documentació* (Universitat de Vic, Spain) with the aim of bridging the gap between the undergraduate student and the professional world. In this study my students of medical translation were put in direct contact with the potential demands of potential clients, as well as made directly responsible for their work with the teacher acting as counsellor but not as problem-solver: Students were required to hand in a translation to be assessed for acceptance not only by the teacher but also by medical specialists (González Davies 1998).

A pedagogical approach that draws ideas from translation theory and practice, on the one hand, and from recent trends in teaching, on the other, can offer more efficient translator training that respects teaching styles and the prevailing learning styles of the group. Translation as a pedagogical tool and translation as a professional activity can be reconciled in classes where a theoretical background is directly applicable to practical translation, a point already highlighted by Nida and Taber (1969). For instance, Nord's functionalism and Newmark's diagram of degrees of fidelity (1988) can be introduced by systematically assigning a potential client profile to every student translation and by occasionally changing the text type and/or readership, e.g. ask for the translation of a specialised medical text for the health supplement in a newspaper.

Reflective teaching – observing and improving one's own teaching methods (see Richards & Lockhart 1994) – and action research – class-based research (see Nunan 1990) – can be carried out by teachers in the classroom to trigger insights about their teaching and later reflection on it, with the obvious aim of improving the overall quality of teaching. This can be done, for instance, by keeping a (written or audio) journal and exploring the teaching context: how we teach and why we do so in this manner; by comparing what was expected from a lesson and what actually happened (lesson plans compared to lesson reports or to specific questions prepared by a group of teachers); by taping (video) or recording (audio) the lessons for a less subjective report or reflection; by gathering information through classroom observation and student questionnaires. Reflective teaching is not about evaluating students, but about observing and improving teaching methods, and starts from the premise that teaching is a lifelong process based on a constant updating of pedagogical theories and on classroom observation. Reflective teachers monitor and evaluate their actions and attempt to adapt their teaching methods to different students. They reconsider the knowledge acquired at different stages of their professional life and accept the need for new input after analysing the pros and cons.

Action research is research carried out in the classroom and is a logical outcome of reflective teaching: the implication is that teachers should fix their attention on a certain aspect of their teaching or of their syllabus, or that they propose a hypothesis and follow its evolution systematically, e.g. "if I explain the aims of each activity in the classroom, will the students become more involved in the learning process so that I'll be favouring motivation?" Action research involves three steps: reconnaissance, implementation and analysis of the results.

In this approach, the teacher becomes a key figure. The teaching style, assumptions about translation, and priorities as to what should be included in the syllabus will certainly shape the learning process as much as age, personality, motivation to teach, and the professional and academic background of the teacher.

Student type is another factor to consider and respect. According to Ellis (1985) there are four types of students: active, passive, experiential and studial. Obviously, the ideal student holds characteristics of all four. The predominance of one student type or another will also condition the pedagogical orientation and the possible resulting translator types for, as Séguinot (1991:85) observes: "It appears ... that there is more than one kind of successful translator in much the same way that there are basic types of writers." Activities for the different types of students can be included so that as many styles as possible are catered for, although one or two styles usually predominate.

2.4 Task-based learning: Integrating function-, process- and product-based teaching

Different tasks can be assigned to students, placing the emphasis on the translation process, its function or the product. Once these are clearly delimited in the syllabus, the linguistic and extra-linguistic expectations of the activities can be established, as well as the translational processes to be explored by students and the type of product they should be capable of generating at the end of the course, thereby relating their translation competence and performance.

To this end, Penny Ur's definition of *task* in Foreign Language Learning, which emphasises both the learning process and the product, points to a concept which might also be applied to translator training: "Each task should consist of a thinking process and its outcome in the form of a tangible result. It is not enough just to think out a problem or explore the ramifications of a conflict; the results must be written down, ticked off, listed, sketched or tape-recorded in some way" (Ur 1996:34). In this manner, the activities presented to the students should include a "thinking process" and a "tangible result".

In *task learning*, a chain of activities are related to each other and are sequenced in such a way that they lead to a final product. For example, if we would like students to practise translating paroemias from Spanish into English, a text such as Gato Perez' song *Lo que me da la gana*[4] can be used, but not as a loose activity to be carried out in a void. A couple of previous sessions can be devoted to introducing the notion of paroemia, translation strategies and degrees of fidelity when translating paroemias and songs, the actual translation of fixed sayings and proverbs, a reflection on cultural differences and world views which can be deduced from the students' own work; and then, the final activity would revise and consolidate all the previous: the translation of the song followed by peer editing and, if possible, its recording to prove the translated text also keeps to the music![5]

This pedagogical approach works even more efficiently if it includes the following approaches to translator training:

- Function-based: awareness of *why*, *where*, and *when* the translation assignment is carried out. The students have this information before doing their translations (Nord 1997b).
- Process-based: *how* the students acquire the skills to become competent translators. Here procedures are the most important component. An awareness of the translation strategies and solutions used by professional translators is reinforced by students' reflection on those they use themselves in their assignments. This approach increases their self-confidence as translators and contributes to greater coherence, quality, and speed in their translations. Theorists do not agree on a definition of "strategy" (see, e.g. Newmark 1988; Hatim & Mason 1990; Nord 1991; Baker 1992). For pedagogical purposes, it can be presented to students as *a procedure which has been chosen consciously to solve a translation problem which does not allow an automatic transference* (Lörscher 1991: 76) *and which can be present either in a text segment (micro level) or in the text as a whole (macro level)* (Scott-Tennent & González Davies 2000: 108).
- Product-based: *what* the students achieve. Here the emphasis lies on the final translation produced by the student. This is the approach adopted almost exclusively in so-called traditional translation classes.

There seems to be general agreement – although no conclusive experimental research has been carried out – that sound encyclopaedic knowledge improves the global quality of a translation even more than linguistic knowledge. In other words, the more that is known about what lies behind the words, the better aspects such as intention, function, effect, or style will be grasped. Encyclopaedic knowledge implies recognising the cultural references embedded in the text,[6] as well as intertextual references,[7] and being aware of the importance of familiarisation with the subject dealt with in the text.

Also, an awareness of the cognitive skills needed to optimise the relation between linguistic competence and performance and encyclopaedic knowledge favours reflection on translation. In other words, minding the process improves the product. This relates to one of the as yet unanswered questions in translation research: "What goes on in the mind of the translator?"[8]

From the pedagogic perspective, there are several points around which teachers can plan a class that can help them to design more adequate activities and worksheets for the established objectives. For instance, before introducing translation activities, the following points might be considered:

1. *Linguistic and translational level of the students*: Undergraduates, postgraduates or professional translators?
2. *Translation aims:* The translation aims specify whether the activity has been designed to improve translation skills (e.g. resourcing), to practise translation techniques (e.g. subtitling) or to become aware of cognitive processes (e.g. accessing semantic fields through Mind Maps).
3. *Direction*: Direct (L2 to L1) or reverse translation (L1 to L2), or both.
4. *Linguistic aims:* These should take into account that language improvement and contrast between language pairs are essential for translators.
5. *Non-linguistic aims*: e.g. subject or encyclopaedic knowledge required.
6. *Text type*: Written or oral on the one hand, and descriptive, argumentative, narrative, etc. on the other.
7. *Approach to task*: Bottom-up, top-down, or both, which – according to various studies on reading and on translating (Lörscher 1992; Baker 1992) – are the ways in which competent readers, professional translators and bilinguals deal with texts.
8. *Student grouping*: Individual, pair or group work, or a combination of these.
9. *Timing*: How much time will this activity take up? The timing will depend mainly on the characteristics of the group, the length of the text or recording and the translation direction (reverse translation activities usually take longer than direct translation).
10. *Sequencing*: At what stage in the syllabus is it most coherent to carry out a given task?

As it seems that background or encyclopaedic knowledge is more relevant to a successful outcome than dictionary knowledge, to activate contextualising skills, extralinguistic awareness and decision-making, a topic-based anthology for internal use – designed by the teacher so that teaching styles are respected – can be useful to guide students through the different issues to be dealt with during the course. Students can complement it with an assignment of their choice on one or more of the topics.

Teaching material which aims at the acquisition of translation skills, rather than at the perfecting of a constraining language pair, can be applied to a variety of texts and languages. This material can be both written and audio-visual and can be prepared not only by the teacher but also by the students. Most translation techniques used in professional translation, such as sight translation, prove to be excellent learning techniques and, moreover, are highly motivating because the students realise that they are performing "real world" tasks. The texts to be translated can include multiple text types and can be accompanied by worksheets and complemented by activities to highlight interesting points. For example, to illustrate the translation of artificial languages, activities such as the following based on the film *Bladerunner* can be presented:

1. Look at the words and expressions and try to fill in the blanks BEFORE you watch the film excerpt in English. Then watch the film and correct your text.[9]

    > The . . . . . .'s name was Garth. I'd seen him around. That . . . . . . he talked was . . . . . . , ... talk, a . . . . . . of . . . . . . , Spanish, German, ... I didn't really need a translator. I knew the . . . . Every good . . . . . . did.

    Gibberish, charmer, lingo, Cityspeak, cop, gutter, Japanese, mishmash, what-have-you.

2. Translate the text. Concentrate on the register and the lexis. You can (should!) be as creative and flexible as possible. Watch the dubbed version and compare your translation.[10] Discuss the different options with another student.

3. How would you transfer the Cityspeak Garth uses just before this scene? Which languages does he use?[11] Watch the dubbed version and compare it with yours and that of another student. Discuss translation options and degrees of fidelity.

When preparing an anthology the following guidelines may prove useful:

a. *Topic-based organisation*, i.e. a selection of texts on chosen topics and subtopics (e.g. scientific translation of medical texts on neurology, psychiatry, etc.) to which a minimum of four or five sessions are devoted, and which run as smoothly as possible from one to another. These texts should also provide the students with updated information on subjects related to translation issues, the translation market and specialist areas.

b. *Text type choice* specific to the discipline(s) dealt with in the course in order to familiarise the students with different text typologies and their conventions in both languages involved in the teaching.

c. *Professional and pedagogic material* which includes the following:

  – texts to be translated in different ways in order to practise different translation techniques and modalities, for instance, synthetic translation, backtranslation, or straightforward translation.
  – texts which enhance complementary translation skills such as summary-writing and note-taking.
  – activities and worksheets to reinforce the languages involved through, for instance, work on reading comprehension or writing skills.
  – texts and activities which raise the students' awareness of the linguistic, extralinguistic and cognitive/translational components to be borne in mind before rendering a text into another language, such as reader-oriented translations, culture-bound texts or discussion of different solutions to a translation problem.

3. Evaluation

A pedagogical approach that values, guides and maximises the individual's potential and that considers both the process and the product of translation paves the way for reflective learning oriented towards building the students' "self-concept as translators" (Kiraly 1995).

Evaluation is always a delicate subject in which subjectivity plays an important part. Quite a few scales for translation assessment have been published (see, among others, Farahzad 1992: 271–279 and Pym 1992: 279–291; Sainz 1994: 133–143 and Ibrahim 1994: 151–157; Mahn 1989: 100–109; Valero 1997: 199–210; Kussmaul 1995: Chapter 6; González Davies 1998, 2004; González Davies, Scott-Tennent, & Rodríguez Torras 2001). In all these, one person evaluates. However, in an interactive context it makes sense that, to a certain degree, all the participants should take part in the evaluation of the work carried out. Therefore, an evaluation process along these lines will call for reflection on four questions:

  1. WHO evaluates?
  2. WHAT do we evaluate?

3.   HOW do we evaluate?
4.   WHEN do we evaluate?

In a conventional class, a final exam and, sometimes, a series of set translations would be evaluated by the teacher. This can be done not only through an exam, but other procedures can be used such as a systematic observation of the students' participation and attitude in class (e.g. observation sheets, class diaries, register of important events), observation and analysis of the students' work (e.g. class notebooks, peer preparation of activities and translations, self-evaluation sheets), discussion among the participants (e.g. semi-formal interviews, discussions and debates, round tables), specific tests (e.g. translations, course papers, exams).

Both the process and the product can be assessed at all times and, especially, the students' progress. This can be measured by establishing three main moments of evaluation: (1) *initial*: at the beginning of a course certain activities will determine the students' level from different points of view, (2) *continuous*: the students hand in or observe each other's work over the course, (3) *final*: this can be either a test, course paper, class presentation, or a combination of several possibilities.

In a pedagogical approach that builds translation skills gradually with the students' participation, evaluation should perhaps lay emphasis on pedagogical aspects in the first years of undergraduate training and on professional demands in the final period. It would also make sense to include the students in the process by means of self- and peer-evaluation.

4. Conclusion

The main pedagogical and translational points underlying the approach to translator training which have been presented here are based on a need for Pedagogy Studies to inform translator training. The teaching method I have proposed revolves around teacher/student and student/student interaction in a way that enables students to experience, negotiate and discuss translation issues. Texts and procedures are grouped around thematic areas and text types and evaluation is carried out according to both pedagogical and professional criteria. In short, it is based on the belief that catering for the specific needs of students can help them acquire advanced translation skills.

Function-based, process-based and product-based teaching are dealt with in the procedures outlined in this chapter and are designed to improve the linguistic, encyclopaedic and cognitive knowledge of students. Their awareness of translation components and constraints is thus also raised, and translation strategies and solutions are analysed and discussed. Contacts with the professional world are also encouraged so that students become aware of themselves as translators.

In order to reach an optimal standard in translator training, an understanding between theorists, practitioners and teachers is needed; workshops and sessions should be organised in which teaching materials and experiences are exchanged. Alongside this, an awareness of existing pedagogical approaches, reflective teaching and action research in the classroom can also lead to more effective training. Finally, more empirical research will also enable a better understanding of both the teaching and the learning process.

Notes

1. For a discussion on innate/non-innate translators, see Kiraly (1995:15–16).

2. There are exceptions such as Hervey, Higgins and Haywood (1995), Kiraly (1995, 2000), Hurtado (2000) or González Davies (2003). Notice the relatively recent dates.

3. For a survey on approaches to translation training, see Kiraly (1995:22–33).

4. *Lo que me da la gana* (first lines): Soy pobre como una rata/ pero disfruto como un camello/ trabajo como un caballo/ cuando me pongo serio./ Canto como un canario/ temprano por la mañana/ después de hacer de lagarto/ hasta las seis de la madrugada./ Lo que me da la gana, hago lo que me da la gana/ ya que los animales guían mi conducta humana...

5. Example of students' translation (2000): "I do my own thing: I'm as poor as a street rat/ but I live life to the full/ I work like a dog/ when I have to/ I sing like a bird/ after a big night in town./ I do my own thing/ because animals are what I've always believed in ..."

6. The mass media provide good examples which are easy to find and can represent a real challenge. Compare the following which have been graded from more to less problematic for undergraduate students working in the language combination English/Spanish/Catalan:

a. Complete cultural correspondence: "El Ángel Caído" (*La Vanguardia*, 13.4.96) could be translated as "The Fallen Angel".

b. Partial cultural correspondence: "Los desayunos de la Moncloa" (radio programme – Antena 3) – This was a useful example to establish correspondences between 10 Downing Street and La Moncloa on the one hand, and Buckingham Palace and El Palacio de La Zarzuela, on the other. Also, of course, to introduce the issue of text naturalisation and exoticising.

c. No cultural correspondence: To understand expressions such as "terrorismo de bodeguilla" uttered by Minister Álvarez Cascos, October 1996, or "Rahola i Colom planten un PI" (referring to internal problems in the Catalan political party "Esquerra Republicana" which led to the creation of a new political party "Partit per la Independència"), students have to be really aware of Spanish and Catalan politics.

7. For instance, how many students would recognise the inversion of the speech of Shakespeare's Shylock in this extract from a book by P. D. James (1980: 125): "They had a look of ordinariness which, in some dreadful way, wasn't ordinary at all; they were shells of flesh from which not only the spirit was missing. If they were pricked, they wouldn't bleed"? Also, the elaboration of Mind Maps in multicultural classes is very revealing as to the organisation of the world according to the cultural background of students.

8. A pilot study was carried out at the *Facultat de Ciències Humanes, Traducció i Documentació* (Universitat de Vic, Spain) to determine the teachability of translation strategies and solutions. This research project was an empirical study to observe the effects of a specifically designed syllabus on the students' application of translation strategies and solutions. The project was carried out through three clearly differentiated stages. First, the existing literature on translation strategies was studied, three types of translation problems were chosen and a theoretically optimal methodology was designed in order to teach the strategies to solve those problems. Then, a pilot study was conducted with two groups (experimental and control) of undergraduate translation students. The subjects in the experimental group were trained in the selected strategies, whereas the control group did not receive this specific training. Finally, data analysis and interpretation were carried out, and conclusions were drawn in order to optimise preparation of a second study and decide on our future approach to this particular area of research (Scott-Tennent & González Davies 2000).

9. KEY: charmer/ gibberish/ Cityspeak/ gutter/ mishmash/ Japanese/ what-have-you/ lingo/ cop.

10. KEY: *charmer* – hombre encantador/ *gibberish* – jerga/ *Cityspeak* – Interlingua/ *gutter talk* – argot/ mishmash – mezcolanza/ *Japanese,etc.* – francés, inglés, italiano, español/ *what-have-you* – lo que sea/ *lingo* – idioma/ *cop* – policía.

11. Dubbed version in Spanish: Monsieur, écoutez-moi. Tendrá you que m'acompagner, signore./ He say you arrested./ No, friend, no equivocado, hombre. No hay más que un bogeyman./ He say you Blade Runner./ Le Captain Brian, il me ordené que le lleve aunque sea como fiambre.

References

Bacardí, M. (Ed.). (1997). *Actes Congrés Internacional sobre Traducció 1994*. Barcelona: Universitat Autònoma de Barcelona.

Baker, M. (1992). *In Other Words*. London: Routledge.

Brewster, J. (1996). "Task-based learning. The challenge for teachers and trainers." *A.P.A.C. of News, 27*, 34–38. Barcelona: Alhambra-Longman.

Brumfit, C. & Johnson, K. (Eds.). (1979). *The Communicative Approach to Language Teaching*. Oxford: Oxford University Press.

Candlin, C. (Ed.). (1978). *The Communicative Teaching of English*. London: Longman.

Chaudron, C. (1988). *Second Language Classrooms: Research on Teaching and Learning*. Cambridge: Cambridge University Press.

Delisle, J. (1988). *L'analyse du discourse comme méthode de traduction*. Ottawa: University of Ottawa Press.

Dollerup, C. & Loddegaard, A. (Eds.). (1992). *Teaching Translation and Interpreting. Training, Talent and Experience*. Amsterdam and Philadelphia: John Benjamins.

Dollerup, C. & Lindegaard, A. (Eds.). (1994). *Teaching Translation and Interpreting 2*. Amsterdam and Philadelphia: John Benjamins.

Duff, A. (1981). *The Third Language*. Oxford: Pergamon.

Ellis, R. (1985). *Understanding Second Language Acquisition*. Oxford: Oxford University Press.

Farahzad, F. (1992). "Testing achievement in translation classes". In C. Dollerup & A. Loddegaard (Eds.), *Teaching Translation and Interpreting. Training, Talent and Experience* (pp. 271–279). Amsterdam and Philadelphia: John Benjamins.

Gardner, R. & Lambert, W. (1972). *Attitudes and Motivation in Second Language Learning*. Rowley, MA: Newbury House.

Gile, D. (1995). *Basic Concepts and Models for Interpreter and Translator Training*. Amsterdam and Philadelphia: John Benjamins.

González Davies, M. (1998). "Student assessment by medical specialists: An experiment in relating the undergraduate to the professional world in the teaching of Medical Translation in Spain". In H. Fischbach (Ed.), *Translation and Medicine. ATA Scholarly Monograph Series* 10 (pp. 93–102). Amsterdam and Philadelphia: John Benjamins.

González Davies, M., Scott-Tennent, C., & Rodríguez Torras, F. (2001). "Training in the application of translation strategies for undergraduate scientific students". *Meta, 46*(4), 737–744.

González Davies, M. (Coord.). (2003). *Secuencias. Tareas para el aprendizaje interactivo de la traducción especializada*. Barcelona: Octaedro.

González Davies, M. (2004). *Multiple voices in the translation classroom. Activities, tasks and projects*. Amsterdam and Philadelphia: John Benjamins.

Hatim, B. & Mason, I. (1990). *Discourse and the Translator*. London: Longman.

Hervey, S., Higgins, L., & Haywood, L. (1995). *Thinking Spanish Translation*. London and New York: Routledge.

Holec, H. (1979). *Autonomy and Foreign Language Learning*. Oxford: Pergamon.

Hurtado. A. (Ed.). (2000). *Enseñar a traducir. Metodología en la formación de traductores e intérpretes*. Madrid: Edelsa.

Ibrahim, H. (1994). "Translation assessment: A case for a spectral mode". In C. Dollerup & A. Lindegaard (Eds.), *Teaching Translation and Interpreting 2* (pp. 151–157). Amsterdam: John Benjamins.

James, P. D. (1980). *Innocent Blood*. London and New York: Penguin/Faber & Faber.

Kiraly, D. C. (1995). *Pathways to Translation*. Kent: Kent State University Press.

Kiraly, D. C. (2000). *A Socioconstructivist Approach to Translator Education. Empowerment from Theory to Practice*. Manchester: St. Jerome.

Krawutsche, P. (1989). (Ed.). *Translator and Interpreter Training and Foreign Language Pedagogy. ATA Scholarly Monograph Series* 3. Binghamton: Suny.

Kussmaul, P. (1995). *Training the Translator*. Amsterdam and Philadelphia: John Benjamins.

Legutke, M. & Thomas, H. (1991). *Process and Experience in the Language Classroom*. London: Longman.

Lörscher, W. (1991). *Translation Performance, Translation Process, and Translation Strategies. A Psycholinguistic Investigation*. Tübingen: Narr.

Lörscher, W. (1992). "Process-oriented research into translation and implications for translation teaching". *TTR, 5*(1), 145–161.

Mahn, G. (1989). "Standards and Evaluation in Translation Training". In P. Krawutsche (Ed.), *Translator and Interpreter Training and Foreign Language Pedagogy. ATA Scholarly Monograph Series* 3 (pp. 100–109). Binghamton: Suny.

Newmark, P. (1988). *A Textbook of Translation*. Hemel Hemstead: Prentice Hall.

Nida, E. & Taber, C. R. (1969). *The Theory and Practice of Translation*. Leiden: E.J. Brill.

Nord, C. (1991). *Text Analysis for Translation*. Amsterdam: Rodopi.

Nord, C. (1997a). "Alice abroad. Dealing with descriptions and transcriptions of paralanguage in literary translation". In F. Poyatos (Ed.), *Nonverbal Communication and Translation* (pp. 107–129). Amsterdam and Philadelphia: John Benjamins.

Nord, C. (1997b). *Translating as a Purposeful Activity*. Manchester: St. Jerome.

Nunan, D. (1988). *Syllabus Design*. Oxford: Oxford University Press.

Nunan, D. (1989). *Designing Tasks for the Communicative Classroom*. Cambridge: Cambridge University Press.

Nunan, D. (1990). "Action research in the language classroom". In J. Richards & D. Nunan (Eds.), *Second Language Teacher Education* (pp. 81–98). New York: Cambridge University Press.

Pym, A. (1992). "Translation error analysis and the interface with language teaching". In C. Dollerup & A. Loddegaard (Eds.), *Teaching Translation and Interpreting. Training, Talent and Experience* (pp. 279–291). Amsterdam and Philadelphia: John Benjamins.

Richards, J. & Lockhart, C. (1994). *Reflective Teaching in Second Language Classrooms*. Cambridge: Cambridge University Press.

Sainz, Mª J. (1994). "Student-centred corrections of translations". In C. Dollerup & A. Lindegaard (Eds.), *Teaching Translation and Interpreting 2*. Amsterdam and Philadelphia: John Benjamins.

Séguinot, C. (1991). "A study of student translation strategies". In S. Tirkkonen-Condit (Ed.), *Empirical Research in Translation and Intercultural Studies* (pp. 79–88). Tübingen: Gunter Narr.

Scott-Tennent, C. & González Davies, M. (2000). "Translation strategies and translation solutions: Design of a teaching prototype and empirical study of results". In A. Beeby, M. Presas, & D. Ensinger (Eds.), *Investigating Translation* (pp. 107–116). Amsterdam and Philadelphia: John Benjamins.

Shreve, in Kiraly (1995:xiv).

Ur, in Brewster (1996:34).

Valero, C. (1997). "Cómo evaluar la competencia traductora: Varias propuestas." In M. Bacardí (Ed.), *Actes Congrés Internacional sobre Traducció 1994*. Barcelona: Universitat Autònoma de Barcelona.

CHAPTER 4

Audiovisual translation

Francesca Bartrina and Eva Espasa

Every text is a mirror picture of its source culture as far as its verbal form and physical form are concerned.   (Schröder 1992:323)

The epigraph from Schröder can be read as a ray of hope in this era of globalisation. The role played by audiovisual translation in contemporary international communication invites translator trainers to contemplate the different possibilities available when training translators for the modern mass-communication market. In this chapter we outline a course on audiovisual translation, sequenced along a threefold, progressive axis: starting with the translation of drama texts, then proceeding to dubbing (taking into account the increasing difficulties of specific genres) and, lastly, subtitling.

1. The priorities of constrained translation

The term *constrained translation* was first used by Titford (1982). It was reintroduced by Mayoral, Kelly and Gallardo and applied to translations "in which the text is only one of the components of the message or when it constitutes only an intermediate stage for a speech read aloud or dramatised" (1988:356). The authors take into account the different "noise producing" circumstances in the translation process and the different degrees of constraint found in the translation of different types of messages. They appeal to the concept of synchrony, i.e. the agreement between signals emitted for the purpose of communicating the same message. Synchrony can be of time, space, content, sound and character.

Constrained translating refers to situations in which the text to be trans-lated is part of a more complex communicative event which attempts to convey a message by various means, such as pictures, drawings, music, etc. The translation of the linguistic part is crucially conditioned by the other elements and poses a set of problems that are specific enough to require special attention. We find this concept very useful when applied to the training of translators and interpreters. In the training programme at the University of Vic, students working in the English/Spanish/Catalan combination take two courses on constrained translation. In their third year they take "Constrained Static Translation", where image and space are the main concerns; in their fourth year they take "Constrained Dynamic Translation" – translation for the theatre, dubbing, subtitling – where time and movement also play a role, together with image and space. We concentrate on the following skills, which can be useful for both audiovisual translation and other types of text transfer: cognitive skills, professional skills, technical skills, (re)contextualisation, creativity and speed.

In the "Constrained Static Translation" course the topics of the texts to be translated fall within four broad areas: culture, tourism, comics and advertising. Training in these areas helps students develop the skills necessary for later approaching "Constrained Dynamic Translation", also referred to as "Audiovisual translation".

2. Translating audiovisual and multimedia texts

An *audiovisual text* has two main features: (1) it is received through two channels, acoustic and visual and (2) the synchrony between verbal and non-verbal messages is essential. This approach to audiovisual texts provides the necessary link between theatre and film translation, as they both "involve a systematic interaction between oral, written and non-verbal communication" (Lambert 1994:23). In consequence, audiovisual translation can be taken to include theatre translation, dubbing, subtitling, voice-over, simultaneous interpreting and half-dubbing.[1]

In contrast to stage translation, other types of audiovisual texts require projection on a screen and are thereby based on reproducible and recorded material. In this sense the label *Multimedia Translation* also refers to texts that require a computer screen and interaction between the receiver and the text. The localisation business, for example, can be the paradigm of the need for technology; and, in this context, the term *Multimedia* would also include the Internet, CD-ROMs, etc.

In a sense *all* texts are multimedia texts, because "no text consists of a mere set of linear characters" (Schröder 1992:317). Schröder insists upon the need to analyse multimedia texts as *complete* units with their verbal and non-verbal elements. It is our opinion, also, that the term "text" should no longer be applied exclusively to the verbal parts of the communicative utterance: "Instead, the term 'text' should stand for the whole of all communicative utterances which together become coherent in a communicative situation and form an indivisible functioning whole" (Schröder 1992:318).

Audiovisual translation, with all its specificity, must be framed within the evolving requirements of multimedia translation. Audiovisual and multimedia translation are becoming more and more inseparable: Films are digitalised and DVDs are taking over the industry. Multimedia support is appearing in all sorts of communication: marketing, education, entertainment. In this sense, we are as optimistic as Chris Pollard regarding the future of audiovisual translation, due in great measure to the growing impact of DVDs: "With an estimated output of more than 700 feature films per year, the demand for qualified media translators will increase manifold in the very near future" (*L.T.* 1998:11).

Audiovisual translation should not be considered a kind of specialised translation, although the different audiovisual genres could present specialised terminology, e.g. scientific, technical, legal or economic (Chaume 1999:210). The specificity of audiovisual translation consists in its mode of transmission, rather than in the topics it covers. In audiovisual texts there is semiotic interaction between the simultaneous emission of image and text and its repercussions for the translation process. One characteristic of audiovisual texts is its redundancy: oral and written messages are conveyed with sound and image.

Obviously, the choice of the theatrical and screen material that are going to be covered in the classroom is an essential question that determines the success of the activities. The works selected should provide the occasion for as many audiovisual translation strategies as possible.[2]

3.   Connections between theatre translation and audiovisual translation

As we have pointed out, audiovisual translation – in our teaching context – is included in the wider field of constrained translation. The following features of audiovisual translation are *not* present in stage translation: (1) technical reproducibility, (2) total subordination of text to audiovisual components in the film, components which – contrary to stage translation – cannot be changed, (3) presentation on a screen, (4) extremely tight deadlines, more so – in most instances – than when translating for the stage.

Other differences between theatre and audiovisual texts can be seen in the relation between performance and audience reception, as well as the obvious spatial limitations. Törnqvist mentions the following characteristics of a theatrical production (in Mateo 1997:100):

1. A stage performance involves a two-way communication process: the actors may respond to reactions from the audience.
2. A theatre visit is a social event: the reactions are those of a mass audience.
3. Every stage performance is unique, unrepeatable.
4. A stage performance is determined by the spatial facilities available.
5. The spatial limitation necessitates abundant use of proxemics and the distance from stage to auditorium requires special kinesics and paralinguistics.
6. A stage performance has a plurimedial and unrepeatable nature and it is therefore difficult to notate.

These differences notwithstanding, translating for the stage shares specific features with audiovisual translation: to start with, a semiotic density which leads to the negotiation/selection of the most relevant signs (verbal versus non-verbal, visual versus acoustic) to be privileged in translating. We have developed a course which we believe prepares students for the professional demands for both quality and quantity of work. By forcing them, within the context of the course, to meet tight deadlines, to find their own sources of documentation and to take global, consistent translation decisions, students are establishing their autonomy as prospective freelance translators. In the course each student is *commissioned* to translate an entire, unpublished play and present a "credible" brief, e.g. translating for the National Theatre of Catalonia or the Spanish Drama Centre, to be evaluated at the end of the term.

Training in theatre translation is excellent preparation for dubbing and subtitling. The emphasis in stage translation should be on the following elements, which are common to drama and to screen texts: (1) Concision, (2) Fictitious orality, (3) Negotiation of the translation with other professional agents (actors and technicians).[3]

3.1 Concision

Stage translation requires the use of direct, concise language because, as with dubbing, the text is received immediately and there is no time for the viewer to "reread" the audiovisual text (with the exception of video rewinding). Concision can be a criterion for controlling the overall duration of translated drama texts, which "operate against the clock of performance" (Pujante & Centenero 1995:93). Concision on stage does not require the exact precision it demands in dubbing and, therefore, provides good preparation for learning to produce concise dubbed and subtitled texts. In stage translation, it is rather a question of not rendering a two-hour long original as a three or four-hour long translation (Pujante 1995:12). It is worth remembering that translations from English to Romance languages, such as Spanish and Catalan, tend to be longer than the original. Therefore, a concise stage translation can avoid lengthening the performance duration which might lead to potential cuts by stage directors. Having said this, concision is not exclusive to drama – it can be as important in other literary and audiovisual text-types – or it may be at odds with very rhetorical drama writing. It is always necessary to consider the *degree* of orality and concision in different text types (see Formosa 1999:81–82).

We choose for translation contemporary dramatists, such as Caryl Church-ill, Lillian Hellman, Tony Kushner, David Mamet, and Harold Pinter, who tend to use concise, direct language. It is worth mentioning that these authors have generally worked for both the stage and the screen.

3.2 Fictitious orality[4]

Both drama and dubbing texts share the paradoxical "ordeal" of having to (re)create realistic, credible *oral* texts, even though the source texts are *written*, as is the translation which is handed to the client (the theatre company, the dubbing studio or the subtitling agency). Audiovisual and theatre texts are written texts to be spoken *as if* they had not been written, as if they were spoken *spontaneously*.[5] This "*as if*" conditions the entire project: verisimilitude is a usual requirement, even though fictional texts are never true to life. In Elam's words, "drama presents what is very much a 'pure' model of social intercourse, and the dialogue bears a very limited resemblance to what actually takes place in 'everyday' linguistic encounters" (1980:178). This also holds true for dubbed and subtitled texts. For example, the Catalan TV stylebook emphasises that dubbed scripts are "written [texts] to be spoken *feigning spontaneity*" (TVC 1997:11, our emphasis).

As with concision, this requirement of orality is subject to other factors, including the complexity or specificity of the original texts: the priority of recreating fictitious orality sometimes clashes with professional or institutional restrictions governing register and dialect acceptability. For example, when translating into Catalan, interference from other languages, especially Span-ish, is often considered unacceptable. Therefore, in a teaching environment, debates frequently arise in class regarding the acceptability of certain translation decisions, particularly in reference to register and language interference and the tension between credible versus normative language. The Catalan TV stylebook shows this tension in its insistence on the standard language and the restrictions it places on dialectal expressions, learned words, and anachronisms (TVC 1997:11). However, this stylebook recommends *both* standard language *and* register variation, depending on the communicative situations shown on screen, and both are seen as compatible (TVC 1997:12).

Professional and institutional factors, such as those mentioned above, are recreated in the classroom; and students negotiate their translation solutions, taking into account the available norms on audiovisual translation, for example, stylebooks, in-house norms of translation agencies or of dubbing studios. The classroom becomes a site for negotiation of these factors and the students' own criteria. The translation solutions that are reached are as important as the *criteria* for those decisions, and *the ability to defend those solutions* before prospective clients.

3.3 Negotiation of the translation with other professional agents

In teaching stage and audiovisual translation – as well as the translation of other genres – it is essential to situate the translation within a complex communication system. In stage and audiovisual translation, the translated text is one link in a chain of agents and components: e.g. the actors who will speak the text, the adaptors who will have to take into consideration the technical restrictions of space and time, the requirements of lip synchronisation. All of these are "orchestrated" by a director who will give relative prominence to each aspect. Usually the director has the last word regarding the interpretation and negotiation of the text. But the first decisions are taken by the translator, since translation always involves interpretation, and only at a later stage will these be negotiated. Therefore, we consider that it is essential that translator trainees become familiar with the professional and technical restrictions to which their translations will be subjected. They can thereby anticipate these constraints and take them into account when making translation decisions, especially regarding synchrony and synthesis.[6]

As can be seen by the above, the task of stage and audiovisual translators is complex, but – in the case of audiovisual translation – this does not amount to greater social and authorial consideration of their work. In the Spanish context, audiovisual translators do not own the copyright of their work, nor do their names or those of the dubbing actors appear on the credits of dubbed films.

An exception is the case of films shown in theatres, where the translator's name does appear at the end of the credits. We hope that foregrounding professional aspects of audiovisual translation in the classroom will, at least in the long run, contribute to the production of better translations and to greater social consideration of translators and to the authorial recognition of their task.

The following sections summarise the dynamics of our classes on dubbing and subtitling. It is our hope that this chapter will also contribute to acknowledging the importance of audiovisual translation within the academic world.

4. Teaching dubbing

Teaching dubbing necessarily covers both theoretical and professional aspects. The pedagogical aspect of the course includes discussions of theory, debates on theoretical articles, and workshops on each modality of translation. Within the broad field of dubbing, the genres are sequenced according to increasing difficulty: documentaries (voice-over);[7] cartoons, TV series, TV films, and, finally, feature films for the cinema (see Agost & Chaume 1996). Thus, in documentaries the emphasis is on isochrony; in cartoons on creativity; in TV series and films on verisimilitude and familiarity with script-writing conventions. Finally, feature films provide students with practice in all of these, in addition to the different types of synchrony (see Agost, Chaume, & Hurtado 1999: 188).

In our course, because dubbing is taught mid-term – after theatre translation and before subtitling – theoretical aspects are primarily dealt with by comparing the specificity of each modality. Other aspects that are explored are, as we have seen, the fictitious orality in drama and in audiovisual translation, the various agents involved, and historical and ideological translation policies. In our teaching situation, students become acquainted with these by discussing relevant bibliography on the European, Spanish and Catalan audiovisual translation context (Whitman 1992; Ávila 1997; TVC 1997; Agost 1999; Díaz Cintas 2001; Chaume 2003), on the history of audiovisual translation (Izard 1992; Benet 1999), and on the specificity of theatre translation (Mateo 1995, 1996; Bassnett 1998; Aaltonen 2000). The ideological implications of audiovisual translation are also considered, with class discussions on translation policies (on dubbing versus subtitling, Danan 1991; on censorship, Ballester 1995; on globalisation and mass media translation, Lambert 1994; Gambier & Gottlieb 2001).

A key theoretical aspect in teaching dubbing is the notion of synchrony. A historical overview is given of the typology, established by Fodor (1976),

Table 1. Types of synchrony (Whitman 1992: 19)

Visual/optical synchrony:
– lip synchrony/phonetic synchrony
– syllable articulation synchrony
– length of utterance synchrony (gap synchrony or isochrony)
– gesture and facial expression synchrony (kinetic synchrony)
Audio/acoustic synchrony:
– idiosyncratic vocal type
– paralinguistic elements (tone, timbre, pitch of voice)
– prosody (intonation, melody, tempo)
– cultural variations
– accents and dialects

of content, character, and phonetic synchrony. The historical importance of Fodor's contribution is widely acknowledged, but its professional feasibility is questionable: content and character synchrony are, arguably, common to other types of translation. They can only be seen as specific to audiovisual translation when there is a close connection between image, sound and text which might pose a translation challenge because of word-image discrepancies or which might require the elimination of the text due to audio-visual redundancies. The same would apply to phonetic synchrony, which has been hailed as the paradigmatic dubbing scenario.

The need for synchrony can vary historically and culturally and from country to country. Whitman, while establishing more specific types of synchrony, (see Table 1) acknowledges that "exacting and meticulous lip synchrony is an animal threatened with extinction, especially since this is probably the easiest to distract the audience away from with other sensory input" (1992: 54).

Consequently, according to Whitman (1992: 53):

> it is important [...] that the synchronies not be seen as discrete units. They overlap, coincide and are mutually influential. The fundamental questions that must not be lost sight of are essentially: What in fact does the audience notice? What dyssynchronies do they register as jarring or annoying? What distracts them in their perception of inconsistencies and what do they forgive?

It is important, therefore, to keep in mind the overall relevance and frequency of dyssynchronies, rather than specific instances.

For teaching and professional contexts, it can be useful to summarise the different types of synchrony according to the following categories, as suggested by Agost, Chaume and Hurtado (1999: 184):

- Phonetic synchrony: adapting the translation to the actor's lip movements
- Kinetic synchrony: adapting the translation to the actor's body movements
- Isochrony: adapting the translation to the duration of each utterance by the actor.

The relative importance of synchrony in the translation task as a whole is a good example of the connections between theoretical and professional aspects. The professional requirements of each translation modality are taught through presentation and discussion of different guidelines, such as in-house style guides for dubbing and subtitling, and specific bibliography on dubbing and copyright restrictions (for the Spanish/Catalan context, see Agost 1999; Ávila 1997; TVC 1997; Chaume 2003). Students are first introduced to the peculiarities of different source texts, such as pre-production and post-production scripts. On the source-text side, students are introduced to technicalities: camera shot abbreviations, specifications of special effects, time codes, etc. From the target system perspective, students are introduced to the different dubbing symbols used in dubbing studios. These symbols may vary from one geographical area to another and from dubbing studio to dubbing studio (some of which may only use "on", "off" and pause symbols). In class we use an eclectic combination (following Ávila 1997:81; Agost 1999:68, and in-house dubbing studio norms). The symbols we use are either in Catalan or Spanish, according to the target language. The following symbols are ones we use in Catalan:

(ON)	The dialogue and the character's lips are visible on screen.
(OFF)	The dialogue is not visible on screen but the character's voice can be heard.
(DE) [d'esquena]	The character's back faces the audience.
(SB) [sense boca]	The character is visible, but not his/her mouth.
(DC) [de costat]	The profile of the character's mouth can be seen.
(ALHORA)	The characters speak simultaneously.
(AD LIBITUM)	Many characters speak simultaneously and their words can hardly be understood.
(LL) [lluny]	The characters are far off and their vocalisation is not particularly noticeable.
(CP) [canvi de pla]	Change of shot. This sign may be used at the beginning, in the middle or at the end of a sentence.
(G) [gest]	Sound gesture from a character, such as a breathing sound or a grunt.
(R) [riure]	Laughter.
(X) [xisclar]	Scream.

(A) [abans]	The dubbing actor starts speaking before the original sound track.
(T) [trepitja]	A character starts speaking before another has finished.
(IE) [inici d'efecte]	Start of sound effect (telephone, radio, television, loudspeaker, etc.).
(FE) [fi d'efecte]	End of sound effect.
(AMB) [ambient]	Background voices (bar, office, street, etc.).
//	Long pause.
/	Short pause.
...	Very short pause. It also indicates hesitation.

Let us briefly consider the different stages of a dubbing seminar:

1. Reading the film script. As in subtitling seminars (see Section 5) we tend to work from scripts, preferably post-production scripts, to avoid spending class-time in transcribing/translating directly from screen. The importance of reading the script lies in anticipating translation difficulties, cultural referents, etc. This provides the student with ample time to begin the resourcing process, which might involve third parties.

2. Viewing the entire video.

3. Checking text-image correspondence. It is essential that the text matches the images. If necessary, this involves noting down what is said but not included in the script, in order to be translated later.

4. Noting down the time codes (TCR) whenever there is a pause longer than five seconds or a change of character or scene.

5. Writing down any relevant text appearing on screen, which will be translated later and included as a written note called "chyron".

6. Writing a list of characters, including their name and sex, to help organise the casting of dubbing actors.

7. Viewing the video again, while noting down the dubbing symbols on the original script.

8. Translating the text. After the first viewing, the most general translation decisions will be taken, regarding register, idiolect, politeness of characters, etc. Furthermore, while translating, the dubbing symbols will be added to the translation script. Thus, decisions regarding synchrony can be included in the translation process: for example, the choice of certain words because there are visible, (semi)labial consonants (p, b, m, v, f...) or open vowels (a, o...).

9. Checking through the translation with the on-screen images. Although we prepare translators, not dubbing actors, our students become aware of the need to anticipate synchrony by practising it themselves, by reading it in front of the original images and sounds.

Apart from practising these professional aspects in a workshop situation, students are given guidance regarding local dubbing studios and subtitling companies, local exams for audiovisual translation, information on fees, and useful Internet addresses (on documentation support, specific newsgroups for audiovisual translation, and on translators' associations). We also organise seminars with audiovisual translators, visits to dubbing studios and to local cinemas with electronic subtitling systems.

5. Teaching subtitling

As in dubbing, subtitling is also a way of translating what is being said in an audiovisual text, but it has two characteristic features. First, there is a change of code, from the oral to the written form. Second, the oral message of the source audiovisual text is present in the translated product. The oral and written messages are received simultaneously, allowing for comparison between source and target-text. The special features of the subtitling mode determine the existence of some constraints (or priorities) in the translation process.

Ivarsson identifies three main types of subtitling: chemical, optical and laser, the three most common methods for "impressing", "copying" or laser "writing" the titles onto the film copies. Under the category of "other kinds of subtitling", he mentions (1992: 35):

1. Multilingual subtitling, used in countries with more than one official language: Finland (Finnish and Swedish) or Belgium (French and Flemish).
2. Teletext subtitling, in the viewers' native language.
3. Reduced subtitles or captions which are often written simultaneously with the showing of live broadcasts.
4. Simultaneous subtitling.
5. Surtitling for the stage (theatre, opera …).

In the classroom, we deal mainly with film subtitling because other audiovisual genres (documentaries, cartoons and soap operas) have already been covered in the dubbing classes.

The priorities of subtitling are:

a. Synthesis. Reductions are inevitable in subtitling. As Díaz Cintas points out, reduction can be partial (condensation or concision) or total (elimination or suppression), depending on different factors (2001: 124):

> Los niveles de reducción varían, dependiendo de la naturaleza lingüística y el *tempo* del original, los cambios de planos, la complejidad del texto, la situación de los actores, la acción de la película y el medio de difusión, aunque se acepta de modo general que un 40% del texto original suele desaparecer.

However, provided that the audiovisual text is seen as a whole, the necessary redundancy is supplied by the other elements of the text: the image and the sound.

b. Readability. This is a quality criterion in subtitling, and it can be considered the basis for fluency in this kind of translation. As James says: "subtitling is a skill which demands a great deal of time, effort and meticulous work in order to produce subtitles which are accurate, credible, easy to assimilate and which flow smoothly" (1998: 245).

c. Orality. As Brondeel remarks: "Written subtitles should be made to "sound" like their spoken equivalents" (1994: 29). For our students this is the third stage in orality: Our course first approaches the aspect of orality in theatre translation, then in dubbing and lastly in subtitling.

Classroom activities require the simultaneous use of the video tape and a copy of the script (or dialogue list). In the professional world, subtitlers – and translators of dubbed texts – are sometimes asked to take down the text from the screen, but the use of scripts is more convenient and less time-consuming for teaching purposes.

Students are guided through the following stages in the subtitling process.[8]

5.1 Viewing

Students should:

a. view the *audiovisual text* and see if there is any non-verbal information that should be translated. Essential written information in the images (signs, notices, etc.) should be written down in order to be translated.
b. check the correspondence between the written script and the text that is spoken in the film.
c. decide if songs are relevant. If so, they should be translated.

d. solve any linguistic ambiguity or polysemy by taking into account image-text correspondence.
e. take notes and make decisions on politeness between the characters (for example, in Spanish *Tú* or *Usted*).
f. search for the necessary information on specialised language, slang, etc. In this sense, we encourage our students to use the tools offered by Internet.

5.2 Spotting (also known as timing or cueing)

At this stage, we discuss what a subtitling unit is, when a subtitle should start and finish. The duration of subtitles must adhere to a regular, viewer reading rhythm: they usually remain on the screen about six seconds. No subtitle should appear on screen for less than one second or, with the exception of songs, stay on the screen for longer than seven seconds. As a general rule, we recommend that a subtitle of one line should remain on the screen at least four seconds and a subtitle of two lines about six seconds – if they remain longer, they tend to be reread by the audience.

The subtitle should appear when the spoken utterance of the dialogue is heard. The segmentation of the subtitles should take into account the following aspects: the start and finish of a character's utterance, the semantic units of the dialogue, the rhythm of speech and the changes in camera shots. Spotting must reflect the rhythm of the film. As Gottlieb states: "In order not to work against the rhythm of the original, hereby delaying the viewing process, subtitles must be presented in synchrony with the dominant auditive (phrasing) or visual (cutting) signals" (1994:115). The in-and-out-times of subtitles must follow the speech rhythm of the film dialogue, taking cuts and sound bridges into consideration. Subtitling also requires synchrony, since the subtitles are conditioned by their synchrony with both the acoustic and the visual elements.

5.3 Translating

In subtitling one must translate what is being said on the screen and what appears in the written form, taking into account the information given by the iconic dimension of the image. But the translation is going to be strongly determined by the technical priorities (or constraints) of subtitling.

We apply the following typographical conventions:

– Each subtitle unit must be semantically self-contained.
– Each line should have a maximum of 32 characters (including spacing and punctuation).

- There should be a maximum of 2 lines per subtitle unit. Wherever two lines of unequal length are used, the upper line should preferably be shorter to keep as much of the image visible as possible and in left-justified subtitles in order to reduce unnecessary eye movement, although preferences may vary in different professional contexts.
- Subtitles should not be shorter than 4 or 5 characters; if they are shorter they are reread and disturb the audience's reading rhythm (Díaz Cintas 2001: 113).
- Obvious repetition of names and common comprehensible phrases need not always be subtitled.
- Redundant elements, such as performative verbs, vocatives, repetitions, etc. can be suppressed (Marqués & Torregrosa 1996).
- There must be a close correlation between film dialogue and subtitle content; source language and target language should be synchronised as far as possible.
- Abbreviations known by the audience can be used, and numbers should be given in figures rather than in letters.
- It is important in a classroom context to insist on strict typographical norms, in spite of the fact that there are differences within the professional world.[9] Examples of these conventions are the following:

  - Individual speakers in a dialogue should be indicated by a dash at the beginning of each line.
  - The segmentation of the subtitle, from line to line, and from subtitle unit to subtitle unit, should respect grammatical units. Therefore, an article cannot be separated from its noun, an auxiliary from the main verb or a link-word from its sentence.
  - Dots (…) indicate that a subtitle unit continues on the following screen, which will also start with dots.
  - Italics are used for voices off-screen, such as those coming from TV, radio, songs, etc.

5.4 Editing

This is a very important part of the subtitling process. Technical and linguistic corrections need to be made in order to guarantee the final quality of the product. Subtitles are presented in a written form and must therefore follow the conventions of written language. We insist that trainees not omit this stage.

A comparison between subtitles and transcribed dialogue will never be relevant. As Gottlieb points out: "In judging the quality of subtitles, one must examine the degree to which the subtitled version *as a whole* manages to convey the semantic gestalt of the original" (1994: 106). Subtitles do not constitute an independent written text: they must always be considered together with the complete audiovisual text. The same is true of playscripts and dubbed texts.

6. Conclusion

In conclusion, our approach to teaching audiovisual translation includes professional, technical and pedagogical aspects, all of which are framed within wider cultural and ideological issues. We argue for greater social visibility for the translator, for better integration between translation and adaptation tasks on the basis of a wide notion of text, which includes audiovisual and non-verbal aspects. Consequently, translation cannot be considered as mere text-transfer, but as a multimedia activity which takes into account the fascinating semiotic density of audiovisual language.

Notes

1. Often theatre translation is not included in audiovisual translation because the definition of audiovisual excludes, for some scholars, texts which are not projected on a screen; see Note 3 below, and Sokoli (2000: 12–26).

2. Many on-line resources can be a good source of material for teaching. Some Internet possibilities for finding scripts are included at the end of the reference list.

3. The connections between theatre translation and dubbing have also been analysed in Espasa (2001). The prerequisites of concision, orality and the complex communication chain have been examined by Mateo (1995, 1996) and Massip (1997) regarding stage translation. For audiovisual translation, see Agost (1999), Ávila (1997), Izard (1999), Whitman (1992), and Zabalbeascoa (1993).

4. See Chaume (1999: 217) on what he terms "prefabricated orality". On linguistic variation in translation, see Agost (1998); as regards orality in dubbing, see Dolç and Santamaria (1998). All of these studies acknowledge the fictitious nature of this orality and the influence on it by professional and institutional restrictions.

5. We follow Gregory and Carroll's (1978) account of the complexity of oral and written channels, which has been applied to translation by Hatim and Mason (1990: 49), and – as regards dubbing – the Catalan Television stylebook *Criteris lingüístics sobre traducció i doblatge* (TVC 1997: 11, 13).

6. In this sense, we think that it is essential for translators to assert their authority regarding the final translated product; see Bartrina (2001:73).

7. We include voice-over as a preparatory exercise for dubbing, with the main emphasis on isochrony, or equal duration of original and the voiced-over translation (Agost, Chaume, & Hurtado 1999:183).

8. For detailed tasks for every stage see Bartrina and Espasa (2001) and Bartrina and Espasa (2003).

9. We follow the norms elaborated by different subtitling studios and the European Association for Studies in Screen Translation (ESIST, at: http://www.esist.org), as well as the ones available in different publications on subtitling (e.g. Marqués & Torregrosa 1996; Díaz Cintas 2001:111–122 and Díaz Cintas 2003:157–192).

References

Aaltonen, S. (2000). *Time-Sharing on Stage: Drama Translation in Theatre and Society.* Clevedon: Multilingual Matters.

Agost, R. (1998). "La importància de la variació lingüística en la traducció". *Quaderns. Revista de traducció, 2,* 83–95.

Agost, R. (1999). *Traducción y doblaje: palabras, voces e imágenes.* Barcelona: Ariel.

Agost, R. & Chaume, F. (1996). "L'ensenyament de la traducció audiovisual". In A. Hurtado Albir (Ed.), *La enseñanza de la traducción* (pp. 207–211). Castelló: Publicacions de la Universitat Jaume I.

Agost, R., Chaume, F., & Hurtado, A. (1999). "La traducción audiovisual". In A. Hurtado Albir (Ed.), *Enseñar a traducir. Metodología en la formación de traductores e intérpretes* (pp. 182–195). Madrid: Edelsa.

Ávila, A. (1997). *El doblaje.* Madrid: Cátedra.

Ballester, A. (1995). "The politics of dubbing in Spain". In P. Jansen (Ed.), *Translation and the Manipulation of Discourse: Selected Papers of the CERA Research Seminars in Translation Studies 1992–1993* (pp. 159–181). Leuven: CETRA.

Barbe, K. (1996). "Dubbing in the translation classroom". *Perspectives: Studies in Translatology, 4*(2), 255–274.

Bartrina, F. (2001). "La previsió del procés d'ajust com a estratègia de traducció per a l'ensenyament del doblatge". In R. Agost & F. Chaume (Eds.), *La traducción en los medios audiovisuales* (pp. 65–73). Castelló: Publicacions de la Universitat Jaume I.

Bartrina, F. & Espasa, E. (2003). "Traducción de textos audiovisuales". In M. González Davies (coord.), *Secuencias. Tareas para el aprendizaje interactivo de la traducción especializada* (pp. 19–38). Barcelona: Octaedro.

Bartrina, F. & Espasa, E. (2001). "Doblar y subtitular en el aula: el reto hacia la profesionalización mediante la didáctica". In E. Pajares, R. Merino, & J. M. Santamaría (Eds.), *Trasvases culturales. Literatura, cine, traducción* (pp. 429–436). Gasteiz: Universidad del País Vasco-Euskal Herriko Unibertsitatea.

Bassnett, S. (1998). "Still trapped in the labyrinth: Further reflections on translation and theatre". In S. Bassnett & A. Lefevere (Eds.), *Constructing Cultures: Essays on Literary Translation* (pp. 90–108). Clevedon: Multilingual Matters.

Benet, V. J. (1999). *Un siglo en sombras: Introducción a la historia y la estética del cine.* Valencia: Ediciones de la Mirada.

Brondeel, H. (1994). "Teaching Subtitling Routines". *Meta, 39*(1), 26–33.

Chaume, F. (1999). "La traducción audiovisual: investigación y docencia". *Perspectives: Studies in Translatology, 7*(2), 209–219.

Chaume, F. (2003). *Doblatge i subtitulació per a la TV.* Vic: Eumo.

Danan, M. (1991). "Dubbing as an expression of nationalism". *Meta, 36*(4), 606–614.

Díaz Cintas, J. (2001). *La traducción audiovisual. El subtitulado.* Salamanca: Ediciones Almar.

Díaz Cintas, J. (2003). *Teoría y práctica de la subtitulación: inglés – español.* Madrid: Ariel.

Dolç, M. & Santamaria, L. (1998). "La traducció de l'oralitat en el doblatge". *Quaderns. Revista de traducció, 2*, 97–105.

Elam, K. (1980). *The Semiotics of Theatre and Drama.* London: Methuen.

Espasa, E. (2001). "La traducció per al teatre i per al doblatge a l'aula: un laboratori de proves". In R. Agost & F. Chaume (Eds.), *La traducción en los medios audiovisuales* (pp. 57–64). Castelló: Publicacions de la Universitat Jaume I.

Fodor, I. (1976). *Film Dubbing: Phonetic, Semiotic, Esthetic and Psychological Aspects.* Hamburg: Helmut Buske.

Formosa, F. (1999). "La traducció teatral: del drama a l'escena". *Revista d'Igualada, 2,* Anoia, Septembre, 79–84.

Gambier, Y. & Gottlieb, H. (Eds.). (2001). *(Multi)media Translation: Concepts, Practices and Research.* Amsterdam and Philadelphia: John Benjamins.

Gottlieb, H. (1994). "Subtitling: Diagonal Translation". *Perspectives: Studies in Translatology, 2*(1), 101–121.

Gregory, M. & Carroll, S. (1978). *Language and Situation: Language Varieties and their Social Contexts.* London: Routledge and Kegan Paul.

Hatim, B. & Mason, I. (1990). *Discourse and the Translator.* London: Longman.

Hurtado Albir, A. (Ed.). (1996). *La enseñanza de la traducción.* Castelló: Publicacions de la Universitat Jaume I.

Ivarsson, J. (1992). *Subtitling for the Media. A Handbook of an Art.* Stockholm: Transedit.

Izard, N. (1992). *La traducció cinematogràfica.* Barcelona: Generalitat de Catalunya.

Izard, N. (1999). "Traducció audiovisual i creació de models de llengua en el sistema cultural català. Estudi de cas del doblatge d' "Helena, quina canya!" Doctoral thesis, Barcelona: Universitat Pompeu Fabra.

James, H. (1998). "Screen translation training and European cooperation". In Y. Gambier (Ed.), *Translating for the Media* (pp. 243–258). Turku: University of Turku.

Lambert, J. (1994). "Ethnolinguistic democracy, translation policy and contemporary world (dis)order". In F. Eguíluz et al. (Eds.), *Transvases culturales: Literatura, Cine, Traducción* (pp. 23–36). Vitoria-Gasteiz: Universidad del País Vasco.

L.T. (1998). "DVD will increase demand for media translators". *Language Today,* November 1998, 10–11.

Massip, C. (1997). "Traduir teatre". *El Pou de Lletres,* summer 1997, 50.

Mateo, M. (1995). "Constraints and possibilities of performance elements in drama translation". *Perspectives: Studies in Translatology, 3*(1), 21–33.

Mateo, M. (1996). "El componente escénico en la traducción teatral". In M. Edo (Ed.), *I Congrés Internacional sobre Traducció. Abril 1992, Actes* (pp. 907–917). Barcelona: Universitat Autònoma.

Mateo, M. (1997). "Translation strategies and the reception of drama performances: a mutual influence". In M. Snell-Hornby, Z. Jettmarová, & K. Kaindl (Eds.), *Translation as Intercultural Communication. Selected Papers from the EST Congress – Prague 1995.* Amsterdam and Philadelphia: John Benjamins.

Marqués, I. & Torregrosa, C. (1996). "Aproximación al estudio teórico de la subtitulación". In M. Edo (Ed.), *I Congrés Internacional sobre Traducció. Abril 1992, Actes* (pp. 367–379). Barcelona: Universitat Autònoma.

Mayoral, R., Kelly, D., & Gallardo, N. (1988). "Concept of constrained translation. Non-linguistic perspectives of translation". *Meta, 33*(3), 356–367.

Pujante, Á. L. (1995). "Traducir Shakespeare: mis tres fidelidades". *Vasos comunicantes,* autumn 1995, 11–21.

Pujante, Á. L. & Centenero, M. Á. (1995). "Las canciones de Shakespeare en las traducciones alemanas de A. W. Schlegel". *Cuadernos de Filología Inglesa, 4,* 93–106.

Schröder, H. (1992). "Semiotic aspects of multimedia texts". *Koiné: Annali della Scuola Superiore per Interpreti e Traduttori "San Pellegrino", II*(1–2), 315–325.

Sokoli, S. (2000). "Research issues in audiovisual translation: Aspects of subtitling in Greece". Unpublished research paper. Barcelona: Universitat Autònoma.

Titford, C. (1982). "Subtitling – Constrained translation". *Lebende Sprachen, XXVII*(3), 113–116.

Törnqvist, E., in Mateo (1997: 100).

[TVC] Televisió de Catalunya (1997). *Criteris lingüístics sobre traducció i doblatge.* Barcelona: Edicions 62.

Whitman, C. (1992). *Through the Dubbing Glass: The Synchronization of American Motion Pictures into German, French and Spanish.* Frankfurt: Peter Lang.

Zabalbeascoa, P. (1993). "Developing translation studies to better account for audiovisual texts and other new forms of text production (with special attention to the TV3 version of *Yes, Minister*)". Doctoral thesis. Lleida: Universitat de Lleida.

Internet resources for finding scripts

http://www.imbd.com
http://www.script-o-rama.com
http://www.personal.redestb.es/jmuñoz/scripts.html
http://www.geocities.com/moviscriptandscreenplays
http://www.easyweb.easynet.co.uk/shadelet
http://www.phrases.shu.ac.uk/meaning/106875 (The Phrase Finder)

CHAPTER 5

Computer-assisted translation

Richard Samson

> In the information age, translation, seen as a knowledge-based activity, re-
> quires a completely new strategy with regard to the logistics of information.
> This reflects a paradigm shift in the methodological-practical aspects of trans-
> lation that is not only restricted to the professional world of translating, but
> that also influences the areas of teaching and researching. (Austermühl 1999)

1. Introduction

The possibilities afforded by computers in rendering the translator's work more
efficient and more effective are diverse and far-reaching. Change has been
relatively sudden and all-embracing, as professional translators who have been
active over the past 15 years can testify. Translator training programmes must
rise to the challenge of providing up-to-date serviceable skills for students.
What skills do students need to have learnt by the time they graduate?

As for the title of this chapter, what do we refer to when we talk about
"computer-assisted translation" (CAT)? In this chapter I will be arguing for
a wide definition of CAT, and for its implementation across a broad range
of studies. The justification for this approach is that all professional translation nowadays is done in a digital environment involving some kind of
computer platform.

Obviously, for professional specialists CAT is often taken to refer only to
a more or less clearly defined set of highly-specialized tools such as translation memories and on-line database systems. While not excluding such applications, a broader view of CAT will include more general-purpose applications without which the translator will find it impossible to develop skills
in these more specialized tasks. Such skills may be taken to comprise what
has been called "computer literacy", an expression which indicates nicely what

is involved: that computer use is a general but not universal skill. Computer know-how is a defining feature of a new social group, just as reading knowledge once was.

Such general purpose skills, at the present stage, include acquaintance with the following tasks, amongst others (referring to PCs[1]):

- Configuration of the user's workstation
- File management
- Digital text production (word processing)
- Basic Internet use

These skills are cross-curricular and, as has been stated repeatedly over recent years, involve a paradigm shift that affects the whole of the educational system. Teachers are no longer the most important sources of knowledge for their students. Rather, teachers are now guides and counsellors to students who no longer have too little but too much information available and need to know how to manage the situation, how to find what they want in order to tackle whatever task they have in hand at any particular moment. The skills they need are skills for managing change and learning on an on-going basis.

This paradigm shift is self-evident. It does not need to be argued for. Yet it causes more disorientation among teachers than among students, almost none of whom can remember the pre-Internet era. Students of any discipline actively seek to improve their skills in the four areas identified above, with varying degrees of success, without any relevant formal instruction.

The fact that students perceive the need for developing their computer literacy makes the instructor's task a good deal easier. Since students will not need to be convinced of the utility of these studies, the teacher can harness the students' pre-existing motivation. As the students move forward in their computer studies from more general skills to more specific applications, they will reap the harvest of their increasing comfort and flexibility with the computer. A useful parallel with language study might be drawn. Foreign languages are all complex and different, yet acquisition of the first few foreign languages facilitates acquisition of further languages. Similarly, skills acquired in early computing contexts facilitates further development with other applications.

I will outline several observations, proposals and teaching procedures that might be of assistance to those interested in pre-service translator training in an undergraduate context. In line with my preceding comments, I will not be restricting my remarks to highly specialized professional translation applications.

2.   Appraising the situation

2.1   A personal view

The spreading use of computers in translation and translator training has caused considerable disorientation within the profession and consternation within the academic community. At best, this is merely a generational problem for those who went through school and college at a time when computers were merely a peripheral concern. But, in all likelihood, the problem is serious and long-term because developments in computer applications that are relevant to translation activities are continuing at an ever-faster pace, driven by innovation within the commercial sector. The challenge now lies with universities and other training institutions to keep pace with these changes.

The cutting edge for innovation is the so-called localization sector.[2] Localization refers to the adaptation of a product for local distribution, be it a car, a home appliance, a computer program or whatever. Translation often plays a key role in localization processes. The localization market is one of the fastest growing areas of translation around the world and is of enormous importance in commercial terms, particularly in the area of software localization. Witness these recent remarks from the President of the American Translators Association:

> Software developers have been working more closely than ever with translators and translation companies. Obviously, part of this initiative is due to the booming software market. More importantly though, we know that translators play a key role [...] and it is important to note that the software industry will "absorb" more and more translators/linguists in general. The key for associations, universities, training programs, and employers is to re-think and re-design the training and the curriculum of translation programs to meet the linguistic and technical needs of the localization industry, since a sizable number of future translators will be working directly or indirectly for the software industry.
> (Muriel Jérôme-O'Keeffe, President, American Translators Association, 1999)

This growth has given rise to new specializations and job profiles, such as project managers, localization translators, quality control specialists, software developers and engineers, each of them playing a part in a large team. The demands of working in these conditions are many, but perhaps most significantly translators need to be conversant with a variety of general and specific computer skills.

Yet localization is not the only language sector which has seen great innovation as a result of the computer revolution. Other areas where professional practice has been thoroughly overhauled include publishing, journalism (where whole jobs such as type-setting have disappeared) and lexicography (where corpus collections, concordancers, taggers, etc. are now in general use). The broad range of applications for the digital treatment of text has given rise to the so-called language industry, taking in disciplines other than translation *per se*. Bearing in mind the range of professional job prospects for translation undergraduate students, and the interdisciplinary nature of these skills, such applications cannot be ignored in translator training courses.

I am writing from the perspective of a teacher of fourth-year undergraduate students in a specialized translation degree course in Spain. Within an academic environment of this kind the priorities must be firmly established, if useful work is to be done in the limited time available. Clearly, it is impossible to prepare students for specific and varying job profiles within the localization or publishing sector in a pre-service context. There are several reasons for this difficulty. Principally it is because students generally start from a low baseline in their computer studies. In addition, as I have stated, the digital treatment of text is a rapidly developing field. Change is constant.

Be that as it may, any reticence on the part of translator trainers can only exacerbate difficulties for graduates entering the job market, who will suffer a computer literacy deficit that increases in approximate proportion to the entrenched out-dated practices of their teachers. As translator trainers, not only are we in danger of missing the boat, we may find ourselves swimming after it as it gets ever further ahead. If this happens, technical translation activities and other jobs of legitimate interest to our students will become the preserve of computer engineers or other technicians with foreign language skills, rather than career opportunities for university-trained translators. Deficient computer skills are a blight on all professionals in today's world. Companies in the language industry frequently bemoan the lack of qualified job candidates that bring together both translation and computer skills.

2.2 A wider view

More than a dozen undergraduate degrees in translation have been set up in Spain over the last ten years, since the Spanish government promoted translation courses from a three-year *diplomatura* to a full four-year *licenciatura*, qualifying graduates for a range of posts. Training programmes of such recent creation hardly have any excuse for being behind the times. Yet are the universities rising to the occasion? Are they up-to-date? Are they keeping pace?

For the writing of this chapter, I undertook some fieldwork on translator training institutions in Spain. The methodology used, admittedly *ad hoc*, was inspection of the curricula of these institutions, information which is in the public domain, broadly circulated and published on institutional web sites.

The questions I sought to answer were these:

1. How much computer training is provided in core (obligatory) subjects on these translator training programmes?
2. How many subjects, and of what duration, are devoted to general computer literacy?
3. How many subjects, and of what duration, are devoted to other computer skills?
4. What evidence is there for the inclusion of computer skills in other subjects?

The evidence, though only sketchy, is hardly encouraging. The minimum requirement in computer skill credits for official recognition of the degree course in Spain[3] is four credits.[4] These credits are divided up as follows:

> *Informatica aplicada a la traducción*   4 credits
> (Computers and Translation)

There is a further requirement in terminology, though it is not clear to what extent these studies need be computer-related:

> *Terminología*   8 credits
> (Terminology)

That is the minimum. As for the maximum, the undergraduate courses in Spain with most obligatory credits in directly computer-related subjects (excluding terminology) offer only 9 or 10 credits, at the present time. One university offers as many as 28 credits in obligatory and optional courses on computer-related subjects (including terminology). But, clearly, optional courses can be avoided if students choose to do so.

It is important to be clear about the figures here. The specialist translation undergraduate degree course in Spain with the most obligatory credits in computer-related studies offers 10 credits. These credits are equivalent to a total of 100 hours, out of a minimum of 3000 hours of classroom instruction over the whole degree course, less than 4%. Even a student opting for all the computer course options in the university offering the most credits of this kind would only reach just over 9% of their total studies in this speciality.[5]

The fourth question above, on the inclusion of computer skills in other subjects, is difficult to answer on the basis of the evidence available. Indeed, despite the attempts at standardization implicit in the official degree study plan, there is great variability from institution to institution; and there may even be variation from class group to class group.

The amount of instruction in computer skills is likely to be a function, in the first instance, of access and, secondly, of the preferences of the teacher involved. As most teachers received their own training before the advent of the computer tools discussed in this chapter, I would tentatively venture to suggest that the inclusion of computer skills is the exception rather than the rule. As Pym states (1999: 127–137):

> However, although the word "localization" does appear here and there in the programmes of the 280 or so translator-training institutions of which I am aware, the only actual training courses I have found are in Ireland, in departments of computer science. This could mean that our translation schools simply do not have enough of the computers and experts needed to teach localization. Alternatively, it might mean that the best solution is to send our translation students to the computer-science departments for their enlightenment.[6]

This may be a tongue-in-cheek remark, and in any case since Pym wrote this the situation has changed for the better, I think. Even so, most new specialized courses in "computing and translation" in Spain are now being offered at the postgraduate level. Without doubt, this option causes minimal disruption for staff and administrators responsible for undergraduate teaching. But it does beg the question. What is being done to integrate appropriate computer skills in four-year translation courses at the undergraduate level?

Far be it for me to call into question the worth of specialist postgraduate courses. But training in computer skills, both general and specialist, cannot be systematically postponed for the convenience of practitioners of out-of-date instructional methods and curricula. I am proposing a committed and challenging approach in which all teachers at the undergraduate level are encouraged to engage with new technologies, both general and specialized, and include them at the heart of their courses.

3. Proposals

In this section I make four recommendations for translator training programmes. These are:

- that programmes be practical and varied
- that programmes be cross-curricular
- that institutions provide adequate staff training
- that institutions seek suitable commercial partnerships.

I will take these subjects in turn, focusing on the first two recommendations,
which are those that fall most directly within the scope of the translator trainer.
This is not to underestimate the importance of the remaining proposals.
Nonetheless, staff training and institutional partnerships are most likely to
correspond to higher level decision makers.

3.1 Training courses must be practical and varied

Training must be hands-on practical training, at suitable work stations in a
properly equipped computer room with video projection facilities or alternatively screen sharing collaboration software.[7] Appropriate training methodology will combine aspects of task focus, student autonomy, resourcing in a
coherent digital text environment.

And students must, during their university studies, work with a variety
of relevant applications (operating systems, word processors, spreadsheets,
databases, audiovisual presentations, Internet, automatic translation, translation memory programs, design and authoring programs, etc.) that will give
them a foundation of know-how sufficient to render subsequent pre- or in-
service training a question of specification and fine-tuning, rather than a totally
new task and an insuperable obstacle.

3.1.1 *Hardware and software*

The single most important pre-requisite for all computer training is access.
Students must be able to use computers, whether in the classroom, in a general
purpose computer room or at home. Computers are only tools. To learn how
to use a tool, the best method is to use it yourself under expert guidance. Given
only this, many students will informally train themselves in whatever aspects
are suitable to their needs.

Furthermore, the computers made available must be modern enough to
run the software used, and Internet access must be easy and fast. Computers

that run too slowly for the software installed to work effectively in real time can give students a false impression of the possible benefits of computer use and lead to frustration.

In practical terms, what does this mean? While it is difficult and dangerous to give guidelines on paper in relation to computer technology, since circumstances change so fast, it is possible to give some indication of what is required and what is likely to be required in the foreseeable future.

As regards machines, economy range PCs are nowadays sufficient. Unless extensive use of high-quality sound and image is contemplated, there is no need for machines of any special power.[8] Mac computers are a viable alternative. Furthermore, it is necessary to have total networking and Internet access: all computers must be included in the network. Ideally, it is also desirable for students to be able to have a reserved workspace folder on a local server computer, so that they can store their work in a secure and accessible fashion.

As regards software, my own experience, as will be clear from the examples given, is with the various versions of MS Windows, MS Office and other commercial solutions. This option is no longer by any means a foregone conclusion. Institutions entering the field should at least give due consideration to the non-commercial options which have made great advances over the last few years. For example, the LINUX operating system and OpenOffice suite of general programs are a feasible alternative, at least for non-specialist applications.

In general, it is not important precisely which programs students use in their training. Depending on the kind of application, there are usually a variety of broadly equivalent alternatives available. (For example, in word processing: Microsoft Word, Lotus WordPro, OpenOffice, Corel WordPerfect, etc.)[9] The graphic interface philosophy that underlies modern program design is now universal. Generally speaking, therefore, an understanding of a particular kind of application's options and its ease of use can be acquired by students with any of the programs available. This is at least the case with applications such as word processors which have reached a high level of standardization over recent years.

3.1.2   *Methodology*

The methodological approach used in the "Computing for translators" courses referred to in this chapter is based on demonstration and practice, in a paper-free environment. All course materials are distributed via computer networks and all course assignments are sent by e-mail. The course is administered through a virtual classroom whose web pages and other on-line resources are made available to registered users and the class becomes a virtual, as well as a physical, community. Students are presented with a wide variety of resources and are encouraged to choose their own learning and practice activities by engaging in a conscious experiential learning cycle where they first observe a target professional skill in action, then reflect on their own abilities, inspect the learning resources made available to them, and go on to decide which activities to pursue in the light of the progress they need to make, and finally submit themselves to evaluation, choosing again from a variety of options. Great emphasis is placed on maximizing student autonomy, providing them with clearly identified destinations and a choice of paths to follow.

The methodology I am proposing here is collaborative and student-centred.[10] This kind of methodology is in marked contrast to the transmission model, the traditional approach in which the teacher declaims and the students listen and take notes. In this more modern approach, methodology is differentiated and individualized. Students are encouraged to take more responsibility for their own learning, and the teacher becomes more of a counsellor and guide and less of a knowledge source. Within this model it is possible and appropriate for the teacher to help students undertake projects that involve applications where the teacher is not in fact an expert. This way of working might be considered irresponsible or fraudulent within a traditional transmissionist paradigm of education; but I would argue that in fact it is no longer possible, with the presently distant and expanding horizons of knowledge available to students, for teachers to maintain their traditional role (of expertise in all aspects of their field). Collaborative work between a teacher and students, none of whom knows the answers at the outset, can in my opinion restore much-needed excitement to the educational task.

But these are not the only justifications for an alternative methodology. Students invariably come to computer training from a variety of different starting points. They need to assess their own knowledge in the light of the goals established for the course and invest their time appropriately. Projects worked on should include choice and be open-ended so that students can tailor their studies and investment to their interests and needs.

Explanations and demonstrations, one-to-many, from the teacher to the class should be reduced to a minimum and, if possible, be given in response to a specific request from the class group. This in turn guarantees enhanced motivation.

The translator computer training course described in this chapter is divided into a series of modules, each centred around one or more projects. The materials needed for each project are available to registered users on a web site.

In fact, nearly all primary documentation is provided by this means. No paper documentation is distributed. Apart from the obvious advantage of imbuing the work with a "digital culture", this decision brings other benefits:

- The course may be pursued at a distance. Attendance at class may be optional. Class sessions tend to become individual one-to-one tutorials.
- Students do not need to carry course materials around with them on paper, since wherever they are they have access to the materials via Internet.
- There is no extra cost to course participants for course materials.
- Extra material may be introduced at will.

Examples of this methodology, including materials, are given in the Appendix. I have chosen the detailed example given there, a digital subtitling project, because of its brevity and simplicity. It also serves to show how cheap or free software may be put to use on a training programme of this kind. Some other projects I have developed for use in translator training are listed in outline in the same Appendix.

3.1.3   *The bottom line*

What is the bottom line in terms of computing skills for graduates of translation courses? What is the minimum level of computer know-how that students should have attained by graduation? These questions are of fundamental importance and can help trainers gauge the success of their instructional programmes.

In my view, the bottom line, corresponding to broad computer literacy, includes the following items (a more detailed version of the list given in the Introduction):

- knowledge of computer components and basic maintenance requirements
- ability to install hardware and programs
- personalization of the operating system interface and setting up of preferences
- file management, file formats and security (back-up and antivirus)
- basic word processing skills, including appropriate use of layout functions, spell-checkers, etc.
- basic Internet skills, including WWW navigation and e-mail use.

Only once these basic skills have been acquired will it be possible to work on more advanced aspects.

3.2 Instruction in computer skills must be cross-curricular

A glance at the preceding list and the inventory of relevant computer applications in the Appendix will indicate the scale of the challenge in training
translators in computer skills. If this task is to be accomplished with any success, it is vital that the relevant skills be taught throughout the curriculum in
appropriate subjects. Training in general computer skills must come to occupy
a central place within overall training, no longer marginalized to peripheral
specialized subjects.

Furthermore, the planning and distribution of computer skills instruction
across a range of translation subjects provides translation department teaching
staff with a new opportunity for creating coherence across the courses that
students take. The benefits of this are not to be underestimated since in
emergent multi-disciplinary studies such as translation it is all too easy for
individual subjects to be taught in "splendid isolation" and for the sum
of the parts, from the student's point of view, to remain fragmentary and
kaleidoscopic.

Undergraduate degree courses invariably include subjects such as "Computers and Translation" (broadly speaking, along the lines of the course described in the preceding section and the Appendix) and various courses in
specialized translation such as "Audiovisual Translation", "Legal and Administrative Translation", "Literary Translation", "Technical Translation", etc. Traditionally, these subjects have been taught as separate specializations. In particular, for our purposes here, the role of computers has all too often been reduced
to basic word-processing, that is, a means for producing attractive hard copy of
assigned exercises on paper. In fact, even basic word-processing skills are all too
often taken for granted rather than taught, with the result that students may resort to a variety of substandard practices (such as, in word processors, use of
the space bar to align text). This cosy situation of non-instruction or merely
basic instruction is no longer tenable, and constitutes in fact a grave disservice
to students.

Furthermore, study plans usually provide for a number of preparatory
subjects, such as "Translation Theory", "Linguistics and Translation", "Language and Culture", etc. which are intended as a foundation for all general and
specialized translation courses. Their role is similar to the one I perceive for
CAT studies, not as a separate specialization, but as a cross-curricular field to
be introduced early in the degree programme and developed in the various
specialized translation courses subsequently. (Within this framework there is

also room for specialist CAT courses in subjects such as software localization, dictionary preparation, etc.)

Some CAT teachers might see the presence of CAT skills in other specialist subjects as a relinquishment of their own specialist area. Similarly, translation teachers may perceive the increasing use of computers in their subjects as a technical (and soulless) encroachment on disciplines of the Humanities, whose aspirations lie elsewhere. Nonetheless, as I have stated in Section 2, it is my view that CAT skills, in the broad sense of computer literacy, are a cornerstone in translator training and need to be introduced in a general way early on and developed in more specialized instruction in other subjects appropriately. To use an in-vogue word, I am appealing for the *mainstreaming* of computing in undergraduate translation studies, just as ecology and gender issues have been mainstreamed before.

Some examples of how CAT skills can be incorporated into other specialist translation subjects follow.

3.2.1 *Interpreting*

Trainee interpreters can be shown how to use database management systems, such as the European Commission's EUTERPE database, or other databases that the training institution may have acquired, to prepare specialized bilingual glossaries before and during interpreting practice. Interpreting departments may also acquire and teach the use of various stand-alone CD ROM-based interpreting training materials.[11]

3.2.2 *Literary translation*

Trainee literary translators can be shown how to use the Internet (WWW, translator mailing lists and newsgroups, etc.) as a resource for locating bibliographic material and resolving problems in texts to be translated. This use of the Internet is now absolutely standard among professional translators and most students find the Internet, particularly the WWW, an attractive resource. But students need to be given specific instruction in how to conduct advanced searches on the WWW in order to be able to locate specific resources efficiently. The use of mailing lists and newsgroups is an attractive option too, but is not as intuitive as the WWW and therefore needs a careful introduction. One option is to set up a mailing list for course participants.

3.2.3 *Administrative translation*

Students can be shown how to gain access to sample documents, parallel texts and on-line databases.

3.2.4 *Audiovisual translation*

Students can be given practical experience in the preparation of digital translation subtitles for selected sequences of film. Without such an experience, translation practice is inevitably reduced to pen, paper and word processor, dealing with genre but hardly touching on issues of process in the production of screen subtitles. Professional subtitling packages, hardware and software, are expensive and not adapted for classroom environments. However, there are now a variety of inexpensive solutions that can be effectively adapted for educational use. (See Appendix.)

3.2.5 *General translation*

Students can be given the experience of working in a totally digital text environment. Instructors should provide texts to be translated in digital format and students should be shown how to respect that format in their translation work. This means a decisive move away from resources based on paper and photocopies (which still unfortunately predominate in many academic contexts). Students need to be able to deal with basic tasks of file management, printing, spell-checking, layout, etc.

Students can also be given useful experience in digital text editing, proofreading and supervision, using readily available tools such as those incorporated in most modern word-processing software. These tools can also be used in exciting ways to allow students to edit other students' work by the inclusion of commentaries, rather than rewriting of the original, thus permitting a collaborative mode of work for groups of students.

Students can also be given projects to compare the efficiency of traditional paper-based research in libraries and reference books with innovative digital research environments. Such projects help students develop their own understanding of the strengths and weaknesses of the instruments at their disposal and provide instructors with ample opportunities for intervention and feedback. Furthermore, the general translation class is an appropriate venue for an introduction to terminology management.

As the diverse use of computers becomes more fully integrated into general and specialist translation classes, it will become possible, in specific computer skills courses, for time to be devoted to more specialized applications.

3.3 Staff training

None of the initiatives outlined in the preceding section will be possible unless training institutions adequately retrain their own teaching staff. It is unfortunately the case that many experts in specialist fields and experienced adult educators are even more disoriented when it comes to computers than their students, who at least have the relative advantage of having grown up in the information technology era. Institutions must, therefore, ensure that all translation teaching staff be provided with attractive opportunities for in-service training in basic and specialized computing skills.

3.4 Partnership

The use of computers in language applications ranges now from very basic general-purpose applications such as word processing to highly specialized applications such as translation memory systems. In order to stay abreast of developments and provide appropriate instruction, translator training institutions must seek to establish partnerships with the commercial sector, in particular with the language industry, to ensure that relevant software and hardware is made available to them and to provide suitable work/study opportunities for their students.

Institutions must also ensure that sufficient access to computer work stations is provided to students and that the computers are new enough to run the applications under study.[12] General purpose computers have a useful lifetime of about 5 years at the moment. This is not because they wear out after that time. Indeed, computers are in general very resistant to wear and tear. But after that time period they are no longer powerful enough, experience demonstrates, to run the most up-to-date applications.

As computer skills become more centrally integrated into training programmes, institutions will need to move away from the traditional blackboard and chalk set-up to classrooms with networked computers and/or a video-projector.

It will probably only be possible for training institutions to meet these various challenges if they develop suitable commercial partnership arrangements.

4. Summary

– I have given a broad definition to CAT (computer-assisted translation) in an educational context.
– I have argued that computer skills need to be given a high profile in translator training programmes in both general and specialist subjects, coming to occupy a central role in this multi-disciplinary field.

- A certain amount of evidence has been gathered to lend support to the notion of an existing deficit in computer skills training in translation courses in Spain.
- I have proposed that, given sufficient computer access, training in computer skills constitutes an excellent opportunity for the implementation of an alternative teaching approach based on student-centred collaborative project work.
- I have outlined proposals for instructional programmes based on this approach and given examples, referring to projects that have been successfully piloted with my own students.
- I have outlined proposals for the integration of computer skills into general and specialized translation courses.
- I have also made recommendations for institutions that seek to enhance the computer skills component of their translation training.

Appendix: Sample projects

The project I have selected for detailed presentation here is on subtitling.[13] The study guide ("complete user guide") for this project is available at http://www.uvic.es/fchtd/especial/en/ptg/dvsc.html (opened 22 October 2003).[14] This web page forms part of a more wide-ranging project, the "Poor Technology Group", which includes other educational solutions and is described more fully at http://www.uvic.es/fchtd/especial/en/ptg/ptg.html (opened 22 October 2003). The subtitling user guide referred to above is fairly typical of the study guides that I use in my teaching. It serves as a key document for the subject, a kind of do-it-yourself guide. These study guides usually include the following sections:

- Observation and reflection: viewing of a professional process or product followed by some questions about the subject and some specialized terminology, allowing the students to gauge their entry level knowledge.
- Gathering resources and deciding what to do: bibliography, on paper and electronic, providing a wide range of materials for students to consult.
- Action: materials and activities specifically put together for this class. These activities comprise the "bottom line".
- Assessment: details of the project options for work to be submitted for assessment.

This structure is intended as a flexible framework for students to be able to use to their advantage in a variety of ways. Many students choose to go straight to the Assessment section and refer back to the preceding sections as needed if they find that they cannot do what is asked for in the assignment. If some students ask for specific instruction in class then I use the corresponding notes from the Action section, which have been written for self-study or class use in this way. This four-section division of materials is loosely based on the experiential learning cycle of action, reflection, theorizing and pragmatism.[15]

For the sake of convenience extracts from this guide are reproduced below. For full details refer to the web page given above.

*

Introduction
The purpose of this project is to provide the audiovisual translator with realistic practice in digital video subtitling but in a "normal" PC environment. In this approach the subtitles are "scripted" by using the video's audio track to set times by using a freeware application called Sub Station Alpha (SSA). SSA subtitles can be played back in another freeware application called ViPlay along with the original video. The purpose of this "readme" file is to provide the student with sufficient documentation to undertake a video project without the need for constant supervision. The project is supplied on CD together with all the necessary software and examples.

Software installation
ViPlay: In My PC or Windows Explorer, open the programs folder. Execute (double click) the ViPlay "exe" file, following the on-screen instructions.

DirectX: Included on the CD is a version of this Windows add-on for multimedia performance improvements. The latest versions are available at this page: http://www.microsoft.com/windows/directx/default.aspx (opened 22 October 2003).

In My PC or Windows Explorer, open the programs folder. Execute (double click) the DX81eng.exe file (if you are using the CD version), following the on-screen instructions. (The computer will reboot at the end of the installation process, therefore close all other programs first.)

Sub Station Alpha: In My PC or Windows Explorer, open the programs folder. Execute (double click) the Sub Station Alpha "exe" file, following the on-screen instructions. Clearly, you only need to install software once on each computer.

Hardware installation

The only "extra" hardware required for this project is a set of headphones or speakers. These should be connected to the sound card at the back of the PC. The appropriate jack is usually indicated by a green surround. Check that your headphones/speakers are working correctly by playing any sound on your computer. If you cannot hear the sound then either you have made the wrong connection, or you need to adjust your computer's volume controls, or both.

The complete subtitle editing process

a. Raw material: Get a copy of the film (VHS or DVD).
b. Translation: Familiarize yourself with the video material by watching it a few times. Prepare the subtitle text in outline on paper.
c. Digital files: Get a copy of the film in .mpg format. Get a copy of the film audio track in .wav format. The files should have the right format. In the case of the .wav file this is 8-bit mono, 11025 Hz. The .mpg and .wav files included on the CD all have the right format for this project. It is important to respect these formats. You will need to take your original DVD or VHS material to the University Audiovisual Service with a recordable blank CD for the digital files to be recorded onto. Ask your teacher to contact the Audiovisual Service for you. If in doubt about formats, take this CD to the University Audiovisual Service and tell them that you want the files to have exactly the same specifications as the samples here.
    If you are working on a classroom project then steps (a) to (c) have probably been carried out for you by your teacher.
d. Preparing the subtitle script: Use the Sub Station Alpha program to make your complete subtitle script.
e. Playback: Use the ViPlay program to play back your finished work.

Post-editing and production processes

After preparing your SSA subtitle script you should send it to your teacher/supervisor in .ssa format. Your teacher can evaluate your subscripts from this script. For short fragments of subtitles this is probably enough. Playback in ViPlay is excellent and allows for optimization of the subtitle appearance. On most computers the film is best played at less than full-screen size, since unless you have a powerful computer, the processor will not be able to keep up with the demands of refreshing the image and the film will as a result appear jumpy. If you produce a full subtitle script (i.e. for a whole film), then you may wish to have a Video CD version that you can play on a TV in a standard DVD player. To do this the subtitles and the film must be recoded and combined and then recorded onto a CD. This process can be carried out for you if your teacher/supervisor requests it and sends the materials to me at rsamson@uvic.es.

About subtitling

The following selection of web pages provides information on good subtitling practice in both professional and amateur contexts.

http://accurapid.com/journal/04stndrd.htm (opened 21 October 2003)
"A Proposed Set of Subtitling Standards in Europe." This page also contains an excellent bibliography of paper-based resources. Fotios Karamitroglou.

http://www.accurapid.com/journal/09av.htm (opened 21 October 2003)
"Audiovisual Translation at the Dawn of the Digital Age: Prospects and Potentials." Fotios Karamitroglou.

http://www.eswat.demon.co.uk/substation.html (opened 1 December 2002)
The home web page of Sub Station Alpha, the subtitling program used here. At the time of the final revision of this chapter in October 2003 the web page was no longer available, though references to the program abound on other pages.

http://www.screen.subtitling.com (opened 21 October 2003)
A commercial digital subtitling system.

http://www.cpcweb.com/Subtitling/sub_splash.htm (opened 21 October 2003)
A commercial digital subtitling system.

Technical approaches to subtitling have been totally changed by the digital revolution. It is now possible for subtitles to be set up in a totally digital environment, with all the flexibility and power that such environments offer. It would be nice to simply type the subtitles onto the moving image with an edit, start and stop button and fine playback controls. Programs that do this are available but they are both expensive and require special equipment, which means that students cannot practise with these programs on ordinary computers.[16] By contrast, SSA is a subtitling editor that is not only economic on computer resources, but also free and easy to use.

SSA background information

SSA is a freeware subtitling program developed by manga enthusiasts for private use. If you search for SSA on the WWW you will find many related resources. In the words of the program's author, alias Kotus:

Sub Station Alpha (SSA) is a freeware program for video titling and subtitling which runs under Windows on a PC. It works in "real-time" – adding subtitles to live video via a "genlock". Real-time subtitling with a dedicated subtitling program like SSA is generally much easier, faster, and cheaper than using digitised video and a general purpose non-linear editing program. However, future versions of SSA will also allow subtitles to be written into the individual frames of digitised video.

It was originally aimed at anime "fansubbers", and is intended to make subtitling quick and easy, and produce high-quality subtitled video. It is equally useful for adding titles and credits to videos, and for making karaoke videos. In SSA subtitles are synchronized by reference to the audio track alone (without images). The subtitles, once created, can be "played back" in SSA with the accompanying images, but not very satisfactorily. "Play back" gives you the opportunity to view your work as anybody else would see it. Since the "play back" options in SSA are not very easy to operate, we propose you play back your subtitles with the ViPlay program.

In the following sections, I have indicated how SSA can be used with the materials on this CD-ROM for subtitling practice in a university context.

Example assessment task
Your task is to produce timed on-screen same-language subtitles in SSA format for the sound file supplied to you. You should send the SSA file (not the sound file) to me at rsamson@uvic.es as an attachment to an e-mail message with the subject field "SSA" by (deadline).

*

The web page from which the above extracts were taken is merely one component of the courseware. Equally important is the class mailing list, which facilitates two-way communication at a distance. (By contrast, the web page is basically a unidirectional teacher-to-student communication.) Among the mailing lists I have used for my courses have been those administered at E-groups, now absorbed into Yahoo! The use of a mailing list encourages students to appeal for help and to help each other. The teacher can really move from the position of "sage on the stage" to "guide on the side", only intervening if students do not manage to resolve difficulties among themselves. The mailing list allows students to work and get help at a distance. Since students have easy access to the e-mail addresses of all course participants, they can use the one-to-many dialogue of the mailing list or more private one-to-one dialogues with other course participants.

The dynamics of working in this way, with multiple digital information resources, flexible permanently open channels of dialogue, a project focus, together with class meetings for group instruction, guided study and tutorials, can help students move rapidly from a novice level, through introductory sessions and the establishment of a collaborative working environment, to more advanced autonomous modes of work that reflect professional practice.

At first, many students are disoriented by the range of possibilities on offer and the reluctance of the teacher to fill the available class time with lock-step transmissionist exercise sequences. A collaborative way of working can, at first sight, seem uncooperative and even subversive since it runs counter to much tradition and experience in training institutions. But over the course of time students tend to realise that the extra responsibility and freedom they have can only work to their advantage.

In summary, a well-resourced digital learning environment with a clear project focus and permanently open channels of communication is an enhanced situation for effective learning.

Other projects (in outline): An inventory

Translation students need to be prepared in basic computer literacy and in a variety of more specialized skills that will prepare them for the future and further developments in information technology. At my institution I have organized the material into two courses, the first focusing on general computer skills and the second dealing with more specialist skills for translators and other language industry professionals. This kind of organization is flexible, and in my case responds to the constraints of available time and other institutional factors. In the list below I have given outline information on most of the projects I have prepared to date, for both general and specialized courses.

Subtitling
Sample project (details given above): Provide timed, on-screen same-language subtitles for a song. Featured application: Sub Station Alpha.

Operating systems
Sample project: Write a multiple-choice test on operating systems and Windows 95/98/XP. It should consist of 15 original, appropriate questions, each with three suggested answers to choose from. Featured application: Windows 95/98/XP.

Word processing
Sample project: Make a template of your own including the following features: default text style of Courier New, 10 point; styled numbered headings 1, 2 and 3 of your choice; personalized Standard and Format toolbars; two macros of your choice, each with a toolbar button on the Standard toolbar. Featured application: Microsoft Word.

Spreadsheets
Sample project: Eight students have taken the same computer course, consisting of the four subjects: (1) Operating Systems, (2) Word Processors, (3) Spreadsheets and, (4) Internet, each with equal weight. To pass the course they need to pass each subject separately (>50%), whether through the set assignment or the corresponding section of the final exam. If they do both, then the higher of the two grades counts. The final grade, a whole number out of ten, is the average of the subject grades. Invent the results of the eight students and make a spreadsheet with columns for each subject and assignment or final exam. The final grade for each student must be calculated automatically. Featured application: Microsoft Excel 97.

Internet
Sample project: Send fully documented answers (citing the resource used and copying any relevant text) to the following tasks to me at rsamson@uvic.es:

a. I want to see the proceedings of the European Parliament in both Spanish and English.
b. I want to know what Marmite is.
c. I want to know what FOB, CIP and ACV mean in a commercial context.
d. I want to know if anything by Quim Monzó has been published in French.
e. I want to find out if I can join any virtual translation agencies and find translation work over the Internet.
f. I want to find out what associations there are for translators in Spain.
g. I want to find out if it is more usual to say "the same way as" or "the same way that" in English.

Featured applications: browser, newsgroups, mailing lists, ftp, WWW, search engines, Copernic.

Relational databases
Sample project: Organize the data given to make a database with three tables: customers, products and orders. Then design the queries and forms specified. Featured application: Microsoft Access 97.

Audiovisual presentations
Sample project: Make a slide presentation about your final year translation research project. The presentation should include a minimum of 5 slides (including the title slide), a change in the background, a graphic (clipart, wordart, etc.), a change in the slide transition or animated text. Featured application: Microsoft Powerpoint 97.

Automatic translation
Sample project: Try to fool a translation machine with at least 25 sentences of your own choice, in a language pair of your own choice. Write a short research report on your experiment. Featured applications: Globalink Power Translator, Babelfish (http://world.altavista.com, opened 21 October 2003), etc.

Terminology databases
Sample project: Make a bilingual terminology database for a translation project and use it on-line to translate the documents given. Featured applications: Trados Multiterm, STAR TermStar.

Translation productivity tools (translation memories, format management)
Sample project: Import, align and translate the given texts using each system and write a report assessing the relative advantages and disadvantages of each. Featured applications: Trados Workbench, STAR Transit, Atril Déjà Vu, Wordfast.

Desk-top publishing
Sample project: Using the supplied image files, create a print-ready file with the appearance of the supplied pdf file. Featured application: Adobe PageMaker.

Web page editing
Sample project: Design and publish a personal web page, including a translation resources directory. Featured application: Netscape Composer.

The above list of projects is wide-ranging but by no means complete. It reflects the projects that I have used with trainee translators.

Other areas for projects might be:

Image editing

Scanning of images, conversion between image formats and retouching of images are essential tasks in publishing. In a training context they can be worked on in the context of preparation of images for inclusion in web pages.

Video editing

Video editing will become increasingly important across a range of applications now that low-cost digital video is feasible.

Electronic document distribution

Adobe Portable Document Format (PDF) has become a standard for electronic document distribution worldwide.

Software localization

Translators in the localization sector may need to work with packages such as Alchemy Catalyst.

Concordancing

Students can conduct short research projects into issues of language use, working with their own or other available corpora.

Projects in the above and other areas can be drawn up in response to demand and further developments in the technical translation field.

Notes

1. I refer throughout this chapter to PCs. Although it is possible that students will use other kinds of computer, PCs are the most universal standard, and the cheapest, for the kinds of application discussed here.

2. I have tended to use the -iz- spelling rather than the -is- one, unless citing other sources.

3. Official recognition means that the degree course is "homologada", that is, it conforms within limits to the study plan set out and approved for all institutions of higher education by the Spanish government. Institutions are free to set up courses that follow other study plans but in that case the degree will not serve as an entry level civil service qualification. In practice, to date all undergraduate translation courses in Spain conform to the official plan.

4. One credit is equivalent to ten hours of classroom time.

5. These figures may have varied since the original survey was carried out in 2000.

6. "Localizing Localization in Translator-Training Curricula". A. Pym (1999). First published on his web page. (Later published 1999 in *Linguistica Antverpiensa*, *33*, 127–137.)

7. Robin Good offers excellent independent news and reviews of collaboration software at http://www.masternewmedia.org/online_collaboration_and_exchange.htm (opened 21 October 2003).

8. Until recently, powerful processors, RAM memory and hard disk memory were all relatively expensive. But at present entry-level PCs in general all have specifications well beyond what is needed for programs for the digital treatment of text.

9. The following names, mentioned in this chapter, are registered trademarks: Lotus WordPro, Corel WordPerfect, Microsoft Word, Microsoft Excel, Microsoft Access, Microsoft Office, Microsoft PowerPoint, Microsoft Windows, Netscape Commmunicator, Netscape Navigator, Yahoo!, Sololingue, Microsoft FrontPage, Alchemy Catalyst, Adobe PageMaker, Atril Déjà Vu, STAR Transit, Trados Workbench, Trados MultiTerm, STAR TermStar, Wordfast, Globalink Power Translator, Copernic, Google, Altavista. Sub Station Alpha, OpenOffice, ViPlay and Linux are freeware.

10. For an excellent up-to-date discussion of this kind of approach to translator training, including a chapter on computer skills, the reader is referred to Kiraly, 2000. *A Social Constructivist Approach to Translator Education*. Manchester: St. Jerome.

11. See, for example, http://www.uvic.es/fchtd/especial/en/ptg/int.html

12. The number of computers per student will vary depending on circumstances. At the present time it is desirable, in my opinion, to have at least one computer for every ten students or so, but in the future it will probably be the case that more and more students will come to the training institution with their own portable computers. This raises new issues of access to software and also means that it will become increasingly important for institutions to ensure adequate networking of their facilities, including classrooms and halls of residence, so that students may "hook up" wherever they may be on campus.

13. In this regard, readers may also be interested in consulting Section 5 on "Teaching subtitling" in Chapter 4 of this volume: "Audiovisual translation" by Francesca Bartrina and Eva Espasa.

14. The reader is advised that, while the electronic references in this chapter were correct at the time of going to press, they are inherently less stable than paper references. Very often a broken link can be traced by searching the host site or, failing that, conducting a search on data included in the link.

15. See, for example, Honey, P. and Mumford, A. (1986).

16. Since this chapter was written, cheap and free software that does precisely this has become available. For details consult the "Poor Technology Group" web page at http://www.uvic.es/fchtd/especial/en/ptg/ptg.html

References

Austermühl, F. (1999). "Between Babel and bytes. The discipline of translation in the information age". *AREAS Annual Report on English and American Studies, 16,* 439–450. Trier: WVT Wissenschaftlicher Verlag Trier. (Available as an abstract at: http://www.hit.uib.no/AcoHum/abs/Austermuehl.htm, opened 14 July 2003.) Scholarly discussion of the on-going important and far-reaching changes in academic and professional practice occasioned by the digital revolution.

Honey, P. & Mumford, A. (1986). *Using your learning styles.* Maidenhead: Peter Honey.

Kiraly, D. (2000). *A Social Constructivist Approach to Translator Education.* Manchester: St. Jerome.

Pym, A. (1999). "Localizing localization in translator-training curricula". *Linguistica Antverpiensa, 33,* 127–137.

Further reading

Abaitua, J. (2003). Proyecto de creación de material docente. http://www.serv-inf.deusto.es/abaitua/konzeptu/ (opened 14 July 2003). Project for the creation of teaching materials in hypertext format at the University of Deusto. Extensive pioneering work in the Spanish context (in Spanish).

Austermühl, F. (2001). *Electronic Tools for Translators.* Manchester: St. Jerome.

Bowker, L. et al. (2001). *Bibliography of Translation Studies* (4th ed.). Manchester: St. Jerome. Selected annotated references arranged under specific headings. Ideal for course designers.

Canali De Rossi, L. (2003). "Robin Good's Sharewood tidings – Ideas, tools and resources for effective communication and learning with new Media Technologies – Communication skills and tools". http://www.masternewmedia.org/ (opened 14 July 2003). A wide-ranging independent news and review resource with a section on translation and internationalization.

Esselink, B. (2000). *A Practical Guide to Localization* (2nd ed.). Amsterdam and Philadelphia: John Benjamins. A vital resource for those interested in CAT in the narrow sense, particularly translation in localization projects. Wide coverage of issues for project managers and translators.

Feder, M. (2001). *Computer Assisted Translation (CAT) Tools and a Bibliography.* http://elex. amu.edu.pl/ifa/interp/cat.htm (opened 14 July 2003). An extensive list of links to computer-assisted translation sites and a CAT bibliography. The list features the following CAT categories: Terminology Management Systems (TMS), Machine Assisted Human Translation (MAHT) and Machine Translation (MT).

Localization Industry Standards Association. http://www.lisa.org/ (opened 14 July 2003). LISA is now the leading organization for the localization and internationalization industry. Its mission is "promoting the localization and internationalization industry and providing a mechanism and services to enable companies to exchange and share information on the development of processes, tools, technologies and business models connected with localization, internationalization and related topics."

Sandrini, P. "Translation Links". http://homepage.uibk.ac.at/~c61302/tranlink.html (opened 14 July 2003). A good example of a translation resource directory, in this case hosted at the University of Innsbruck. There are many directories of this kind on the WWW, not all of them as up-to-date as might be. To find more pages in a similar vein, try searching for ["translation resources" links] at Google.

CHAPTER 6

Teaching conference interpreting
A contribution

Daniel Gile

1. Introduction

This chapter highlights fundamental principles and suggests guidelines for organisations which plan to develop a conference interpreter training program or to improve existing programs, if these are considered unsatisfactory. Trends are indicated and explained and evaluations of specific strategies and methods are made, but no "universal" training model is suggested, due to the following:

a. At this point, in spite of the ever-increasing volume of research on interpreting (see *Target*, 7, 1 (1995); Gile 1995a, 1995b; Tommola 1995; Gambier et al. 1997; *The CIRIN Bulletin*), there is too little evidence that would make it possible to determine that any combination of concepts and methods in a set program is "better" than others in absolute terms, or even in particular environments.

b. There is too much variability in environmental parameters, including admission conditions, the students' age, previous academic experience, mastery of their future working languages, class size, instructor qualification, access to a multilingual environment outside the program, academic requirements at the local institution, etc. Such variability suggests that when optimising a syllabus, adapting to environmental constraints may be more important than attempting to comply with a standard model.

Another point is that conference interpreting being a complex skill, a vast amount of publications has been devoted to interpreter training over the past 45 years (see Gile 2000). A single chapter cannot do justice to all the ideas, methods and experiments reported in the literature, or indeed cover all aspects of training. The more humble ambition of this chapter is to highlight important didactic issues and to make some specific suggestions which may not be easily collected elsewhere, especially as regards non-standard environments. For a more comprehensive view of facts, opinions and methods in the field of conference interpreter training, readers are referred to the appended bibliography.

Finally, some skills taught in conference interpreter training programs, in particular consecutive interpreting, are also useful to community interpreters, court interpreters, etc., but my qualifications do not extend beyond conference interpreting, which is therefore the focus of this chapter. Leaders of training programs with a different focus are invited to assess the relevance and applicability of principles explained here to their own environment and to read the relevant literature.

2.   Translation and interpreting

One preliminary point to be made concerns the relation between translator training and interpreter training. Should they be offered in parallel, or one as a preparation to the other, or separately? It is sometimes claimed that translation and interpreting require different and incompatible skills and personalities. At this time, no research finding has confirmed this idea: there are many interpreters who also do translation work and vice-versa, both as freelancers and as employees of international organisations, though many of them do prefer one or the other. Be that as it may, both translation and interpreting rely on good mastery of the relevant working languages, on extralinguistic knowledge ("knowledge of the world"), and on the ability to understand messages expressed verbally and to reformulate them, overcoming obstacles by making appropriate decisions. A large part of these difficulties and of the strategies implemented to solve them are common to translation and interpreting. This is why many syllabuses start with basic training in translation, or in translation and liaison interpreting, and follow up with specialisation in either conference interpreting or some specific form of translation. Such a system is particularly common and makes much sense when translation and interpreting training starts at first year undergraduate level, with a full four-year syllabus:

–   During the preparatory phase, students learn to view translation not as a language-to-language "transcoding" process, but as a comprehension operation followed by a reformulation operation governed by communication-oriented aims, with specific translation strategies designed to achieve them. (A necessary condition being that their instructors have the same view – see Section 5.1.) This saves time at the specialisation phase.

– The translation process leaves the translator with much more time than the interpreting process to find solutions to problems (generally hours or days, as opposed to seconds or milliseconds in interpreting – see below). When studying translation during the non-specialised phase of a syllabus, students probably learn more in terms of language, terminology and relevant extralinguistic knowledge, and probably set the sights for problem resolution in terms of language quality and precise information restitution higher than in an interpreting-only syllabus. Moreover, this work is done without the overwhelming difficulty of cognitive load which is inevitably associated with interpreting (see further down).

– The preparatory phase helps qualify interpreting students for professional translation work. This is no small advantage, since many eventually fail to become conference interpreters, or live in a market where they have to do translation work in addition to interpreting.

At most institutions where conference interpreting is taught at graduate level only, over a period of one to four semesters, the prevailing model is special-isation in conference interpreting without translation, as time is short and much has to be learned, especially in terms of cognitive skills. Differences between translating and interpreting which justify this separation lie in the following areas:

a. Mastery of the passive language(s)

Translators need to understand written texts and have some time to solve comprehension problems, using dictionaries, other documents, or human sources. Interpreters need to understand speeches, which they perceive essen-tially through the speaker's voice, instantaneously, with practically no pos-sibility of consulting documents or human sources. The mastery of speech comprehension as required for interpreting relies on better 'intuitive' knowl-edge of language-specific transitional probabilities ('having a feeling' for what words and structures are most likely to follow what words and structures) than the one needed for translation, as well as on much familiarity with accents and intonation patterns. Such mastery is based on much practice in listening, while the mastery of passive languages required for translation is acquired through reading. In liaison interpreting, the task is made easier by the fact that the interaction is generally face-to-face between two persons, with the possibility of asking for further clarification. In conference interpreting, especially in the simultaneous mode, speeches are often fast, technical, linguistically more complex; and this difference between the type of mastery required from translators and interpreters becomes an important skill element.

b. Mastery of the active language(s)
As regards active language mastery (the native language, called "A-language", and active foreign languages into which the translator or interpreter works, called "B-languages"), translators are professional writers and need high-level grammatical and stylistic skills, but can read their target texts and correct them again and again. Interpreters are not constrained by the same grammatical and stylistic standards, but must make instant decisions with respect to words, syntactic structures and pronunciation, with virtually no possibility of going back. Again, the type of skills involved differ significantly from the translators'.

c. Cognitive skills
Translation and liaison interpreting are less constrained by time at cognitive level (less than one second), and do not require particularly demanding cognitive abilities. Conference interpreting is associated with a very high cognitive load, due to the fact that it involves several parallel operations, each of which takes up much processing capacity. In fact, most of the errors and omissions in conference interpreting can probably be traced to cognitive failure, due to either high processing capacity requirements that the interpreter cannot meet, or errors in processing capacity management (further indications on the cognitive dimension of interpreting are given throughout this chapter, and more extensive discussions are found in many texts published in the nineties – for a "soft" initial approach, see Gile 1995a, b, 1999 – for a review of research into conference interpreting cognition, see Gile 2003; Setton 2003). Mastering conference interpreting necessarily includes the acquisition of specific attention-sharing skills, which are not required for translation. This may be the most important difference between the two which justifies specialisation in conference interpreting.

In cognitive terms, in the field, translators without specific training in interpreting can perform well in liaison interpreting, but only rarely, or after much experience, do they manage to perform equally well in conference interpreting (socio-psychological skills, which are important in community interpreting, and sometimes in court interpreting, are not discussed here). Specific training which would give them the ability to achieve high-level conference interpreting performance may mean too much effort and too much time for what they will gain from it as translators. This is why the specialisation paradigm is not really challenged.

3.   The content of conference interpreter training

3.1   Interpreting exercises as the main pillar of training

Virtually all training programs are built on interpreting exercises, in both consecutive and simultaneous, with some sight translation and other peripheral exercises. In some programs, there are other lectures and tutorials in fields such as economics, international institutions, parliamentary procedure, the language of international organisations, the professional environment of conference interpreters, interpreting theory, research methods, etc. However, they are generally considered marginal with respect to the acquisition of interpreting skills proper.

For language skill enhancement and the acquisition of relevant strategies (deliberate actions aimed at overcoming difficulties and achieving specific aims) and cognitive skills, interpreting exercises are universally considered the most efficient. Some teachers also recommend the use of preparatory attention-sharing exercises ("shadowing", i.e. repeating the source speech with a short time lag, counting backwards while listening to the speech, etc.), but their usefulness is strongly challenged by many, who claim that attention-sharing skills are acquired during consecutive and while practising simultaneous, or even that some of these exercises, in particular shadowing, are counterproductive because they differ too much from actual interpreting.

3.2   Learning stages and progression

3.2.1   *Stage one: Consecutive without notes*
In most programs, training starts with a brief period (one to several weeks) of exercises in consecutive without note-taking, sometimes called "memory-enhancement exercises". One of the formal aims of these exercises is to train the students' memory, but as such, they are probably of little use, since interpreters do work with notes, and the effects of this training on memory are likely to fade away after a short while. On the other hand, they are very useful for the purpose of demonstrating to the students how memory works, and in particular the fact that if they listen carefully and understand the logic of the speech, its content will be stored in their memory even without a conscious effort to memorise

it, although recalling it actively may be problematic unless they have cues. The purpose of the notes will be to provide such cues, not replace storage in memory.

As is explained further in Section 3.2.2 below, such exercises need not be conducted with a target language different from the source language. Students can be asked to reword the source-language speech into a target speech in the same language. The advantage of this procedure is that the mechanisms of memory and the importance of the comprehension of the "logic" of the speech can be demonstrated: in such exercises, students cannot incriminate language switching in the problems they experience (in particular misunderstandings and logical contradictions).

3.2.2   *Stage two: Consecutive with notes*

The next stage is the introduction of "true consecutive", that is, full consecutive rendering of segments of several minutes with note-taking (consecutive interpreting involves rewording the full content of the source speech, not producing a report, a summary or comments on the source speech). Consecutive is considered by many the "highest" form of interpreting, above simultaneous, essentially because it requires the comprehension phase to be completed before the formulation phase, since most traces of the linguistic form of an utterance disappear from memory after a few seconds at most, and are replaced by traces of its content. The short time lag between perception and production in simultaneous allows production from verbal traces, whereas in consecutive, production is done from traces of the content. Therefore, simultaneous interpreting is partly possible at word-identification level without deeper comprehension, whereas it is generally impossible in consecutive. The notes in consecutive do not change this, firstly, because note-taking often lags behind the speech by a few seconds, and secondly, because notes are made up of single words or symbols for ideas, not full sentences. Therefore, they are useful as cues to help recall the content of the speech, and do provide useful information on names, numbers and other specific items, but they do not represent the whole speech. Experience shows that students who do not truly understand speeches cannot reconstruct them from their notes.

For these cognitive reasons, the fundamental skills of consecutive interpreting can also be taught in the monolingual mode. In fact, when students mistakenly attribute their difficulties to language switching, it is helpful, in the beginning stages of consecutive with notes, to conduct a few exercises of A-into-A interpreting, so as to shift the focus back to essentials.

In some markets, particularly in Western Europe, consecutive tends to be replaced by simultaneous, which has led some trainers to suggest that it should be eliminated from the syllabus. However, the majority of instructors feel it remains valuable regardless of its actual use in the marketplace (it should be stressed however that in many markets, and in particular outside Western Europe, consecutive accounts for a large share of interpreting assignments, and that it is still present even in Western Europe). The value of consecutive in training is due to the fact, explained above, that it fosters analysis and reformulation, as opposed to transcoding, and to its power as a diagnostic tool: the performance of a student in consecutive makes it possible to locate strengths and weaknesses, in particular regarding faulty comprehension or insufficient mastery of the target language. In simultaneous, such diagnosis is much more uncertain, since inadequate output can result from different factors, including faulty management of processing capacity, and it is difficult to discriminate between insufficient analysis, poor language-separation capacity, and insufficient mastery of the source and/or target language. Most importantly, however, many interpreting trainers believe that it is risky to let students go into the simultaneous mode before the principles of analytical listening and reformulation from the content rather than the form have been thoroughly mastered, lest they choose the easy way by transcoding without the required analysis, and thus never progress beyond mediocre performance.

Consecutive is taught in most conference interpreter training programs, but it is given more or less weight depending on the institution. In some, such as ESIT (École Supérieure d'Interprètes et de Traducteurs) and ISIT (Institut Supérieur d'Interprétation et de Traduction) in France, it is practised for a full academic year before simultaneous is introduced. In others, it is given less weight, and taught at the same time as simultaneous, from the start. No data from research is available to demonstrate the superiority of one option over the other.

3.2.3   Stage three: Simultaneous and consecutive interpreting, sight translation

Simultaneous interpreting is seen by students as the culmination of their training. Indeed, when it is taught after consecutive has been fully mastered, it provides them with the final technical skills required to enter the labour market. In the standard model adopted in postgraduate programs at ESIT and ISIT in Paris, simultaneous is taught during the second year of studies, along with exercises in consecutive. These are valuable in order to help maintain the proper approach in students, check the status of their progress, and correct lapses.

The transition from consecutive to simultaneous is a sensitive and critical one. In consecutive, the cognitive load during target-speech production is low, because the interpreter paces him/herself, and attention need not be shared on operations other than note-reading, which partly interferes with, but partly helps speech production. In simultaneous, target-speech production is paced by the rate of delivery of the source speech, and the presence in the interpreters' working memory of both languages increases cognitive load. Consequences of this difference are:

- Frequent dramatic drops in the linguistic quality of the output in simultaneous, especially in B-languages. This is why in many training programs, simultaneous is taught only into the students' A-language, and why many professionals who accept assignments into their B-language in consecutive refuse such assignments in simultaneous (also see Section 3.7).
- The temptation to reduce cognitive load by bypassing content analysis, and transcoding directly from verbal memory.

As soon as signs of such weaknesses surface, it is desirable to take the students through intensive exercises in consecutive to put them back on the right track.

At some time during the second half of this last stage of interpreter training, exercises in "simultaneous interpreting with text" are introduced: the speaker is reading a text and the interpreter has a copy in the booth. This type of exercise is relevant insofar as it corresponds to a frequent situation in professional life. It is introduced late in the syllabus because it is associated with an additional difficulty, due to the combined use of the source speech as it is heard and the written text: speakers often read faster than they speak normally, without hesitation pauses, and interpreters are tempted to use the text rather than the speech as a basis for reformulation, which entails the risk of lagging even further behind and of missing the speaker's improvised deviations from the text.

3.2.4   Sight translation

Simultaneous with text is distinct from sight translation, which is also taught to student interpreters, and consists in reading aloud a source-language text in the target language. In sight translation, the translation operation is not paced by a speaker, which, at first sight, seems to make the cognitive load lower than in interpreting. This leads some trainers to consider that it can/should be taught early in the syllabus. The problem is that in sight translation, students see the source-language text while they translate it, hence the temptation to translate word-for-word, which goes against the fundamental comprehension-reformulation approach which they are taught. It is better to teach sight translation at the same time as simultaneous interpreting, once consecutive has been mastered. To reduce further the risk of word-for-word translation, students can be given the text for advance preparation, and be required to be very fast in their reformulation phase. This should help induce meaning-based rather than form-based translation.

3.3 Source speeches in training

In principle, except in the case of simultaneous with text, source speeches used for interpreting exercises are impromptu speeches (as opposed to speeches read from text). In the very beginning of their training, students are asked to prepare short self-presentations (one to several minutes), statements of opinions on topical or other matters, short presentations on non-specialised subjects. Papers may be prepared in advance, but they should never be read from texts or learned by heart before the presentation. Otherwise, their informational density may be too high for interpreting to proceed smoothly, especially at this early stage of training. Instructors may also make their own interventions to be interpreted by students, the advantage being that they have better control of the difficulty of the speech they make than students, and can regulate it on the basis of the response in the classroom.

During the consecutive interpreting stage, speech segments to be interpreted become gradually longer, up to about ten minutes, sometimes more. It should be understood, however, that length is not of the essence in consecutive. Interpreting a segment of fifteen minutes does not require better skills or memory than interpreting a segment of five minutes; the difference lies in stamina. Therefore, in class, instructors may prefer shorter speech segments, which provide them with the possibility of assessing, testing and correcting more students. On the other hand, the automation of cognitive skills and stamina build-up require much practice, more than can be given in class (with generally not more than two to three one-hour sessions per week and per language combination). This is why students in conference-interpreter training programs are required to set up informal groups of two to four or five people and practice on a daily basis. Nevertheless, classroom sessions are indispensable for checking and correction, in order to guide students, help them overcome specific obstacles they may encounter, and prevent them from acquiring and automating the wrong responses.

The large number of source speeches required for training (hundreds per year for each language combination if students practice regularly both in and outside the classroom) rapidly becomes a problem. Neither the students', nor the instructors' and guest lecturers' interventions cover more than a fraction of the requirements. Inevitably, after a few weeks, both students and instructors start using written texts, either transcripts of speeches if available, or articles from periodicals, a convenient "renewable speech source". However, the prose read from such texts does not have the characteristics of impromptu speech, in particular as regards information density and delivery features, and is more difficult to interpret than actual interventions made orally. One answer to this problem is "oralising", which consists in paraphrasing while reading, changing both vocabulary and syntactic structures, thus introducing the required features of impromptu speeches into the text. However, "oralising" is a rather difficult exercise, which beginners do not manage to carry out very successfully. Another way of obtaining the same results consists in choosing a text, reading it and taking notes similar to notes taken in consecutive, and then constructing the source speech to be interpreted on the basis of these notes, rather than reading the text. The advantages of this method over "oralising" are that the end-product is truly the result of "online formulation", and that the exercise also provides some training in note-taking, without the stress associated with cognitive load in actual consecutive (see Section 3.4).

Other important sources of material for practice are audio and video recordings of speeches made by students, instructors, guest lecturers, as well as speeches and interviews broadcast on radio or television. The Internet now provides further convenient possibilities, including internet radio and actual conference speeches, for instance on the European Parliament's EbS – Europe by Satellite (see de Manuel Jerez 2003). The main advantages of such recordings are:

- The variety of voices, accents and other delivery patterns in authentic speeches that students can get accustomed to, as opposed to the limited range of "styles" offered by their instructors and fellow-students.
- The fact that such speeches can be transcribed and/or played again for closer scrutiny of specific phenomena or problematic segments.
- The possibility for instructors to acquaint themselves with them prior to exercises, so as to be able to concentrate on the students' target speeches and detect problems more accurately. This is particularly important in simultaneous interpreting, as explained below.

- The possibility for students who do not have enough partners with the same language combination or who cannot take part in informal group training sessions to practice on their own.
- The possibility for students to practice in simultaneous interpreting even when there are not enough practice booths available.

Simple audio cassette players are an acceptable substitute for practice purposes. Recordings can be copied and shared by several institutions, so as to increase the number of suitable materials even in countries where it is otherwise difficult to find source speeches for particular language combinations.

The main drawback of recordings put forward by opponents to the use of this type of material is that there is no live presence of a speaker, meaning that some extralinguistic cues presumably used by interpreters in authentic situations are lost. This is particularly salient in the case of audio recordings (as opposed to video recordings). However, so far, the few studies conducted on the actual contribution of body- and face-language have not confirmed the importance of the role of such visual cues (see Anderson 1979; Balzani 1989; Tommola & Lindhölm 1995; Alonso Bacigalupe 1999). In any case, the advantages of recorded speeches as listed above make them valuable for training, if only as additional material, in combination with live speeches in and outside the classroom.

Source speeches used for practice in simultaneous are basically the same as those used for consecutive, the only difference being that longer stretches (up to 30 minutes, the standard length of an interpreting turn in the booth) are required to build up the students' stamina. Recordings of speeches are particularly valuable to trainers in simultaneous for cognitive reasons: as mentioned earlier, cognitive load in both consecutive and simultaneous interpreting is extremely high, very close to saturation at any time. In consecutive, instructors can focus on the source speech at the same time as the student, and then focus on the student's target speech and assess it. In simultaneous, it is virtually impossible to listen carefully to the source speech and to the student's target speech at the same time and detect all the problems. Familiarising oneself with the source speech prior to the exercise or following the student's target speech while checking it against a transcript of the source speech are the only ways to be able to make a comprehensive assessment of the student's performance.

3.4 Note-taking in consecutive

The weight of consecutive interpreting in conference-interpreter training programs also makes it necessary to devote attention to the principles of note-taking. As is the case for other important issues, much has been written about note-taking for consecutive since Rozan's (1956) classic handbook, and this section will only highlight three particularly important points.

Beginners, who struggle with the difficulty of intensive analytical listening, tend to consider that note-taking will solve what they perceive as memory problems. As soon as they are allowed to take notes, many take too many at the expense of listening, and their performance drops dramatically. One way of preventing this from happening is to introduce note-taking gradually, by allowing them only one word/sign/symbol per idea initially, then two, then three, and removing restrictions only when notes are no longer a serious hindrance to the analytical listening component in their daily practice.

It should be made clear to beginners from the start that notes taken during consecutive are not a comprehensive or "balanced" or "logical" representation of the content of the source speech. They are only cues that will help them recall content which is basically stored in their memory (except for some names, numbers, etc.). Failing to understand this will inevitably result in students writing more than they need at the expense of the listening component.

Since notes are only cues, there should be no standard requirements for specific parts of the speech (the main concepts, logical links, etc.) to be taken down. Generally, it turns out that notes representing each idea as well as logical links between them are the most efficient. However, this is a matter of statistics, not a general law. Much variability should be allowed depending on the students' personal preferences, no matter how attractive the ideas of consistency in the symbols, specific rules for page-layout, the use of abbreviations, preference for use of the source language or target language, etc. appear to instructors. There are several methods and systems, some with strong rules and a specific set of symbols and abbreviations to learn, others with more flexibility (compare for example Rozan 1956 with Matyssek 1989). None has been demonstrated to be the best in absolute terms. If a system works for the student, it is acceptable. If it does not, suggestions can be made, but it should be kept in mind that cognitive style, writing speed, writing style, and personality features can vary greatly between individuals, that the professional interpreters' notes are far from uniform, and that individuals will optimise their system over time to suit their own profile.

Neither should it be forgotten that the purpose of notes taken in consecutive is to help interpreters reconstruct the speech as soon as it is over, not to be used as a prop over a long period. In other words, while the skills of intensive analytical listening acquired when learning consecutive can be of wide use in everyday life, note-taking in consecutive is task-specific, although some symbols and abbreviations can be exported for everyday use.

3.5 Classroom practice

As suggested above, working sessions in the classroom are essentially tutorials aimed at guiding students into acquiring the appropriate strategies and developing the relevant skills. It should be borne in mind that the learning process is virtually always painful and associated with much stress and feelings of frustration and failure. In many schools, this is made worse by the instructors' tough attitude, rationalised as a good preparation for the stress in the marketplace. Such an attitude is unjustified and counter-productive. Firstly, stress in the marketplace differs from stress in the classroom; it is induced by the difficulty of the interpreting task and working environments, not by the ever-present fear of being judged and criticised by unsympathetic instructors. Secondly, the instructors' tough attitude is demotivating if anything, and thus not in line with sound pedagogical practice. Students are generally well aware of their weaknesses. When they are not, their attention can be drawn to them without making discouraging comments which damage the students' self-image. A more positive attitude, that seeks to adapt the requirements to the gradually developing skills, may be more efficient than the "sink or swim" attitude prevalent in many prestigious schools.

In this mindset, the following suggestions can be made:

- Try to avoid exercises at a level of difficulty far above the current level of performance of a class (or a specific student). However, exercises should be difficult enough to require efforts from the students and to reveal their weaknesses. Determining the level of difficulty of a given source speech before it is interpreted is not easy. The best indicator is past experience with students, hence another advantage of working with recordings. If a source speech turns out to be too difficult, make students listen to it a second time before interpreting it. If it turns out to be too difficult nevertheless, even for professionals, do not hesitate to point this out, so as to avoid discouraging the students by letting them think that the gap between their skills and those of professionals is unbridgeable.

- Do not hesitate to point out weaknesses to students, but make it clear that you are judging the target speech, not the person. Try to make a diagnosis of the reason(s) for a particular weakness, and if possible, suggest remedial strategies to the student. Focusing on the technicalities of a process rather than insisting on the students' "failures" is part of the process-oriented approach favoured by an increasing number of interpreter and translator-trainers (see Gile 1995a).
- In your corrections and diagnosis, try to focus on specific skill/strategy components at the corresponding stages of the syllabus. Mixing correction of cognitive skills, strategies and language performance may confuse the issues. If you feel that a specific weakness outside the focus of your current endeavours deserves a comment, make it separately.
- When weaknesses observed in the classroom are "normal" at a particular stage of the syllabus, do not hesitate to tell the students.
- Try to explain the weaknesses as well as the remedial action you suggest by means of a student-friendly remedial intervention. Clearly, this requires some theoretical comprehension of the cognitive factors involved in interpreting, as well as a philosophy of interpreting as a communication-oriented service activity (see the discussion in Section 3.6).

3.6 The place of theory in the classroom

There are differing views about the contribution of theory in the interpreting classroom. Some consider that it is indispensable for self-improvement. Others claim that interpreting is basically action, and that theory has not been able to improve either training or the practice of interpreting. It is indeed difficult to prove that either of these views is correct, but it seems reasonable to expect a modest amount of theory in the classroom to be helpful, insofar as it places various phenomena encountered by students, as well as strategies recommended by instructors, in a cohesive conceptual framework.

The most relevant and useful elements of theory in the classroom are probably found in two fields: one is the fundamental "philosophy" of interpreting, and the other the cognitive dimension of interpreting, including language mastery.

- The core of "interpreting philosophy" is that interpreting is intended to transmit content (including factual, emotional and other content) from a sender to one or several receiver(s), in a way that will serve the sender's and/or the receiver's aims and interests in a particular communication environment. The transmission process is made difficult by a number of linguistic, cultural and cognitive obstacles, and interpreters use strategies to optimise it. Thus, interpreting weaknesses and strategies can be assessed against communication-oriented criteria.

– Cognitive constraints make the operations involved in interpreting difficult. Understanding the source of these difficulties may make the learning process less painful to students, and explain why certain strategies which may seem intuitively wrong (like taking less notes in consecutive) are recommended by instructors.

Theoretical components from sociology, psychology and cultural studies are probably useful in the training of community interpreters and sign-language interpreters, and legal theory may be useful in the training of court interpreters. However, in conference interpreter training, I feel that their relevance is not sufficient to justify their introduction into short syllabuses.

There are basically two ways of introducing theory in the classroom. One is to give explanations piecewise when a specific phenomenon occurs or a strategy is recommended. The other is to present it in a series of lectures, alongside the tutorials. Over the years, models have been developed. Gile (1995a) presents a set of such models to cover the interpreting (and translation) students' requirements. More sophisticated theory, be it in linguistics, semiotics, cognitive psychology, communication theory or text linguistics is taught in some schools as well, but this is probably linked to academic requirements more than to the learning process in interpreting per se.

3.7 Working into A-languages and/or B-languages

An important issue that regularly comes up concerns the "direction" of interpreting. While some purists, mostly from Western countries, demand that interpreters only work into their A-languages in simultaneous, an opinion held in East-European countries favours working from one's A-language into a B-language, and in the marketplace, a large proportion of the interpreters work both ways. In terms of training, consecutive should not be problematic in this respect, though in non-standard environments (see Section 5), work into one's A-language makes it easier for instructors to make a diagnosis of the student's cognitive and technical skills, as weaknesses in one's B-language output may also have linguistic origins. In the simultaneous mode, for similar reasons, it seems reasonable to start with work into one's A language. Once the required cognitive skills and techniques are up to a satisfactory level, instructors may decide to let students practice in both directions, though many prefer to keep the exercises strictly B-into-A and C-into-A, and leave it to young graduates to gradually extend their skills into interpreting into their B-language(s) in the field, after their training is completed.

4. Checkpoints

One of the most problematic points in conference interpreter training has to do with admission conditions and graduation. In spite of some research done on the subject, it is very difficult to predict upon admission who will reach the required level of proficiency at the end of the syllabus, and failure rates are very high, often much higher than 50% of the graduating class. This generates institutional, financial, but also human problems, since students of prestigious interpreter-training institutions often make strong commitments and may invest three or four years at considerable financial and psychological cost with a damaging result if they do not graduate. Institutional solutions can be found. For instance, in Australia, academic achievement and professional skills are tested separately, meaning that an academic degree can be earned at the end of the syllabus even if cognitive and strategic skills are not up to the required professional level. Such solutions will not be discussed here. This Section focuses on internal checkpoints, which may help reduce the damage if students are found not to have the necessary aptitudes.

In four-year syllabuses, the preparatory years give both instructors and students a better idea of the candidates' aptitudes than admission tests, and probably reduce uncertainty. In two-year syllabuses, there are three important checkpoints: one at admission, one at the end of the first year, and one at graduation.

The checkpoint at admission is problematic not only because it is often difficult to judge a candidate's chances of success on the basis of a test (although a majority of candidates are generally eliminated because of their obviously insufficient mastery of their proposed working languages), but also due to the fact that national legislation does not always allow selection at admission.

The checkpoint at graduation is relatively uncontroversial, insofar as it consists of a set of interpreting-task tests with an assessment committee composed of trainers from the training institution, of other professional interpreters, and of representatives of conference interpreter employers, such as chief interpreters in international organisations, and is thus highly representative of market norms and expectations.

The most sensitive checkpoint is the midway point, where the assessment is internal only, and instructors have to decide whether the student is allowed admission into second year, with or without further tests, whether s/he needs to spend a year overseas or to repeat first year, or whether s/he should be encouraged to turn to another profession. Students may find it less difficult to accept the idea that they will not become conference interpreters if the verdict falls after one year of investment, or after they have repeated the first year without significant improvement, than later. Failing to stop them there and allowing them to be trained in simultaneous (in those institutions where only consecutive is taught during the first year) makes accepting the judgement more difficult, and may induce them to seek employment as conference interpreters even if they have failed the examination. Midway problems are generally of either linguistic or cognitive type. In the case of a student who has achieved the required performance level with respect to technical and cognitive skills and his/her weakness is essentially an insufficient mastery of either an active or a passive language, giving him/her a chance to enhance language mastery while learning the skills of simultaneous may be an appropriate choice. If cognitive weaknesses are identified, including insufficient language-separation ability, it is probably preferable to be strict.

The modalities of the midway checkpoint vary with schools: in some institutions, they consist of a sequence of tests in consecutive interpreting; in others, the procedure is more informal, with the instructors determining the fate of the students on the basis of their achievements in class.

5.   Adapting to non-standard environments

Essentially, the training principles and methods outlined above apply to all cases. However, their implementation in non-standard environments entails some adaptation. Two cases are discussed here: conference interpreting programs in non-standard environments and non-interpreting programs where interpreting is taught.

5.1   Conference interpreting programs in non-standard environments

Institutions may be required to train students in conference interpreting techniques under non-standard conditions, which may be associated with facilitating factors and/or difficulties. For instance, training is facilitated when experienced translators wish to take up conference interpreting. By definition, such a situation is not problematic per se, and need not be discussed here. Difficulties, on the other hand, are often found in countries which have only recently started interacting intensively with the international community, or which have urgent needs without the required infrastructure, tradition, pool of candidates meeting the usual prerequisites, etc. (such was the case of South Africa a few years ago when it required interpreters for its Truth and Reconciliation Commission). The basic strategy recommended here is to adapt the methods so as to achieve feasible objectives in a first phase, and let time and experience do the rest, while planning long-term environmental improvement of the situation. In other words, the principles of interpreting should be learned and internalised by the students as solidly as in standard environments, but improvement of performance towards the desired professional proficiency level should be sought over a longer period, beyond the duration of the training program. The most common environmental difficulties and possible coping strategies are the following:

a. Insufficient language mastery
When the trainees' mastery of the working language(s) is insufficient, adaptation is dual. Firstly, intensive language training should be conducted in parallel with training in interpreting techniques proper. This goes against the principles of the major interpreter training programs, which require full mastery of the languages prior to admission, but is made necessary by circumstances. Secondly, as regards passive languages, source speeches can be adapted to the current level of students in a number of ways:

– Source speeches can be selected and/or prepared by instructors with special attention to linguistic difficulty, i.e. with simplified sentence structures and vocabulary.
– Students can be given texts in advance on the same topic as the speeches so that they can do some linguistic and other preparation.
– Words and structures considered potentially problematic can be explained to students before the actual interpreting exercise.

It is important to remember that interpreting relies on strategic and cognitive skills which can to a large extent be acquired in the course of monolingual consecutive interpreting exercises (also see Section 3.2). This is particularly useful when students with "exotic" languages are trained in overseas institutions where no instructor has the same language combination. In such a case, the student's strongest language shared by the instructor can be used for monolingual exercises. In fact, an entire training program for diplomats in Germany was based on two phases, the first being the acquisition of interpreting skills with German-into-German exercises, and the second the application of these skills to the specific languages that trainees were supposed to use overseas (Feldweg 1980).

When instructors only share one language with a trainee, the help of a non-interpreting native speaker of one of the trainee's other languages can be enlisted. The native speaker can produce source language speeches for the trainee, so that the instructor can listen to and assess the target speech in the shared language. When source speeches in the shared language are used, the native speaker can assess the linguistic output of the trainee in the "exotic" language. This system is far from ideal due to the fact that non-interpreting native speakers generally do not share the interpreting instructors' norms and relevant skills, but if clear instructions are given to them, it can help.

b. Lack of professional conference interpreters as instructors

In some organizations required to train conference interpreters, especially (but not only) in countries in political and/or economic transition, there are not enough professional conference interpreters to serve as instructors. Thus, much of the training is done by non-interpreters, often language teachers. This is a problematic situation. Firstly, such instructors do not know the professional interpreting market and are therefore not in a position to give much-needed advice to the students as regards optimum professional strategies and behaviour. This is regrettable, but not critical, as graduates can pick up the norms in the field. A much more serious problem is associated with the fact that many of them regard translation and interpreting as a language-oriented activity and teach it as such, rather than as a communication-oriented activity. In particular, they tend to judge the output on the basis of linguistic equivalence, disregarding the fact that better service may be achieved by deviating from linguistic equivalence for the benefit of communication (for examples from the field, see Jones 1998). This may cause lasting damage by giving students the wrong foundation for their decisions. Thirdly, instructors do not understand the cognitive processes underlying interpreting and are therefore unable to give proper advice to students in this respect (the issue is discussed further in Section 5.2).

It is very important that such teachers gain some understanding of the professional interpreter's "philosophy" and of the cognitive dimension of interpreting. Discussing the issues with interpreters, reading the literature and observing phenomena in the classroom can give them the proper foundation if they are willing to learn a new way of looking at translation and interpreting.

c. Lack of equipment

In many interpreter training institutions, both in developing countries and in the most highly industrialised countries, there is a lack of equipment, essentially interpreting booths for practice in simultaneous. This need not be a major problem, since cheap cassette players with audio cassettes and appropriate headphones can be used just as well. The implication is that much use be made of recorded speeches, which is no problem per se. The only further requirement is that students find a quiet spot where they can listen to the source speech without interference and make their own target speech undisturbed. If they record their output on a second cassette player, they can also submit it to their instructor for assessment and correction.

5.2   The case of non-interpreting environments

Interpreting is taught in many programs where students are trained in modern languages, but are not expected to become conference interpreters. The advantages to be gained from training in interpreting techniques in such environments can be summarised as follows (not necessarily in the order of importance):

a. Gaining a better grasp of the nature of interpreting (and translation)

However weak the students' cognitive and linguistic foundation may be, training in conference interpreting (in consecutive only) gives them insight into the way interpreters and translators work, the types of problems they come up against, the strategies they use to overcome them and the norms these strategies are associated with. In this respect, students will become better users of interpreting and translation services.

b. Improving analytical listening (and reading) skills

As stressed earlier (see Section 3), the practice of consecutive interpreting demonstrates beyond doubt the importance of analytical listening as opposed to plain word identification. Since the actual words and sentence structures of the source speech disappear from memory after a few seconds, interpreters who rely on words they have taken down while listening without gradually building a mental model of the content of the speech inevitably fail to reconstruct the speech properly. This increased awareness is easier to achieve in interpreting exercises than in translation, since in translation, the source text remains visible throughout the exercise, and reformulation can be carried out on a word-for-word and structure-by-structure basis. In this respect, interpreting exercises can also help student translators acquire an appropriate meaning-based approach to translation.

c. Improving speaking skills

In interpreting exercises, students have to speak in public and *convince* the audience (the teacher and the other students in class), part of which may have understood the source speech as well and will judge the target speech on fidelity and on its intrinsic quality as a speech. Such exercises can only improve their speaking skills, including strategies for overcoming doubts and linguistic weaknesses. The resulting improvement in public speaking can probably be of great benefit to the students in a wide range of professional and personal situations.

d. Improving linguistic skills

Interpreting is one of the rare linguistic activities (along with translation) in which the statement produced has to match the precise content of a previous statement not formulated in the same language. In other words, unlike daily communication situations where speakers can bypass a word-retrieval task when they encounter production difficulties by deviating from what they intended to say initially, interpreters must complete the process. As a result of such repeated efforts, lexical availability is increased. Similarly, the requirement for immediate production should also enhance syntactic production skills in the active languages (although there is more syntactic flexibility than lexical flexibility in expressing specific content, and interpreters are not forced to use specific sentence structures as they are forced to use specific words).

Interpreting exercises into a B-language (in consecutive!) are therefore particularly useful to enhance production skills in foreign-language learners.

e. Learning about language in communication

The difficulties encountered by students in the production of their target speech also make them aware of various phenomena in verbal communication which they might overlook otherwise: word retrieval difficulties, problems in the completion of syntactic tasks, linguistic interference, the role and frequency of filled and unfilled pauses, evasion tactics in production, production errors, etc. On the comprehension side, the full comprehension requirement, which calls for very concentrated listening, should raise their awareness of the importance of various linguistic and non-verbal phenomena, of the need to use extralinguistic knowledge to disambiguate structures, of redundancy and lack of logic in many real-life utterances.

5.3   Limitations and risks

Basically, there are three potential risks associated with the teaching of conference interpreting skills to non-interpreters:

- Efforts required of them may be too demanding for the expected benefit.
- Without an adequate baseline in terms of cognitive aptitudes, language mastery and knowledge of the world, they may gain too little from the training.
- Having been introduced to the techniques, they may seek and find interpreting assignments as conference interpreters without the proper qualifications, and thus damage the reputation of the profession.

My personal experience in training non-interpreting students in basic interpreting skills for many years suggests that these risks can be controlled, essentially by using easier source speeches, by refraining from asking students to spend much time practising besides the tutorials, by refraining from teaching them simultaneous interpreting techniques (see below), and by pointing out to them the difference between their performance and professional performance (however, generally, they become aware of this difference without any prompting).

The actual training techniques and methods to be implemented are much the same as those used in non-standard interpreting programs, with one important difference. Simultaneous interpreting should not be taught to students who will not need to perform conference interpreting. Firstly, all the benefits listed above are gained from consecutive, and simultaneous will not add anything. Secondly, as explained in Section 3.2.3, the introduction of simultaneous may actually be counterproductive, in letting students slip back into word-for-word transcoding. Thirdly, as explained several times in this chapter, it may encourage students without the necessary qualifications to seek conference interpreting assignments.

6.   Conclusion

Visits to training institutions world-wide and a survey of the literature show a wide variety of situations and methods. While some prestigious schools claim theirs are the best, arguing that this is demonstrated by their graduates' successful careers, this rationale is flawed insofar as:

- High proficiency in graduates may result, to a large extent, from strict standards at admission and/or graduation, not from good training methods.
- Good methods may not result in high proficiency in graduates if graduation standards are low, meaning that some schools may be implementing very good training methods and yet do not produce uniformly qualified graduating classes.
- The best methods for one environment may not be best for another.

This is why it is best to keep one's mind open to a wide range of possibilities, including methods that deviate considerably from the ones advocated most often in the literature. Such possibilities include the introduction of other training components as required, when the local environment makes the boundaries between conference interpreting and other categories of interpreting fuzzy and interpreters are likely to have an active mediation role in an environment where business issues, sociological issues, public health issues, military issues or legal issues become salient. Special training may also become useful to adapt to the specific demands of broadcast interpreting, to interpreting by satellite, to interpreting for the Internet, and to take full advantage of new possibilities offered by the most recent technology.

References

Most of the issues tackled in this chapter are discussed in dozens of publications, which cannot be listed comprehensively here. References to specific items from the literature have been included in the body of this text sparingly, when it was felt that they deserved particular attention. Besides these items, the following bibliography is a sample taken from hundreds of existing publications on the topic of interpreter training. Nearly all were written by conference interpreters who teach interpreting, and many address in detail issues only discussed briefly in this chapter. Priority was given to books, both monographs and collective volumes, in such a way that reading even a few of them should give the reader an idea of prevailing views on many training issues. For more specific follow-up reading, bibliographical lists found in these publications should be consulted, along with the *CIRIN Bulletin*.

AIIC (1979). *Enseignement de l'interprétation. Dix ans de colloques*. Geneva: AIIC. [AIIC's official viewpoint of conference interpreter training as it was in 1979]
AIIC (1993). *Advice to Students Wishing to Become Conference Interpreters*. Geneva: AIIC.

Alonso Bacigalupe, L. (1999). "Visual contact in simultaneous interpretation: Results of an experimental study". In A. Álvarez Lugrís & A. Fernández Ocampo (Eds.), *Anovar/anosar: estudios de traducción e interpretación*, Vol. I (pp. 123–137). Vigo: Servicio de Publicacións da Universidade de Vigo.

Altman, J. (1987). *Teaching Interpreting: Study and Practice, Bibliography*. London: CILT.

Anderson, L. (1979). *Simultaneous Interpretation: Contextual and Translation Aspects*. MA thesis, Concordia University, Montreal.

Balzani, M. (1989). "Le contact visuel en interprétation simultanée: résultats d'une expérience (français-italien)". In L. Gran & C. Taylor (Eds.), *Aspects of Applied and Experimental Research on Conference Interpretation* (pp. 93–100). Udine: Campanotto Editore.

Bowen, D. & Bowen, M. (1984). *Steps to Consecutive Interpretation*. Washington: Pen and Booth.

Delisle, J. (Ed.). (1981). *L'enseignement de l'interprétation et de la traduction*. Ottawa: Editions de l'Université d'Ottawa. [Practical training methods at ESIT]

De Manuel Jerez, Jesús (2003). "El canal EbS en la mejora de la calidad de la formación de intérpretes: estudio de un corpus en vídeo del Parlamento Europeo". In A. Collados, M. Fernández Sánchez, & D. Gile (Eds.), *La evaluación de la calidad en interpretación: investigación*. Granada: Editorial Comares.

Dollerup, C. & Loddegaard, A. (Eds.). (1992). *Teaching Translation and Interpreting – Training, Talent and Experience*. Amsterdam and Philadelphia: John Benjamins.

Dollerup, C. & Lindegaard, A. (Eds.). (1994). *Teaching Translation and Interpreting 2 – Insight, Aims, Visions*. Amsterdam and Philadelphia: John Benjamins.

Dollerup, C. & Appel, V. (Eds.). (1996). *Teaching Translation and Interpreting 3 – New Horizons*. Amsterdam and Philadelphia: John Benjamins. [Proceedings from a series of 3 conferences on translator and interpreter training, with papers offering a wide range of descriptions from many countries]

Falbo, C., Russo, M., & Straniero Sergio, F. (Eds.). (1999). *Interpretazione Simultanea e Consecutiva. Problemi teorici e metodologie didattiche*. Milano: Ulrico Hoepli Editore. [Methods and contents from the Trieste School]

Feldweg, E. (1980). "Dolmetschen einsprachig lernen? Bericht über ein gelungenes Experiment". *Lebende Sprachen, 25*(4), 145–148.

Gambier, Y., Gile, D., & Taylor, C. (Eds.). (1997). *Conference Interpreting: Current Trends in Research*. Amsterdam and Philadelphia: John Benjamins.

Gile, D. (1995a). *Basic Concepts and Models for Interpreter and Translator Training*. Amsterdam and Philadelphia: John Benjamins.

Gile, D. (1995b). *Regards sur la recherche en interprétation de conférence*. Lille: Presses Universitaires de Lille. [An analysis of the conference interpreting research scene]

Gile, D. (1999). "Testing the Effort Models' Tightrope hypothesis in simultaneous interpreting – A contribution". *Hermes, 23*, 153–172.

Gile, D. (2000). "The history of research into conference interpreting. A scientometric approach". *Target, 12*(2), 297–321.

Gile, D. (2003). "Cognitive investigation into conference interpreting: features and trends". In A. Collados Aís & J. A. Sabio Pinilla (Eds.), *Avances en la investigación sobre interpretación* (pp. 1–27). Granada: Editorial Comares.

Gran, L. & Dodds, J. (Eds.). (1989). *The Theoretical and Practical Aspects of Teaching Conference Interpreting*. Udine: Campanotto Editore. [Proceedings from an important conference on interpreter training]

Gran, L. & Taylor, C. (Eds.). (1990). *Aspects of Applied and Experimental Research on Conference Interpretation*. Udine: Campanotto Editore.

Jones, R. (1998). *Conference Interpreting Explained*. Manchester: St Jerome.

Matyssek, H. (1989). *Handbuch der Notizentechnik für Dolmetscher: ein Weg zur sprachunabhängigen Notation*. Heidelberg: J. Groos.

Monacelli, C. (1999). *Messaggi in codice. Analisi del discorso e strategie per prendere appunti*. Milano: Franco Angelli.

Rozan, J.-F. (1956). *La prise de notes en interprétation consécutive*. Genève: Georg. [The classic handbook on note-taking in consecutive]

Seleskovitch, D. & Lederer, M. (1989). *Pédagogie raisonnée de l'interprétation*. Paris: Didier Erudition. [ESIT's methods. Many examples, many good ideas, but a dogmatic attitude]

Setton, R. (2003). "Models of the interpreting process." In A. Collados Aís & J. A. Sabio Pinilla (Eds.), *Avances en la investigación sobre interpretación* (pp. 29–89). Granada: Editorial Comares.

Tommola, J. (Ed.). (1995). *Topics in Interpreting Research*. University of Turku, Centre for Translation and Interpreting.

Tommola, J. & Lindhölm, J. (1995). "Experimental research on interpreting: Which dependent variable?" In J. Tommola (Ed.), *Topics in Interpreting Research* (pp. 121–133). University of Turku, Centre for Translation and Interpreting.

Journals

The Interpreter's Newsletter, SSLMIT, Trieste.
Interpreting, John Benjamins.
The CIRIN Bulletin, Paris. http://perso.wanadoo.fr/daniel.gile/
Target, 7, 1 (1995), John Benjamins.

Chapter 7

Training interpreters to work in the public services

Ann Corsellis

Clarification of title is a useful beginning. Public service interpreters work in the context of services which include legal, health, education, housing, environmental health and social services. In some countries they are referred to as "community interpreters." It is a good title and denotes the concept of a community of people from varied language and cultural backgrounds living together. However, in some countries, such as the UK, the term "community interpreter" has attracted connotations of a lower standard or of a different and partial role. The title "public service interpreter" is preferred for qualified professionals who work in these areas and will be used in this chapter, which is a reflection of the more usual practices in the United Kingdom and parts of the European Union.

1. Background

Public Service Interpreting, in the formal sense, is a relatively new branch of the profession. It has developed in order to meet the need for linguistic assistance arising from the increasing movement of people between countries. In London, for example, 30% of schoolchildren speak one of 400 European, Asian or African languages at home. If these children and their families do not have adequate access to the public services, they may be unable to develop or sustain a desirable quality of life, and the social infrastructure as a whole is thereby weakened. Language profiles similar to those found in London exist in other European cities, and people who live in rural areas may be especially disadvantaged if they do not speak adequately the language of the country.

The standards of excellence needed in the public services are the same as those required of interpreters in other areas, especially as irreversible decisions – affecting at times the life or liberty of an individual – may rest upon the quality of interpreting. The fact that those standards are not always available at this time is another matter. It is not possible to wait until the ideal situation exists; there are, for example, court hearings, traffic accidents, illnesses and school parents' evenings which already occur on a daily basis and involve people who do not speak adequately the language of the country in which they find themselves.

The present situation is a midway stage in a continuum of change, and the profession is responding to the pressures of contemporary social needs. In much the same way, conference interpreters responded to the need for their skills after World War II. Internationally, it is interesting to note when and why the development of public service interpreting has taken place in different countries at different speeds. For example, the Swedes and the Australians led the way in the 1960s and 1970s; the UK only made a systematic start in the 1980s; the South Africans have made truly significant headway since the end of apartheid in the mid 1990s.

There are therefore variations in training but common basic approaches are emerging. This process is being supported by on-going communication among people working in the field in different countries. International communication channels include the Critical Link international conferences and publications, as well as projects sponsored by the EU Commission Grotius programme with the aim of establishing equivalencies of standards for interpreters and translators in the legal context, the public service context often used first for development work because of its need for a precise use of language. The central idea emerging is that linguists working in the public services should become regulated professionals, like their colleagues in other public service disciplines such as doctors, lawyers or nurses and for the same reasons. This approach would require them to have nationally (and probably internationally) consistent, accountable and transparent professional structures for selection, training, accreditation and so on, which were adequate for the responsibilities of the tasks they undertake. The debate on the detail of the long-term professional structures is still under way.

What follows is drawn in part from established and tested examples of good practice taken from training programmes from various parts of the world and in part from what is in the process of incremental development.

2. Selection of students for training

The criteria for selection take into account the acceptance of inevitable practicalities while, at the same time, seeking high standards. Applicants will not all have the relevant post-graduate academic qualifications which can normally be expected from those wishing to be conference interpreters. Some will already be working as interpreters in an unqualified capacity; these may be the most difficult to train as they will have developed their skills incorrectly or incompletely. Others will have unassessed language skills.

2.1 Selection methods include

–   interviews by university graduates who are native speakers of both the languages in question. They assess listening and spoken language competence, the range of registers, fluency, voice and interpersonal skills of the candidates.
–   assessment of a short:
    –   interpreted role play on a non-specialist topic (both ways)
    –   written translation on a non-specialist topic (both ways)
    –   sight translation (both ways)
    –   written text, in both languages, on a chosen topic.

The following factors should be taken into account during the selection process.

a.   Languages: students should be selected in the language combinations required in the work place according to the urgency of the demand.
b.   Previous qualifications may have been acquired in another country and their content and status may not be clear. Some candidates may have no formal qualifications or incomplete qualifications. This does not necessarily mean that they are not suitable for training as interpreters at an initial professional level. They may be found to have good levels of language skills, while others, university graduates in diverse philologies, will prove to be entirely unsuitable.
c.   Length of the course: resources available limit the length of the courses. There are likely to be few students with the language combinations required who can afford to pay the fees and subsistence needed to attend full-time university courses, where these exist. Training courses are likely to be state subsidised, part-time and of limited duration. Students are also

likely to have domestic or work commitments, which may include working as unqualified interpreters.

d. Level of training programmes: two levels are emerging as part of the incremental development. The lower one is vocational in nature and is aimed at training for an initial, lower professional level. This would be equivalent to an undergraduate degree in level but not in breadth. There are a few higher, post-graduate MA courses which provide greater in-depth training. It is hoped that the numbers of higher level courses will increase, so that those who have taken the lower level assessment will, in time, progress to the higher one and be given the opportunity to explore the academic theory which underpins their practice.

e. Existing levels of language competence need to be matched against the improvements that can be made in the time available. Interpreting potential should be explored, given that some candidates may be competent in both languages but have difficulty in transferring between them.

f. The professional standing of the candidate should be taken note of. Public Service Interpreters (PSIs) often live within their own language communities and will need to be respected in order to be able to work properly. In some countries, such as the UK, all those who work in the public services are required to disclose any previous criminal convictions before being employed. Legal interpreters may need higher standards of security vetting.

3. Dual training: Public service personnel and interpreter

Reliable interpreting, while an essential pre-requisite, is only one of the elements required to provide public service across language and culture. The public services themselves are responsible for developing the additional skills and structures required. Unless they do so, public service interpreters are constantly under pressure to take on tasks and responsibilities which not only threaten their status of impartiality but for which they are unqualified, unrewarded and uninsured. The quality of service is diminished if interpreters are pressured into taking medical case histories and witness statements or giving medical, legal or other types of advice or information. When this does happen PSIs must learn to insist on observing their own code of conduct, which demands impartiality, and suggest other and better ways of achieving what is needed.

It is extremely beneficial to use the interpreters' training as an opportunity to train the public service personnel in how to accommodate the interpreting process and to introduce the notions of what is required in order to deliver service effectively across cultures. The delivery of public services inevitably involves a multidisciplinary team, such as doctors, nurses, physiotherapists, occupational therapists or police officers, lawyers, judges and probation officers. Traditionally they are trained to work together and to recognise, support and respect each other's expertise. Linguists are the new members of this interdisciplinary team. They need to learn how to work with professionals from other disciplines in the public services and vice versa. There are developments within the public services which would add formal professional training and assessments in these aspects for public service professionals.

4.   Creating a constructive learning dynamic

The following points are aimed at contributing to a constructive dynamic within a training programme that might have difficulties in negotiating the diversity of the trainees. Trainers should:

– recognise that students from different cultural and educational backgrounds will have acquired different ways of learning, e.g. rote learning, and there may be more than one learning convention within a class, which will require some negotiation on the part of both trainers and students.
– provide clear and adequate information about the course, especially for those unfamiliar with the educational system of the country. This would include:
  – aims and objectives
  – content
  – time-table
  – names of trainers
  – assessment procedures.

– encourage students from the outset, particularly those who come from more passive learning traditions, to take control of their own learning. This is an integral part of the working interpreter's professional life and the earlier it starts the better. It has been found helpful to support students in creating their own profiles. This might include:
  – identifying the skills they will require
  – identifying their own strengths and weaknesses in both languages, e.g. comprehension and expression of the written and spoken forms

- identifying the best learning methods for them
- evaluating their own performance.

- develop a class contract which allows students to negotiate, and record for future reference if necessary, how they agree the learning process will be conducted. In this manner their disparate conventions and needs can be accommodated.

5.   Summary of course content

Courses are taught in units of context and subject, with each unit dealing with five recognised, interdependent areas of training. The sequence may be, for medical interpreters for example: ante-natal care, child birth, paediatrics, common surgical and medical conditions, AIDS, community care, geriatrics, and so on.

The five areas of training are: (1) Understanding the working context of the public service (2) Fluency and familiarity with relevant specialist formal and informal terminology in both languages (3) Interpreting techniques and translation skills (4) Codes of ethics and guidelines to good practice (5) Continuous personal and professional development.

5.1   Understanding the working context of the public service

Public service interpreters seldom have much warning of assignments and therefore have little time to prepare. If they are to do a good job they must have solid background knowledge of the services they are trained to work in: structure, procedures, processes and personnel. This information is primarily in relation to the country they are working in, but they also need an under-standing of what is relevant in the country/district of their other language so that equivalencies in terminology can be sought more accurately.

Taking the legal services as an example, interpreters must have a back-ground understanding which includes the structure of the criminal and civil legal systems and the main procedures followed in such contexts as:

- the courts and tribunals
- police stations
- probation
- prisons

- immigration
- customs and excise.

Interpreters should be familiar with the procedures that must be followed in these contexts. They must know, for example:

- the roles and expertise of the personnel who work in the legal system
- the significance denoted by different uniforms and badges of rank
- the formal address required for different members of the judiciary
- geography of the buildings they are likely to work in, such as courts and police stations
- conventions and rules governing professional practice in each, e.g. what to do if a prison inmate asks the interpreter to relay an apparently innocuous message.

The same principles apply to any other service. An interpreter on the way to a medical emergency should not, for example, get lost in the hospital. He or she should also be fairly accustomed to the smells, sights and sounds so as not to be distracted from the interpreting tasks. There is much to be learnt about working as an interpreter in the public services which is rarely taught in the classroom and, in hindsight, is just common sense. Like the members of the other disciplines involved, they will have to know, for example, where alarm buttons are situated. Students should be made aware of the fact that their assignments will be very diverse and that these assignments will require them to be alert to and find proper responses to a great variety of situations.

Methods of teaching include:
- instruction by practising members of the services, such as doctors, police officers or social workers. They are perhaps the best informed on the subjects
- observation visits to places where interpreting assignments are likely to take place. These must be carefully structured. Students might be required to:
  - prepare for the visit in terms of gaining an understanding of the foundation terminology, the roles of people working in the service and how to recognise them, transport systems (to and from local hospitals, for example)
  - complete a fact sheet and their own notes during the visit

- contribute to the de-briefing session afterwards on such matters as: terminology (including acronyms and informal terminology, and the equivalents in the other language), security measures and clothing (e.g. when do interpreters have to wear a mask or gown in medical situations and how do they put them on)

- preparation of background information for particular assignments, including instruction on ways of filing information for future use
- information retrieval exercises, which help students gain confidence in being able to quickly access necessary information.

Students should use also this period as a time to begin developing their own contacts and sources of information.

Three possible assignments might involve, for example, cases dealing with amniocentesis, defective brake linings or the electoral register. Students should therefore:

- be familiar with the layout and cataloguing systems of local and specialist libraries
- know the names of specialists who could be consulted in either language. These might include lawyers, doctors, garage mechanics and local authority officers
- gather lists of relevant web-sites
- know the senior interpreters who could be consulted for specialist expertise
- participate in sessions of information input and discussion of the bicultural aspects of assignments, with the aim of developing comprehensive, culturally diverse attitudes to such matters as birth, child rearing, death, justice, health and healing.

It is, of course, not possible to reach an in-depth cultural understanding of every aspect. Medical anthropology, for example, can be the work of a lifetime. The course should, however, contribute to an overt awareness, and indeed enjoyment, of the existence of implicit cultural issues and a common-sense professional way of accommodating them. Interpreters learn, with experience, to recognise and reflect cultural dimensions within the decoding and re-encoding process. Public Service personnel need to also learn, wherever possible, to accommodate cultural variations in their service delivery. Informal, inter-cultural and interdisciplinary social gatherings are also valuable as a means of easing discomforts and tensions during the course, while promoting mutual understanding.

5.2 Fluency and familiarity with relevant specialist formal and informal terminology in both languages

Conference interpreters are normally required to interpret the standard version of languages. Public service interpreters clearly need to have a written and spoken command of both their languages. In addition, however, they need to have a command of a wide range of registers and dialects in both languages, as well as both formal terminology and informal language used within the service context. PSIs will usually interpret for speakers who come from a variety of ages, are unaccustomed to working with interpreters and may be anxious and under stress. PSIs must therefore have a command of their languages which can, for example, encompass the up-to-date jargon of youth cultures and the language used by those who left their country of origin some years before and which may have shifted and mixed. If this seems a tall order, perhaps it is useful to note that the PSIs' code of conduct allows them to ask for clarification, but if this occurs too frequently the communication flow is hindered.

It should not be assumed that students are necessarily as competent as they should be in their language of habitual use and/or that of their education, which may or may not be their heritage language. Recent educational fashions in some countries, which discourage the teaching of formal grammar and spelling and also diminish extensive reading, have resulted in unhappy consequences for interpreter training. Students from a bilingual background, or who have changed the language of their education mid-stream, may need some consolidation in either or both languages, despite apparent verbal fluency.

Interpreters should be as sure-footed as cats on a china shelf as they transfer utterances. Consider, for example, the following witness statement after a road traffic accident: "I was driving down the street. I came to the traffic lights, which turned green. This chap came tearing across. I would have braked sharply, had I not had my mother in the back seat, who has a heart condition".

As in any interpreter course, training includes the need to build confidence through affirmation and encouragement. Students may, at an initial stage, not make the distinction between the value given to their language skills and their self-worth within their bilingual identity. If their language skills are challenged, they feel challenged as people. It is important to cultivate an enjoyment in what they are doing while drawing rigorous attention to detail.

Methods of teaching include:

- providing access courses. Early selection procedures allow the trainer to spot the weak points in potentially good students. It may be that their

literacy skills in one of their languages, or their study skills, need some work prior to the commencement of the course proper
- identifying terminology in the relevant public services, working up equivalencies and debating how to respond if there are none
- using realia from the services wherever possible
- discussing how individuals, of differing ages, sex and professional/educational and social backgrounds use languages
- having students give presentations, on specific subjects in both languages, so as to promote information retrieval, analysis, logic, coherence and clarity of delivery
- organising all the usual exercises, such as comprehension tests
- supporting students in creating their own glossaries.

5.3 Interpreting techniques and translation skills

Students will need to have practice in the following techniques, in both language directions:
- short consecutive interpreting
- whispered simultaneous interpreting
- sight translation of short texts
- written translation of forms, short reports, letters, information leaflets.

Technology

Unlike conference interpreters, public service interpreting does not normally involve specialised technology. There are, however, various developments emerging which may result in implications for training.

Face-to-face interpreting is almost always the best approach in the public services. In situations where communication is already fragile, all the possible notes of all the tunes from all the participants within an exchange of communication have to be played and heard if there is to be music of any quality.

Two main factors have to be considered when contemplating alternatives to face-to-face interpreting. Firstly, the linguistic difficulty of an assignment does not necessarily correspond with its perceived importance. A straightforward case with a guilty plea in a high court can, for example, be linguistically simpler than dealing with a neighbourhood dispute or a discussion at a school parents' evening. Secondly, the degree of difficulty cannot be predicted. Initial communicative exchanges are also often used to test the waters, as when a patient goes to the doctor complaining of a sore throat; but further consultation reveals the real reason of the visit, which may be an unexplained lump. What starts out as one thing, often ends up as being something much more complex.

The amount of interpreting likely to be required in the public services is beginning to cause anxiety. Inevitably, technology is being turned to, sometimes in order to assist in the quality of the delivery of interpreting and of the public services, sometimes as short-cuts which have to be used with very well informed caution. The use of technological aids should, of course, be explored even though they may be introduced by either entrepreneurs who see a lucrative gap in the market or well-meaning people who may not fully comprehend the interpreting process.

The facilities for simultaneous interpreting through headphones are currently unlikely to be commonly available within the public services. There are indications, however, that increase in access to affordable and appropriate technology may make the use of this approach more likely, not just for court hearings, but also in situations such as social work case conferences.

Videoconferencing is becoming more available and is used, in particular, by Sign Language Interpreters. It is not in general welcomed by spoken language interpreters, because interpreters do not have full access to the non-verbal gestures that imply certain reactions, nor are they able to experience the atmosphere. Pragmatically, it is a way of responding to the need for multiple short assignments and it can be acceptable if used with care in specific situations.

Telephone interpreting is also on the increase in some countries. Australia, which has a long history of telephone communication in order to cover the huge distances involved, is one of the countries with highly developed sophisticated systems of telephone interpreting. The levels of interpreting skills required must be higher for there are no non-verbal signals; therefore situations which require this type of interpreting must be carefully chosen and prepared whenever possible. This has not always been fully recognised or respected in some countries.

Training should therefore, wherever possible, include some experience in these different approaches. The students can then discuss the merits of them objectively, evaluate their own skills in providing these services satisfactorily and also recognise their shortcomings so as to know when to refuse assignments or to suggest alternatives.

a. Interpreting techniques

Methods of teaching include:
- exercises common to all interpreter training, such as memory drills and voice exercises
- interpreted role-plays, more or less taking the place of the language laboratory work done by conference interpreter trainees.

A basic training role-play consists of two interlocutors and a student who interprets between them. One of the interlocutors is a practitioner from the relevant public service. The second is a native speaker of another language, and is usually played by a student – obviously from the same language group as the student "interpreter". The trainer devises beforehand a role-play scenario which is appropriate to the level required and which is intended to address both general skills and specific points. This may include terminology, professional practice or problem solving. The interlocutors are given advance warning of the nature of the scenario but the student may or may not be, depending upon whether, for example, an exercise in information retrieval is called for. Training role-plays normally last about ten minutes and there may be a series of them in a class session. Each student should be given as many opportunities as possible to practice, in order to consolidate lessons learnt and explore new aspects.

Examples of scenarios could involve interpreted exchanges involving:
- a tourist reporting a stolen wallet at the police station
- a woman making an ante-natal visit to the doctor
- parents and a teacher discussing a child's progress at school
- social workers and families discussing care of children/the elderly/the disabled
- police interviewing suspects/witnesses/victims of crime
- patients consulting doctors on a range of illnesses/birth/death.

The subsequent critiques are essential and are conducted by the interpreter trainers but also involve the public service personnel, the role-play participants and the rest of the students. Accuracy, fluency, appropriateness, style, diction, interpreting techniques, note taking, and professional good practice are among the dimensions looked at. This is part of the students' learning process, in that they learn to make objective evaluations of their own and others' performance. As importantly, they learn to take and offer constructive criticism with precision and grace, traits they will be expected to show when they are qualified to practice.

Feedback worksheets focus on the critical process. Sample sheets for reflecting on trainee interpreters' performance are included, as an appendix, at the end of this chapter. A worksheet is also appended to provide an idea of what the public service personnel may be looking for in their own work. As the course progresses the role-plays become more demanding. They involve more participants, more specialised terminology, and more complex situations. They never, however, stop being based upon real-life situations. The mock-court hearings for legal interpreters, for example, are, wherever possible, held in the various types of court rooms, e.g. family, criminal, youth and coroners' courts.

The theory of interpreting, which underpins all practice, is dealt with throughout the course, the depth and approach depending upon the level.

b. Translation skills

Brief mention will be made here of translation, although this chapter is devoted primarily to interpreting. There are not many interactions with a public service which do not involve a form to fill in, such as: operation consent forms, bail forms, forms applying for housing, electoral registers. There may be letters exchanged: such as letters asking the doctor for an appointment, from mothers informing the school that their child is sick, to mothers from schools inviting them to a social gathering, to defendants telling them when their case will be heard.

Information leaflets abound. It is essential that many of them be available to speakers of many languages. Most of them require a careful pre-editing process, through collaboration between translators and the public service, to ensure that the text is accessible and practical for the target readership.

Public service interpreters, therefore, need the skills for accurate translation of short texts, both direct and inverse translation (that is, both from and into one's native language). They should, however, be very aware of their limitations and know how to act responsibly. If they are not sufficiently qualified and experienced to deal with the translation in question, they must learn to refer long or complex texts to a professional translator.

Sight translation
It is a fact of life that, in the public services, interpreters will be asked to sight-translate texts. One of the first things students are taught is when and how to convey to the enquirer the fact that an accurate sight translation is not feasible. The text in question may often be too long or too complex for sight translation. In those cases where a sight translation is required and the text is suitable,

students are recommended to first read the whole text carefully to ensure a full comprehension, then to tell the listener the provenance and nature of the text before beginning translation.

For example:

"This is a letter written by Mrs. Dubois to Doctor Brown, on Tuesday 27th May. The address given is 47 Beech Avenue, Littletown. She writes:

'The pills you gave me last week are making me feel very nauseous. Can I have an appointment to come and see you soon? Meanwhile should I stop taking the pills? I am sorry to trouble you again but I am really feeling most unwell.'

The letter is signed." (Obviously the interpreter would translate a short reply from the doctor.)

5.4 Codes of ethics and guidelines to good practice

Public service interpreters usually work on their own in a wide variety of unpredictable situations. They cannot turn to an interpreter colleague in the booth and ask for advice. Their code and guidelines are not unlike the Highway Code for drivers, whereby, if one follows them carefully, one is unlikely to come to harm or cause an accident. A course must provide trainees with a full understanding of what is required of them and sufficient training to enable them to produce automatic responses under stress. Dithering with uncertainty in a crowded court or by a road traffic accident is not going to help anyone.

The codes and guidelines to good practice are also important because this is a newly formalised branch of the profession and professional status has to be earned if trust is to be extended. The code of conduct is immutable, and any alleged breaches are subject to the disciplinary proceedings of the professional body to which the interpreter belongs.

So far as can be assessed, the codes in most countries include the following core requirements that interpreters:

- interpret truly and faithfully
- observe confidentiality
- observe impartiality
- act with integrity
- not accept assignments which they judge beyond their competence
- deal professionally with any limitations which may reveal themselves during an assignment

- recognise and admit to any conflicts of interest
- do everything possible to safeguard professional standards and support each other.

The code of ethics mentioned above is much the same as for any interpreter. There will, however, be other situations in which public service interpreters, in contrast to other types of interpreters, will be required to intervene in order to preserve the integrity of communication. Public service interpreters may intervene:

- to clarify what they have been asked to interpret
- to ask for accommodation for the interpreting process
- to alert the participants to any perceived non-comprehension by one or more of them, despite accurate interpreting
- to alert the participants to a possible missed cultural inference.

The interpreters interpret subsequent explanations or advice but do not give them themselves.

Good practice guidelines offer detailed information with reference to specific services and situations. The Metropolitan Police force in London provide a good example of dual guidelines; one for interpreters and one for police officers. They cover the processes to be followed in such matters as taking statements.

Good practice guidelines do not have the absolute force of the code of ethics but are intended to be followed, wherever possible, and could be taken into account in the event of any disciplinary proceedings. Students are expected to know and understand any guidelines which apply to the services for which they are training.

Methods of teaching
What may appear to be an obvious ethical or professional stance in one culture may not be one in another. Strict confidentiality may mean one thing in one culture, but something slightly different in another. What is important is that the code used is agreed, public, transparent, accountable and that it complements the codes of conduct of the public services of the country.

In order to reach an informed synthesis, it is helpful to devote time to this aspect of teaching, without neglecting other essential aspects of the course. The most useful approach has been found to include:

- reference to the code of ethics and guidelines in all aspects of the course, such as in role-plays and translation exercises

- small seminars centred around problem-solving activities
- multidisciplinary seminars to promote interdisciplinary mutual understanding of codes of conduct and guidelines.

Many of the elements in the interpreters' code of ethics will also be shared by professionals in other public services, such as doctors, lawyers, nurses and teachers. How the latter deal with implementing their codes correctly may be instructive for the interpreters.

5.5 Continuous personal and professional development

A good professional never stops learning and growing. In their initial training students learn the strategies for implementing this principle. Like interpreters in other fields, they learn how to:

- profile their own strengths and weaknesses
- identify the targets they need to achieve
- identify the sources of information and expertise needed
- use those sources
- evaluate the outcome.

Some of these points were mentioned earlier in this chapter, see Section 4. It is important that these points be continually stressed, throughout training, so that it becomes second nature for students to put them into practice, especially once they qualify as public service interpreters. A more formal framework for continuous professional development is being considered for a variety of reasons, one of which is the fact that situations change very quickly in the public services. For example, an interpreter with a rarer language combination may not be employed on a regular basis and will need to remain up-to-date.

Personal development is perhaps more emphasised in the public service context, where interpreters are physically present during interactions, than in conference interpreting. Most assignments involve the routine of daily life: visits to the doctor, to school parents' evenings, to benefits offices, to courts and police stations in connection with minor offences (such as parking tickets). Even these expose the interpreters directly to the feelings, hopes and anxieties of both of their client groups – the public service providers and the other-language speakers. Interpreters may also be used, usually unwittingly, as the focus of their clients' irritation or frustration at the bilingual nature of the interchange and must learn to deal with this.

There are rare assignments which are more demanding, to everyone involved in them, such as births. These can prove to be very rewarding situations. The growing number of babies whose middle name is that of the interpreter gives testimony to this fact! Other assignments are not so pleasant: death, bereavement, rape and child abuse are just some that might be dealt with; and the interpreters involved are shielded from none of the details.

PSIs are part of the public service multidisciplinary team, and they stand shoulder to shoulder with their colleagues and take their share of the grief on these occasions. Like their colleagues, during the assignments they direct their energies and emotions solely to dealing with the situation itself. They must learn how to deal emotionally with the tragic situations they encounter. Trainers cannot teach students how to cope with these situations. They can only introduce them to the strategies for coping, possibly with the help of trainers and counsellors in the public services. What these strategies may be depends, to some extent, upon individual interpreters and their cultural background. Perhaps the first step is to be overt about emotional reactions and how important it is to deal with them in a sensible and responsible way. Sensitivity is part of an interpreter's, especially a public service interpreter's, professional equipment. It needs to be preserved and extended, rather than blunted, in order to be able to handle whatever may arise.

Management skills

Most public service interpreters are free-lance; some work for local authority non-profit interpreter and translation units. Others work on a salaried basis within, for example, hospitals where there is a demand for a particular language combination. It should be noted that full-time employment by the legal services is not encouraged. Being a "police interpreter" has connotations which impinge on the interpreter's impartiality.

Public service interpreters, like all other interpreters, need to know how to organise their professional lives. It is advisable for trainers to introduce good practice in these matters at the outset, rather than let students pick up tips from others once they have started to practise. One session on straightforward basic procedures should be enough and might include such matters as:

– contracts and letters of agreement
– insurance coverage
– tax information
– diary and time management.

6. Training targets: Assessments

Assessments need to be related to the practical professional context. They differ to some extent from country to country, although efforts are being made to establish international equivalencies. Nationally recognised professional assessments are a first step and these are being implemented in a number of countries. These appear to be offered at first-degree and post-graduate levels in an increasing number of languages and countries.

The methods used may take the form of assessment of simulated assignments or of supervised real-life assignments or a combination of both. Training of examiners (usually practising qualified PSIs) and quality assurance strategies are clearly prerequisites for the task.

7. Registration

Some countries have national registration schemes. In addition to their qualifications and record of experience, applicants for registration are required to submit the details of referees so that references may be taken up. Security vetting may also be required to ensure the absence of criminal records. The Register of PSIs is then made available to the public services. In the UK, for example, the National Register of Public Service Interpreters (NRPSI) is available on CD-ROM or in hard copy for a modest subscription to cover costs. NRPSI Ltd., a non-profit subsidiary company of the Institute of Linguists, regularly up-dates its register. It already has about two thousand interpreters in a hundred languages. The public service personnel can simply look up the details of an interpreter and contact him or her directly, in the knowledge that the interpreter in question has passed the required criteria and is bound by a code of conduct. Secure web-sites are under development.

8. Mentoring, supervision and quality assurance

Public service interpreters rarely work in teams which would include a senior interpreter to whom they could turn for advice. Interesting developments, which have training implications, are, however, emerging in mentoring, supervision and quality assurance. Mentors, usually the more experienced PSIs, can be of great value, especially for the newly qualified interpreters. They can give essential, informed support in what can be an isolated task. Much of this work is done on a voluntary basis, but, in time, a proper structure and payment should emerge. PSI students should be aware that one day they may be required to do these tasks and need to have an understanding of what good practice is in this respect.

Good supervision is intended to make the working PSI's life easier, through proper management and support, and not merely to watch for lapses. The better public service interpreting units provide both supervision and quality assurance. Direct checks on quality assurance take various forms. For example, in some countries, such as England and Wales, all police investigative interviews are tape-recorded and copies of the tapes are given to both defence and prosecution. Where interviews have been interpreted, the interpreting can be checked – and challenged. More could be done in using senior PSIs in supervisory roles. The initial cost implications could be off-set by a consequent rise in standards.

9. Conclusion

Public service interpreting is at an interesting stage of professional development. Its progress thus far has been enabled by the generous support of interpreters from other branches of the profession. What used to be seen as the professional poor relation is blossoming into a rigorous discipline of its own. It is now coming to be seen as one of the most challenging and rewarding aspects of language activity.

Appendix: Sample worksheets for role-plays

1. Role-play – Feedback

> *Introductions   *   Seating   *   Direct Speech

Make notes answering the following questions while you are watching the role-play.

– Did the social worker and interpreter introduce themselves properly?
– Were the seating arrangements suitable for the interpreting situation?
– Did both the social worker and the interpreter use direct speech?
– Any other comment?

2. Role-play – Feedback

Answer the following questions, during and at the end of the role-play.

- Did the interpreter introduce him/herself properly?
- Did the interpreter use direct speech throughout the interview?
- Did the interpreter switch from consecutive to simultaneous at the appropriate moment?
- Was everything said by both clients interpreted?
- Was the interpreter accurate (syntax, lexis, pronunciation, register) and fluent (not hesitant, easily understood) in English?
- Was the interpreter accurate and fluent in the other language? (If you don't speak the language, what impression did you get?)
- Was the interpreter able to understand and transfer public service terminology to the other language?
- Could the interpreter cope with long utterances in the consecutive mode, with the help of notes?
- Was the simultaneous interpretation done effectively and accurately?
- Did the interpreter interrupt either client? If he/she did, was it appropriate?
- Did the interpreter appear to be sensitive to cultural differences/misunderstandings?
- Did the interpreter deal appropriately with any ethical issue?
- Did both clients appear to have confidence in and feel comfortable with the interpreter?
- Did the interpreter ensure that future arrangements were made, if appropriate?
- Any other comments?

3. Role-play – Feedback

(For use when training the public service personnel – denoted as PS)
Answer the following questions, during and at the end of the role-play.

- Had the PS briefed the interpreter beforehand on any unusual terminology or procedures, which could arise during the assignment?
- Did the PS introduce him/herself properly to the other language speaker, describe his/her role and the purpose of the interview?
- Did the PS pronounce the name of the other language speaker correctly?
- Did the PS use direct speech throughout the interview?
- Did the PS encode what he/she had to say clearly, audibly and unambiguously?

- Did the PS accommodate the interpreting process appropriately? (pausing at the right moment for consecutive interpreting and speaking at a comfortable pace for simultaneous interpreting)
- Did the PS respond appropriately to interpreter interventions? (asking for clarifications or accommodations, or alerting all parties to a possible missed cultural inference)
- Did the PS recognise and respect the interpreter's code of conduct?
- Did the PS summarise the outcomes of the interview for the other language speaker, set out the next steps to be taken and ensure that facilities were in place for them to be implemented?
- Any other comments?

I would like to express my gratitude to Anita Harmer for permission to use the first two role-play activities above (Adams, Corsellis, & Harmer 1995).

References

Adams, C., Corsellis, A., & Harmer, A. (Eds.). (1995). *Basic Handbook for Trainers of Public Service Interpreters*. London: Institute of Linguists.

Brennan, M. & Brown, R. (1997). *Equality Before the Law: Deaf People's Access to Justice*. Durham, England: Deaf Studies Research Unit, Durham University.

Carr, S., Roberts, R., Dufour, A., & Stein, D. (Eds.). (1995). *Critical Link 1*. Amsterdam and Philadelphia: John Benjamins.

Corsellis, A. & Crichton, J. (1994). "Crossing the Language and Culture Barrier". *Psychiatric Care*, Nov/Dec, 172–176.

Corsellis, A. (1995). *Non-English Speakers and the English Legal System*. Cambridge: Institute of Criminology.

Corsellis, A. (1997). "West Midlands Probation Service Working Across Language and Culture". Birmingham, UK: The Library, West Midlands Probation Service.

Erasmus, M. (Ed.). (1999). *Liaison Interpreting in the Community*. Pretoria, South Africa: Van Schaik Publishers.

Hertog, E. (Ed.). (2001). *Aequitas: Access to Justice Across Language and Culture in the EU*. Antwerp: Lessius Hogeschool.

Institute of Linguists (2001). Information leaflets on "National register of public service interpreters" and "Diploma in public service interpreting". London. www.iol.org.uk

Jacobs, B., Kroll, L., Green, J., & David, T. J. (1995). "The hazards of using a child as an interpreter". *Journal of the Royal Society of Medicine, 88*(8).

Mason, I. (guest editor). (1999). *Dialogue Interpreting*. Special Issue, *The Translator, 5*(2). Manchester: St. Jerome.

National Interpreting Standards and National Translation Standards for the UK. London: Languages National Training Organisation. www.cilt.org.uk.

Roberts, R., Carr, S., Abraham, & Dufour, D. (Eds.). (1997). *Critical Link 2*. Amsterdam and Philadelphia: John Benjamins.

Part III

The relevance of theory to training

CHAPTER 8

Theory and translator training

Francesca Bartrina

Ignorance, far more than knowledge, is what can never be taken for granted.
If I perceive my ignorance as a gap in knowledge instead of an imperative that
changes the very nature of what I think I know, then I do not truly experience
my ignorance. The surprise of otherness is that moment when a new form of
ignorance is suddenly activated as an imperative.   (Johnson 1989: 16)

1. Theory in the classroom

Johnson suggests a way of learning where any ignorance – any knowledge –
changes the whole conception of what we think we know. This is a good point
of departure for a discussion of the relevance of translation theory to the actual
practice of translation. Knowledge of theory can never be provided to students
as an end per se, but as a starting point for the adoption of the methods
required to ensure continuous learning. Ideally, theory should give university
translator trainees an enthusiasm for learning, practising and thinking about
translation in a specific as well as in an interdisciplinary manner.[1]

Literature on Translation Studies has sometimes questioned the role of
theory in the everyday work of the translator. The question that Jirí Levý
posed in 1965: "Will translation theory be of use to translators?" is still valid
in our discipline, and the answers provided have been unsatisfactory. We find
today, surprisingly – or perhaps not so surprisingly – that many professional
translators and interpreters express their belief in the uselessness of theory in
the actual process of translating. The question examined by Levý will continue
to be valid until everyone involved in the translation chain is convinced that
there is no translation practice without translation theory.

Some theorists, such as Lawrence Venuti, have re-examined the question
within a contemporary context (see Venuti 2000b: 27). I fully agree with Levý

and Venuti that Translation Theory is a way of improving the practice of translation, primarily because it increases the translator's awareness of methodology. The question could, in fact, be changed to: "Is it possible to practise
translation without theory?" The answer is negative if we consider that any decision taken by the translator during the translating process or any comment
on a translation product implies a conception of what translation entails, i.e.
a theory of translation. Any translation choice, any translation judgement reveals a theoretical position. Translation Theory contributes to the recognition
of one's own position in the context of the history of translation and in the map
of reflection on translation and language. Translation Theory aims at systematising translation practices, and it should therefore be considered fundamental
in the training of language mediators as it provides them with the necessary
skills for solving specific problems.

The primary objective of the course outlined below is precisely to train students to translate theoretically and provide them with the necessary theoretical
tools to enable them to defend and justify the decisions they take as translators.

2. Objectives and content

The curriculum of a university degree in Translation and Interpreting – or
any programme, for that matter, that trains translators – should include a
course devoted to Translation Theory. The specific aim of this course would
be to provide a study of the main theoretical concepts underlying the practice
of translation and interpreting. This would include basic linguistic notions
behind translation, mental and behavioural translating processes, and the
consideration of translation as a social, cultural and ideological activity.

If we start with the premise that translation theory and translation practice
should be inseparable, then – ideally – elements of the syllabus described below
for a course on Translation Theory would be re-introduced in subsequent
courses dedicated to translation practice. If students are truly to learn how to
translate theoretically, as part of their general practice as translator trainees and
later as professional translators, theory cannot be relegated to one introductory
course but should be integrated into the syllabuses of all translation courses.[2]

I suggest initiating the course in theory with an introduction to what
translation is, taking into account the considerations that deal with translation
as an art and as a science and the relationship of translation to linguistics and
literature. The debate on translation as an art and translation as a science has
its roots in the disciplines from which it is derived: Literature, Comparative

Literature, Hermeneutics and Linguistics. As Venuti (2000a:4) says: "Any account of theoretical concepts and trends must acknowledge the disciplinary sites in which they emerged in order to understand and evaluate them."

This brings us to the complexity of defining what constitutes a translation, for the concept of translation is culture specific. As Chesterman and Arrojo (2000:152) put it: "One aim of Translation Studies is to discover which kind of texts (in certain cultures at certain times) have been labeled 'translations', as compared with texts that are not called translations. This aim includes the study of who labels the texts, and for what reasons, and whether such attributions change over time."

The questioning of the concept of translation leads us to the considera-tion of translation as a communicative event which can be considered both as a process and as a product. Approaches today often integrate process and product into the study of translation.[3] To consider translation as a commu-nicative event which takes place between two different languages allows us to include the widest range of practices, from literary translation to community interpreting. Kiraly (1995:6) proposes a definition of translation that covers the main concepts we will be dealing with in this chapter:

> A person translating a text for pragmatic purposes engages in a real act of interlinguistic and intercultural communication – the production of a text with a specific textual function, information content, and identifiable readership. A real act of translation presupposes that the translator has cognitive, social and textual skills and access to appropriate stores of linguistic, cultural, and real-world knowledge.

First, we have the determining factors of the person who translates and of the communication act. This brings us to the highly questioned definitions of equivalence, functionality, norms, manipulation, rewriting, domestication and foreignisation and to the different contexts they come from. These concepts could help to establish a typology of translation types.[4]

In contemporary culture, the circulation of texts among languages and cultures is a mass phenomenon. A course on Translation Theory should cover the influence of translation in contemporary society, including consideration of such matters as the use of multimedia technology and the fact that a relatively small number of senders reaches a very large number of receivers. New and old challenges in the field of technology and translation might be considered theoretically. The significance of translation in mass media brings us to the teaching of different theories of translation that take into account all translating and interpreting practices and reflect the presence of translation and interpreting everywhere in everyday life, even when translation occurs in a dispersed, fragmented or hybrid form. Hermans (1999:122) follows José Lambert when he insists on this last point:

> They [the translators] do not necessarily translate entire texts, but may use a combination of partial translation and original text production, so that translation occurs in dispersed and fragmented form. As a result, all kinds of snippets and remnants of translation percolate from public into private discourse. Think, for example, of the vocabulary of European Union directives or of international finance, the terminology of fashion and psychoanalysis in English, computer and sports jargon in numerous languages other than English, all of them shot through with translation, calques, borrowings and loanwords. Translation Studies should deal with fragmentary translations as well as with complete texts.

Hermans also reminds us that sometimes translations disguise their status, as in the case of advertisements, and that many go through numerous intermediate stages. All of these techniques bring to the fore the need for the study of theory.

Some thought on the metaphors related to translation at a particular moment is useful, as it can enlighten us with regard to the predominant attitudes towards translating. In this sense the binary oppositions that have typified thought on translation, viz. original/translation, faithfulness/unfaithfulness, word by word/sense, literal/functional, and the ideas that have surrounded them – such us the identification of culture with a monolingual territory – might be considered with all of their implications. It may no longer be relevant to speak of source text and target text, as many texts are manipulated at many intermediate stages. Translations are often the work of a team, especially in dubbing or in translating for the stage, where the concept of "authority" for the translated discourse is sometimes very confused.

The publication of Nida's, *Toward a Science of Translating* (1964), represents, in great measure, the impulse which led to the application of theory to a systematising of the practice of translation. From that point on, theories of translation have tended to be founded upon predetermined assumptions about what meaning is and what translation entails. For this reason it is necessary to reflect upon certain concepts before entering into the different theoretical approaches to translation. All translations have as their starting point certain ideas about meaning, i.e. what it is and how it functions, be these ideas conscious or unconscious. In fact, any definition of translation makes it obvious that meaning is the fundamental problem behind translation. Students must therefore be encouraged to think clearly and systematically about the changes in the idea of meaning. This is the point of departure in the debate between essentialism and non-essentialism. A thorough study would signify entering the field of the philosophy of meaning, and the course outlined here cannot, due to the limited number of class hours, deal with this area. However, it is important that students be given an overview of various theories, which might include Saussurean linguistics, structuralism, semiotics, post-structuralism, deconstruction and post-colonialism.

The status of translation as text can be dealt with at length. The syllabus can cover areas such as the consideration of translation as text, the question of textuality, cohesion and coherence in translation, speech acts and textual acts, and the concept of relevance. Emphasis might be put on translation practice which incorporates the concept of parallel texts and a clear definition of situationality and informativity. Different text typologies can be discussed and analysed. In the same way, the role of intertextuality and its consequences in translation can be addressed by studying many source and target texts and their contexts. According to Hatim and Mason, every person has an innate capacity to recognise double intertextuality: "our recognition of co-reference within a single text is basically the same as our ability to classify one text in terms of another previously experienced text" (1990:125). This leads us to consider which intertextual relationships assure the continuity of certain social and ideological institutions and how translation practices are related to them.

The psycholinguistic model is concerned with describing the cognitive aspects of the translation process. The consideration of translation as a cognitive process might begin with the definition of experientialism and be followed by an introduction to cognition and translation and to translation memory. If the process of translation is a process of decision-making, a cognitive theory of translation attempts to understand how that decision-making functions. It takes into account the factors that arise during the decision-making, from source and target language textual constraints to audience design. To consider – if not understand – what goes on in the mind of the translator or the interpreter, students might be interested in examining Think-Aloud Protocol (TAP) techniques and uses of the translator's verbalised self-commentary. Aspects such as speed and quality could also be included.

Students need to be aware that the dividing line between theory and practice is becoming more and more blurred in linguistic, text-linguistic and psycholinguistic approaches. According to Neubert (1995:67):

> In the context of translation studies, the binary distinction between the term *applied* and its presumed opposite, *theoretical*, is an artifice. It equates theory

with abstractness and application with concreteness. In other words, the more we deal with language as system (and the less we deal with concrete translation behaviours) the more theoretical our model. This distinction obscures the relationship between theory and practice.

A course on Translation Theory might also wish to emphasise the professional role of the translator, his/her responsibility, and the ethics of translation practice. Translators must learn to constantly re-evaluate their work in relation to the changing political and cultural situations. Students, for example, could be encouraged to become more aware of the role played by gender in translation: the politics of transmission can be influenced by the projects promoted by the translator.[5] The specific conditions of the translating activity have been clearly recognised: the translator is an active creator of meaning and draws attention to the translating process or to his/her own work through the use of footnotes, prefaces and theoretical texts. In this sense, the role played by ideology should not be overlooked, as Álvarez and Vidal (1996:2) have pointed out:

> Contemporary studies on translation are aware of the need to examine in depth the relationship between the production of knowledge in a given culture and its transmission, relocation, and reinterpretation in the target culture. This obviously has to do with the production and ostentation of power and with the strategies used by this power in order to represent the other culture.

The role played by ideology in translation can be dealt with through the discussion of terms such as identity, difference and hybridism. The importance of translation for post-colonialism has caused post-colonial theorists to turn increasingly to translation to appropriate and reassert the term itself. Bassnett and Trivedi, editors of *Post-Colonial Translation: Theory and Practice*, insist upon the importance of translation in the early period of colonisation: "Europe was regarded as the great Original, the starting point, and the colonies were therefore copies, or 'translations' of Europe, which they were supposed to duplicate" (1999:4). First then, there is the role played by translation in facilitating colonisation and, second, there is the metaphor of the colony as translation. Post-colonial studies of translation stimulate the asking of the question: "how do we represent the other?" Spivak (1993:191) suggests that as translators we have to surrender the text in order to allow dissemination and loss of control. She defends a compromise between translator and textuality: ideology is in the rhetoric of the source text also. Students can be encouraged to recognise the positions of power that the practice of translation and interpreting entails.

3. Methodological challenges of on-line courses

Instructors teaching Translation Theory will find themselves more and more obliged to confront new technological challenges in this global era. Perhaps the most revolutionary change, for instructors, has to do with on-line multimedia courses in higher education. As instructors we will need to transfer teaching skills in the face-to-face classroom to those in the virtual environment. This is giving rise to new trends in pedagogy, far from the traditional teaching methods we were accustomed to, and requires the acquisition of new skills in Information Technology. More specifically, in the case of on-line Translation Theory courses, this means that instructors need to stay abreast of new possibilities.

Some questions arise: what kind of supporting material can be developed in continuous on-line assessment? How can we deal successfully with effective elements of the learning process in an on-line environment? Some obvious suggestions are the use of tools such as forums, chats and the permanent update of the on-line material available.[6] The Internet has enormously increased the availability of information and, in the case of Translation Theory, this means that our students have quick access to theoretical readings in on-line journals, articles, papers and conferences proceedings.[7]

4. Course: Translation Theory

4.1 Syllabus

1. What is translation?
1.1. Introduction
1.2. Translation as an art. Translation as a science
1.3. Linguistics and translation
1.4. Literature and translation
1.5. The history of translation
1.6. Translation as a process and as a product
1.7. Translation as a communicative event
1.8. Translation and technology

2. Concepts for the study of translation
2.1. Meaning
2.2. Equivalence
2.3. Function

2.4. Conventions, rules and norms
2.5. Rewriting
2.6. Domestication and foreignisation
2.7. Types of translation

3. Textuality and translation
3.1. Translation as text
3.2. The question of textuality
3.3. Cohesion and coherence
3.4. Speech acts and textual acts
3.5. Situationality and informativity
3.6. Intertextuality
3.7. Text as structure
3.8. Textual typologies
3.9. Relevance

4. Translation as a cognitive process
4.1. Experientialism
4.2. Cognition and translation
4.3. Translation memory
4.4. Think-Aloud Protocols (TAPs)

5. Translation as a cultural event
5.1. Identity in translation: the question of difference
5.2. Hybridism
5.3. Gender and translation
5.4. Ethics and translation

4.2 Methodological proposals

At the beginning of a course on Translation Theory, students are provided with the following:

–   A list of selected readings, together with questions and comments (see below) as a guide to their reading: Hatim, B. and Mason I. (1990); Lefevere, A. (1992); Munday, J. (2001); Nord, C. (1997); Paz, O. (1971); Toury, G. (1995) and Venuti, L. (2000a).
–   Practical exercises to be done in class. The aim of these exercises is to show students the inseparability of theory and practice. The following are included as an example.

1. Consider these statements regarding translation:

> One cannot state that a particular translation is good or bad without taking into consideration a myriad of factors, which in turn must be weighted in a number of different ways, with appreciably different answers. Hence there will always be a variety of valid answers to the question, is it a good translation? (Nida 1964)

> This story of Babel recounts, among other things, the origin of the confusion of tongues, the irreducible multiplicity of idioms, the necessary and impossible task of translation, its necessity as impossibility.
> (Derrida 1985)

> Translation is the forcible replacement of the linguistic and cultural difference of the foreign text with a text that will be intelligible to the target-language reader. (Venuti 1995)

Discuss the different understanding of translation that Eugene Nida, Jacques Derrida and Lawrence Venuti have and that can be deduced from their statements about translation.

2. Comment on the different theories of translation that lie behind the decisions taken by translators, based on your comparison of a source text and two or more translations of that text. One example of this kind of exercise is offered by Robinson in his book *The Translator's Turn*: here he includes his translation of the poem by Jorge Guillén "Desnudo", together with the translation of the same poem by Reginald Gibbons, and comments on the different conceptions of translation that have inspired them (1990: 148–155).

3. Find advertisements of several translation agencies on the Internet and discuss the conception the agencies have of the translator's work based on the metaphors they use to describe the work.

4. Consult a bilingual anthology of translated poetry. Comment on your impressions using the terms "equivalence", "rewriting" and "manipulation".

5. Discuss the way in which cultural difference is expressed in articles from foreign newspapers that deal with an aspect of Spanish culture.

6. On the Internet search for an article in an English publication about the Costa Brava, in northern Catalonia. Propose different translation contexts that could justify a Catalan translation of the article. Based on the article you have found, produce two translations, one a documentary and the other instru-

mental, following the types proposed by Nord in *Text Analysis in Translation* (1991).[8]

7. Locate three "Translator Notes" in examples of literary translations and then answer the following questions:

- What conception does the translator have regarding his/her work?
- In which passages is this conception clear?
- Can we deduce a certain translator's position in relation to the source culture? And in relation to the target culture?

8. Compare the textual markers of coherence and cohesion in a source text and in different target texts and comment on their implications.

9. Take a tourist leaflet. Search for parallel texts and answer the following questions:

- In which aspects are they similar or different?
- Do they satisfy the expectations generated by their text type?
- Do they disappoint these expectations?

10. Look for two magazine advertisements: one which is part of an international campaign and another which refers to a local product. Compare them. Is it possible to translate the second into many languages? Why?

11. Gather together several travel guides for Spain in the same language and in different languages. What do they presuppose that travellers know about Spain and what not? How many of them are translations?

12. Compare two translations of the same literary text. Try to reconstruct the reasoning that went on in the mind of the translator and that led to the solutions chosen.

13. Select an example of the cultural past of your country where translation has played an important role as a cultural enterprise. Then answer the following questions: what role is played by translation in the construction of national identity? Is there any identification between translation and cultural imperialism?

*

The above exercises are aimed at integrating the presentation of different theories into the actual practice of translation. In this sense, the translating experience of students could be used as a starting point that leads them to the theory that is implied by this experience. To achieve this it is important to promote discussion of theoretical issues in class and to devote attention to the contradictory positions that arise in the debates.

5. Conclusion

The application of a particular theoretical concept may be determined by the linguistic, cultural, social and ideological factors that exert their influence on the practice of translation. Knowledge of Translation Theory can motivate specific, practical decisions. Moreover, in the contemporary market environment, translators are asked to justify their decisions to publishers and editors; and they need a theoretical background in order to have the appropriate language skills to do so.

Translators and interpreters need a theoretical field that helps them to be articulate in evaluating all the relevant questions concerning the translating process and the final product, from the ideological consequences of their work to the linguistic choices available in a particular sentence. Furthermore, translators should be aware of the political significance of their work. Translation activity carries social and economic consequences. What is translated and how it is translated are political decisions. As Lefevere (1992) and Spivak (1993) remind us, translation is today a highly institutionalised activity.

Notes

1. I am indebted to my former colleague Neus Carbonell for many valuable insights and for many hours of theoretical discussions during the five years that we taught Translation Theory at the University of Vic.

2. In this sense it can be very stimulating for teachers of an institution to have seminars, as a site for debate, where they can share and discuss their different approaches.

3. The consideration of translation as a process and as a product is dealt with very clearly in Hatim and Mason's *Discourse and the Translator* (1990).

4. In class, we discuss the typologies given by Nord (1991, 1997), House (1981:179–191) and Vidal (1995:47–55).

5. Simon's book *Gender in Translation* (1996) and Von Flotow's *Translation and Gender* (1997) deal with the commitment of writing with a gendered project.

6. Examples of on-line material available to our students for discussion are the web pages on Bible Translation at: http://www.bible-researcher.com/translation-methods.html or http://www.saltana.com.ar/dolet/start.htm.

7. Examples of this sort of material are specialised Translation journals with the full text of the articles available, for example, *Meta* (at http://www.erudit.org/revue/meta/) or the Proceedings of the VII Translation Conference at the University of Vic 2003 (at http://www.uvic.es/fchtd/jornades_2003/inici.html).

8. I think that the two types of translation explained by Christiane Nord are quite useful in the teaching of Translation Theory. Documentary translation is the type of translation process that aims at producing in the target language a communicative-interaction document orientated towards the source culture conditions. Instrumental translation is the type of translation process that aims at producing in the target language an instrument for a new communicative interaction between the source-culture sender and a target-culture audience but is orientated towards the target culture conditions.

References

Álvarez, R. & Vidal, C. A. (1996). *Translation, Power, Subversion*. Clevedon: Multilingual Matters Ltd.

Bassnett, S. & Trivedi, H. (Eds.). (1999). *Post-Colonial Translation: Theory and Practice*. London: Routledge.

Chesterman, A. & Arrojo, R. (2000). "Shared ground in Translation Studies". *Target, 12*(1), 151–160.

Derrida, J. (1985). "Des tours de Babel". In J. Graham (Ed.), *Difference in Translation* (pp. 209–248). Ithaca: Cornell University Press.

Hatim, B. & Mason, I. (1990). *Discourse and the Translator*. London: Longman.

House, J. (1981). *A Model for Translation Quality Assessment*. Tübingen: Narr.

Hermans, T. (1999). *Translation in Systems. Descriptive and Systemic Approaches Explained*. Manchester: St Jerome.

Johnson, Barbara (1989). *The World of Difference*. Baltimore: John Hopkins University Press.

Kiraly, D. (1995). *Pathways to Translation: Process and Pedagogy*. Kent, OH: Kent State University Press.

Lefevere, A. (1992). *Translation, Rewriting and the Manipulation of Literary Fame*. London: Routledge.

Levý, J. (1965). "Will Translation Theory be of Use to Translators"? In R. Italiaander (Dir.), *Übersetzen* (pp. 77–82). Frankfurt: Athenäum.

Munday, J. (2001). *Introducing Translation Studies. Theories and Application*. London: Routledge.

Neubert, A. (1995). "Translation as text". *Rivista Internazionale di Tecnica della Traduzione, 1*, 63–76.

Nida, E. (1964). *Toward a Science of Translating*. Leiden: E.J. Brill.

Nord, C. (1991). *Text Analysis in Translation*. Amsterdam: Rodopi.

Nord, C. (1997). *Translating as a Purposeful Activity. Functionalist Approaches Explained.* Manchester: St. Jerome.

Paz, O. (1971). *Traducción: Literatura y Literalidad.* Barcelona: Tusquets Editores.

Robinson, D. (1990). *The Translator's Turn.* Baltimore: John Hopkins University Press.

Simon, S. (1996). *Gender in Translation: Cultural Identity and the Politics of Transmission.* London and New York: Routledge.

Spivak, G. (1993). "The politics of translation". In *Outside in the Teaching Machine* (pp. 179–200). London: Routledge.

Toury, G. (1995). *Descriptive Translation Studies and Beyond.* Amsterdam and Philadelphia: John Benjamins.

Venuti, L. (1995). *The Translator's Invisibility: A History of Translation.* London and New York: Routledge.

Venuti, L. (Ed.). (2000a). *The Translation Studies Reader.* London and New York: Routledge.

Venuti, L. (2000b). "¿Será útil la teoría de la traducción para los traductores?" Juan Gabriel López Guix (Trans.). *Vasos comunicantes*, 27–35.

Vidal, C. Á. (1995). *Traducción, manipulación, deconstrucción.* Salamanca: Publicaciones del colegio de España.

Von Flotow, L. (1997). *Translation and Gender. Translating in the 'Era of Feminism'.* Manchester: St. Jerome.

CHAPTER 9

Causality in translator training

Andrew Chesterman

1. Introduction

Causality is a central concept in any empirical science. What role does the study of causes and effects play in Translation Studies? Would Translation Studies appear more relevant to professional translators if aspects of causality were made more prominent? How could a causal model of translation be applied in translator training? These are the questions discussed in this chapter.

Contemporary translation theory makes use of three kinds of models. The first is a static model, focusing on the relation between source and target texts, as for instance in contrastive analysis. The second is a dynamic model, which maps the different stages of the translating process over time; typical examples come from communication theory. The third is a causal model, which shows the various causes and effects of translations, kinds of translations and linguistic features of translations. Possible causes and effects range from proximate or cognitive ones to situational and wider socio-cultural ones. Causes, or causal conditions, also vary in strength, from more deterministic ones to merely vague influences (see also Chesterman 2000).

The causal model is the widest of the three, and in fact incorporates the other two, but it is seldom made explicit. Several approaches in Translation Studies are more or less implicitly causal: skopos theory, relevance theory, polysystem theory, critical culture studies, think-aloud protocol studies, and the whole of the prescriptive tradition. An explicit causal model can show how these different approaches are related. It can also highlight the importance of making and testing explicit hypotheses of various kinds. I argue that a causal model of translation also has obvious applications in translator training.

2.   Competing models

Causality has to do with general notions of explanation and understanding. Any theory seeks to describe the phenomena within its field of study. To the extent that we can explain what something is, why it is like that, and what effects it has, we can claim to understand it.

In Translation Studies we have an extensive body of descriptive work, but causality still has rather an unsystematic status in contemporary research. As I shall show, different theories and models focus on different kinds and levels of causality, to the exclusion of other aspects. Furthermore, some approaches seem to overlook causality altogether.

One reason for this is that different scholars work, either explicitly or implicitly, with different models of translation. These models fall into three classes.

2.1.   The first kind of model is a static one, where translation is described as a relation between two texts, a relation traditionally known as equivalence. The basic form of the static model is simply:

$$ST = TT$$

Much time and effort has gone into wondering how this relation of equivalence should be defined. If it is defined as sameness or identity, then of course translation is impossible, and we get the formula:

$$ST \neq TT$$

If it is defined more loosely, as similarity or family resemblance, we allow for a wider range of possible translations, and the formula looks like this:

$$ST \approx TT$$

This last version is the most realistic one and also the most useful pedagogically. Equivalence is made relative, not absolute: relative to the skopos, for instance. Equivalence is also relativised in the sense that it is no longer thought of as being "one" relation, but a cluster of several: equivalence of form, meaning, function, style, sound, etc. (For further discussion of this point see Chesterman 1998a: 16f.)

Static models thus focus on the translation product. The most common theories using the static model are those based on contrastive linguistics or stylistics, such as those of Catford (1965) or Vinay and Darbelnet (1958).

2.2.   The second kind of model is a dynamic one, where translation is seen as a process over time. The basic form of this model is as follows:

A (t1) → B (t2)

Here A and B are states or actions, and "t" denotes a point of time. The model therefore describes a change that takes place between time one and time two. Dynamic (or process) models began to be used in Translation Studies when the machine translation project started: there was a need for algorithms which could explicitly map the transformation of a source text into a target text. Standard models of communication were applied to human translation by scholars such as Nida. Here are some examples of the dynamic model.

a.   Analysis → Transfer → Synthesis (automatic translation)
b.   Sender 1 → Message 1 → Receiver 1/
                          Sender 2 → Message 2 → Receiver 2
     (communication theory; other versions add channel, medium, etc.)
c.   Analysis → Transfer → Restructuring
     (Nida 1964)
d.   Specification → Preparation → Translation → Evaluation
     (Sager 1994)
e.   Routine translation phase → Problem → Solution → Routine phase...
     (a simplification of the model underlying much research using think-aloud protocols)
f.   Problem 1 → Tentative theory / Target text → Error elimination → Problem 2... (Chesterman 1997, after Popper)

Some of these models focus on what Toury (1995: 249) calls the translation event (the communicative situation comprising source text, client's instructions and skopos, etc.), while others focus more on the translation act (the cognitive process in the translator's head).

These variants of the dynamic model represent, in their simplest form, a linear sequence of states or events or phases. Most scholars point out, however, that the translation process is really more like a recursive (or looping, or spiral) one. Nord (1991: 32), for instance, suggests a looping model which we can simplify as follows:

g.   Analysis of the skopos
       → Source text analysis
       → Discovery of translation-relevant source-text elements
       → Transfer

→ Target text synthesis
→ Target text imagined in/checked against the target culture situation
→ Target text proposal checked against skopos ...

This model explicitly consists of a series of recursive loops, as the translator repeatedly checks potential translations against the source text, the target situation and the skopos, moving from analysis to synthesis and back to analysis again, and so on. This is a more complex picture, but it is still basically a variant of the dynamic model, mapping phases over time.

2.3. The third kind of model is a causal one. At its simplest, a causal model looks like this:

Causal conditions >>> Effects

Applied to translations, this can be expanded to:

Causal conditions >>> Translations >>> Effects

That is, translations are seen both as effects (of previous causes) and as causes (of subsequent effects). One advantage of a causal model is thus that it gives a more balanced picture of translations (and translators), not only as products of causal action but also as agents of change, causers of effects. I am taking causation in a very general sense here, covering a wide range of causal conditions from strict determination to vague influence. The causal model can be further expanded to distinguish various levels of causation, some of which may be stronger than others, as follows (based on Chesterman 1998b):

Socio-cultural conditions (norms, languages...)
>>> The translation event (skopos, client, available technology, etc.)
>>> The translation act (decision-making)
>>> Translations themselves: the translation profile (linguistic)
>>> Cognitive effects (in the mind of the reader)
>>> Situational/behavioural effects (observable actions)
>>> Socio-cultural effects (on the polysystem, the target language, etc.)

In this model the translation profile is defined as a linguistic description of a given kind of translation, including its relation to the source text and to the target language. The translation profile – and of course the very existence of the translated text – has both causes and effects, at different levels: at least cognitive, situational and socio-cultural. Although presented thus as a linear chain of causality, the translating process in reality is of course more complex, as I have mentioned above, with causes and effects interacting in complex ways. The causal chain is also, in principle, infinite at both ends. Beyond socio-cultural causes we can continue asking "why", arriving perhaps at individuals with individual needs and preferences; and beyond socio-cultural effects there are also the effects of *these* effects on individuals, and so on.

Let us now take a closer look at some of the ways in which causality is accounted for in contemporary translation research. We shall see that several scholars and approaches refer to either causes or effects, but seldom to both.

3. Manifestations of causality in Translation Studies

An early manifestation of explicit causality appears in Nida's concept of dynamic equivalence, defined as "same effect". This treats translations as causes that have effects on their receivers. In Nida's view, translation assessment should not be based on a comparison of two texts but on a comparison of two sets of effects or reactions: those of the source text readers and those of the target text readers. (There are of course problems here, concerning definitions and measurements of effect, heterogeneous effects, etc., but I will not go into these at this point.)

One of the clearest applications of causality is to be found in Pym (1997). Pym discusses how Aristotle's four classical causes can shed light on translatorial behaviour, as causes of that behaviour. His reasoning is approximately as follows. Aristotle's material cause corresponds to the source text, plus the translator's material tools such as computer, etc. – I would also add the target language, out of which the target text is materially constructed. The source text is thus seen here as one cause of the translation: a translation profile has a particular word or structure *because* of something in the source text. Aristotle's formal cause corresponds to translation norms (as internalised in the translator's mind). The efficient cause is the translator him/herself, including emotional and cognitive state, personality, etc. And the final cause is the skopos of the translation.

Skopos theory itself has an obvious causal dimension. I think we can safely gloss "skopos" as "intended effect." The theory builds on the idea of translations as phenomena that cause effects, and singles out a particular class of effect – an intended effect – to serve as its corner-stone. Insofar as this intended effect is part of the translator's awareness at the time of translating, it also serves as a final (teleological) cause of translatorial action: I translate like this, because I know what the intended effect of the translation is; I want my translation to achieve this effect, and I think this is the best way to do so (the form of this argument is a practical syllogism). All other possible causes are apparently relegated to secondary status (see e.g. Vermeer 1996).

Gutt's relevance-theoretical approach is rather similar (1991). Instead of skopos, the guiding principle is "optimal relevance", and relevance itself is defined in terms of effect. Here, however, the notion of effect – "contextual effect" – is defined rather differently, in terms of mental processing effort. An effect is thus a cognitive event, or change of state, that takes place in the mind of the reader. A translator cannot know what this effect is in advance, of course; but as with the skopos approach, a translator can have some idea of the intended effect, and translate accordingly, i.e. in a maximally relevant way. Here too, we see teleological causality.

Protocol (think-aloud, TAP) research aims to describe the translating process at the cognitive level, and thus also to explain aspects of the translation product in terms of the decision-making process that has produced it. Why this choice of structure or lexical item? Because of such-and-such a reason that the translator mentions at that point in the protocol, such-and-such a justification for a particular decision is made. Reasons of this kind include the translator's awareness and acceptance of translation norms, his/her language proficiency, understanding of the skopos, and so on.

If we continue asking "why?" (e.g. why this justification?) and pursue the chain of causation further, we have at least two possible channels of inquiry. One leads to neurology, chemistry and physics, to a reductive explanation ultimately in terms of atoms, synaptic activity, etc. The other leads out from the translator's head into the translation situation, and then into the surrounding socio-culture. That is, we can either look for further causes at the psychological level or at the socio-cultural level. These do not exclude one another, of course.

This second channel has been the focus of research in the polysystem approach and in much of the cultural turn in recent translation studies. The concept of a norm is, after all, an explanatory one: I translate like this because I am aware of such-and-such a norm, because I wish (or do not wish) to conform to it, and because I think this is the best way to realise this aim of conforming (or not conforming) – another practical syllogism. So norm-theoretical work seeks to establish what the relevant norms are (for a given translation/text type in a given culture at a given period), in order to explain why certain translations have the form that they do. We also look at the socio-cultural effects of certain kinds of translations to see how they have impinged on the target socio-cultural polysystem and what effect they have had on the target language, on the literary system of the target culture, on the target culture's perception of the source culture, etc.

And then we can ask "why this norm?" and move further into cultural and ideological history, or back into the neural circuits of the members of the socio-cultural community. Everything links up to everything else, in an enormously complex network of influences and consequences.

Finally in this brief survey, we should consider the long tradition of pre-scriptive statements. A prescriptive statement is actually a predictive hypothesis of effect. "Translate like this" means something like "If you translate like this, I predict that the effect will be that I (or your client or readers) will like/accept your work." "Do not translate like that" means "If you translate like that, the result will be that I (or the client, or readers) will not like/accept your work." On what grounds are such predictions made? Often, of course, on grounds of evident common sense or experience; but often one wonders whether these hy-potheses have actually been tested. To what extent do they represent any more than the subjective opinion of the prescriber?

A contemporary extension of this kind of thinking can be found in the work of scholars such as Pym and Venuti, who wish to affect the way translators translate. So Venuti, for instance, argues for a resistant, non-fluent style for literary translation (e.g. in Venuti 1995). The motivation for this position is evidently ethical: if we translated like this, intercultural perceptions and attitudes would be more democratic, less hegemonic, the Other would be recognised as such, and the world would be a better place. The structure of the argument is again that of a predictive hypothesis: I predict that, if we translate like this, certain desirable effects will follow. The next stage would then be to test this hypothesis, both on historical and contemporary data.

4. Methodological weaknesses in research and training

4.1.   Quite a lot of work has been done on various aspects of translation causes and effects, then. I think the current state of research has three weaknesses, however. I will outline these first, and then suggest that translator training may suffer from the same weaknesses. Sections 5 and 6 will then offer a remedy.

The first weakness is the lack of adequate links between these different approaches: they are perceived as being very different, often focusing on different text types, with different groups of adherents (the skopos people, the polysystem, the TAP people, etc.). The lack of such links prevents us from developing a united explanatory theory of translation. This weakness is a lack of overall theoretical coherence.

The second weakness is a lack of explicitness. One important way of being explicit in any academic discipline is the formulation of hypotheses. Hypotheses are the basic building blocks of any theory. In translation research, however, not much of the existing research has been crystallised into explicit hypotheses that can be tested in replicable ways. Traditionally four main types of hypothesis are distinguished in the philosophy of science. I will digress for a minute here to outline these.

Interpretive hypotheses are hypotheses according to which a particular concept (such as translation or equivalence or norm) can be defined or interpreted *as* such-and-such. Interpretive hypotheses are building blocks for all research, whether conceptual or empirical; we cannot do without them. Translation Studies is full of them – for instance, I have just suggested that a source text can be interpreted as a cause – but it is worth recalling that they are only means to an end, not ends in themselves. Definitions and interpretations are useful insofar as they allow us to do something with them, to make claims, state arguments, propose explanations, etc. (I return to interpretive hypotheses below, Section 7.)

Descriptive hypotheses are hypotheses concerning the generality of a particular descriptive feature. They typically take this form: all translations (or all translations of a given type or all translators) are characterised by such-and-such a feature. Good examples are hypotheses about translation universals (such as, all translators tend towards explicitation). Descriptive hypotheses tend to be based on static or dynamic models. However, if a descriptive hypothesis of a translation universal becomes well corroborated, it may attain the status of a law (as in Toury's laws of interference and standardisation), and as such serves also as an explanation of some kind: this translation has this feature because all translations do, or: this translator did that because all (or most) translators tend to do that. (Compare the classical syllogism: Socrates is mortal because Socrates is a man and all men are mortal.)

Explanatory hypotheses proper are simply hypotheses that X is caused by Y (but recall that "caused by" in the sense I am using it here may mean no more than "influenced by"). In Translation Studies explanatory hypotheses either start from linguistic features of the translation profile or from given effects. For instance: this profile feature is there because of this specific skopos/because of the translator's ignorance/because of such-and-such a norm, etc. Or: this effect is because of such-and-such a feature in the translation (which in turn was because of . . .).

Predictive hypotheses are ways of testing explanatory hypotheses. They start from causal conditions (e.g. socio-cultural norms, a particular skopos, ideological/ethical factors, translator-specific factors such as beliefs, etc.) and predict profile features. Or they start with profile features and predict effects (as is the case with prescriptive statements discussed above).

The second methodological weakness referred to earlier is that there is too much research that does not propose or test explicit hypotheses. Suggested causal explanations often remain isolated comments on a given case study, and are thus difficult to build on, to incorporate into a more general hypothesis. Additionally or alternatively, they often remain at the level of a general argument, without explicit formulation as a testable claim.

Approaches from hermeneutics and/or post-modernism, for instance, tend not to formulate the issues they discuss in terms of explicit hypotheses, although these issues can often be reinterpreted in such terms. Let's look at an example. A recent paper by Arrojo (1998) argues against an "essentialist" view of meaning and of theory. I think her argument, a combination of interpretive and predictive hypotheses, can be paraphrased approximately as follows. If we see meaning as non-stable, non-absolute; if we see equivalence not as identity of some kind, but as incorporating difference; and if we see translation theory as non-prescriptive [= interpretive hypotheses] – then we shall be able to develop a better theory that takes more account of such factors as the individual translator's ideology, and individual translators will be able to take more responsibility for their decisions [= predictive hypotheses]. We thus have a set of causal (or influencing) conditions, coupled with predicted consequences both for theory and for practice. Although these interesting claims are not presented by Arrojo as specific hypotheses, both these kinds of predicted effects could perhaps be tested, at least to some extent. If translators think thus differently about their work, is this in fact reflected in their translations? If so, how? And if we find some interesting evidence in their translations, how will we be able to tell that its cause is precisely the one we are examining, and not some other possible cause or influence which we have not considered? As regards the predicted consequences for the theory – well, time will tell.

The third weakness is that few of the explicit hypotheses we do find have actually been tested adequately. This means that however plausible they may seem, we still do not know how well they are corroborated by data that are different from the data from which they were originally derived. Some that have been tested may not be as strong as they first appeared. Take, for instance, the claim that smaller cultures will respect the originality of texts from big cultures and therefore translate them in a more foreignising way, allowing an overt influence from the Other, whereas big cultures like the Anglo-American tend to require domesticated texts (see e.g. Venuti 1995). One counter-example to this hypothesis is provided by the history of translation into Finnish. The early Finnish translators by no means held a unanimously respectful view of the originality of their source texts from big cultures (English, German), but were often quite prepared to adapt and domesticate them very freely (see Paloposki 1996). However, it should be noted that hypotheses of this kind are normally stated in probabilistic terms ("tend"), and thus can only be tested in the long run by extensive research. Merely a few counter-examples do not refute a probabilistic hypothesis.

4.2.   Let us now turn to consider the current state of translator training. Does it also suffer from the three weaknesses I have mentioned? Readers may care to ask questions such as the following, with respect to the training syllabus and tradition in their own institution.

As regards coherence: do students see any relation between theory and practice? Between one approach (skopos theory, for instance) and another (text linguistics, polysystem theory, contrastive analysis, TAPs, culture studies, post-colonial studies, etc.)? Between one translation class or course and another? Between advice given by one teacher and that given by another? Between solutions that seem adequate for one text or translation type but inadequate for another?

As regards explicitness: is the (good) advice about thinking of the skopos or the relevance principle actually translated into explicit textual strategies? How explicitly are trainees expected to analyse translations (their own translations, or translations by their peers, or published professional translations)? How explicitly are translation norms and strategies presented or learned? When students read the theoretical literature, are they clear about the kinds of claims (hypotheses) that are being made? Can they paraphrase an article in terms of the specific hypothesis that is being discussed and/or tested and recognise what kind of hypothesis it is?

As regards the testing problem: can students test prescriptive hypotheses? Do they have enough opportunities to test out their own hypotheses about what a good translation might be? Are there adequate opportunities for feedback when such hypotheses are tested, i.e. can the students see the effects of their decisions? Can these tests, these practice translations, be done under real or realistic conditions, so that the feedback is genuine and representative? Do trainees have opportunities to work under different causal conditions and see what the consequences are? (What happens to this translation if we change the skopos or the implied readership? If we postpone or shorten the deadline? What happens to the effect if I change this in the translation?)

5.   Pedagogical application of the causal model

I think a causal model of translation, such as outlined above, provides a good tool for coping with all these three problems. Note that this too is actually a predictive hypothesis, based on an interpretive one. The interpretive one is that translation can indeed be conceptualised (interpreted) in terms of the causal model I have suggested above. And the predictive one is that if such a model is used in translator training, certain beneficial effects will follow. The form of my argument is thus similar to Arrojo's, mentioned earlier, and both hypotheses are open to testing: time and practice will tell. This section presents some arguments which at least support the initial plausibility of the hypotheses.

As regards the coherence problem: the causal model incorporates the static model at its centre, in the notion of the translation profile, for this profile is partly defined in terms of the relation between the translation and the source text (the equivalence relation). But the profile itself goes beyond this static model in that it also takes into account the relation between the translation and the target language (the relation of acceptability or grammaticality or naturalness or textual fit). Making a linguistic profile-analysis of a translation thus means that you have to look in two directions, not just back to the source text.

The causal model also incorporates the dynamic model, in that causes and effects obviously follow one another in a temporal sequence. It is valuable to see how the translator's cognitive decision-processes are preceded and surrounded by situational and other processes, part of a much bigger whole. If the dynamic model is extended at each end, to cover the social, ideological and historical origins of a particular need for a translation and also the later – even much later – socio-cultural consequences of translations, trainees can appreciate the importance of the translator's role in a much larger historical dimension than merely a textual or communicational one. Translations can affect language change and inter-cultural perception, for instance.

Translation students usually take a course, or several, in translation theory, alongside their practical training. In my view the causal model is the widest-ranging of the three basic types, and thus offers the best way of relating different aspects of the theory to each other and to practice. It shows how the different schools and approaches focus on different sections of the causal chain. The simple causal diagram I have used above is a useful first map of the translation-theoretical territory.

As regards the explicitness problem: the causal model makes explicit the relations between different approaches and theories, as I have suggested earlier, by showing how each fits into the larger picture. Distinguishing different levels of causes and effects (cognitive, situational/behavioural, socio-cultural) is a first step towards increasing explicitness in the analysis of the overall translating process; it shows how processes take place within other processes, and these in turn within others. The model can also serve to increase trainees' awareness of the causal factors underlying their translatorial decisions, and also of the effects of the textual manifestations of these decisions. An awareness of these factors enables trainees to see translation – and hence their own work – in a broad context and helps them to make sense of the various theoretical ideas presented to them.

As regards the problem of untested claims: because the causal model highlights the fact that translations do indeed have consequences, it is a natural step then to check what these consequences actually are or to imagine what they might be. The model thus opens up many practical opportunities for simple research projects, for instance testing clients' or readers' reactions to the results of different textual decisions. Fieldwork of this kind can play a valuable role in making trainees aware of the social context of the translator's work. Historical studies of the conditions (such as norms) under which existing translations were produced can also bring more understanding of the causes and influences which affect the form of a translation.

Teaching an awareness of causes and consequences also has an ethical side to it. It promotes a sense of the translator's responsibility, especially in the sense of "emancipatory translation" (discussed in Chesterman 1997: 189f.). The basic point about emancipatory translation is that trainees are of course taught translation norms, but they themselves are responsible for deciding how they will react to these norms. Norm-breaking has certain effects: these may be surprisingly beneficial, if a new and "better" norm is thus introduced, but they may also be negative, e.g. criticism. The pedagogical exploitation of emancipatory translation relies on an understanding of the causes and effects of the translator's decisions, and thus depends on a causal model.

These ideas about the centrality of causality can be applied in practical training in several ways, as general pedagogical principles. In the first place, an introductory course on translation theory can be arranged which throws light on all these aspects of causality quite explicitly. In class good use can be made of "why" questions when a translation is prepared or analysed. Why did the client commission this translation? Why do you think the translator wrote this? If you think there are weaknesses, or particularly good solutions, to what might they be due? Another useful principle is to make explicit reference to the effects of the translator's decisions, both when preparing a translation and when discussing one. If you write this, how do you think a typical reader would react? How might a non-native reader react? It is worth pointing out that students' and teachers' own reactions to a translation are themselves instances of translation effects, caused by the translation in question. And so are published translation reviews and criticisms.

6. Who wants to know what?

If we use an explicitly causal model of translation, in research and in teaching, the main potential applications of the model are evident. It is not just the teacher who will benefit. I will outline here the kind of information about translation that different groups of people tend to be interested in. In each case, the information concerns relations between features of the translation profile, causal conditions, and effects.

What does a translator, or a trainee translator, want to know about translation? First of all, the probable effects of a given translation choice, i.e. of a given feature in the translation profile. For example, if I add an explanation of this term in brackets, how will my client/reader react? We could symbolise this as:

TPx >>> EF?

where TP = Translation Profile feature, x is a specific example of such a feature, and EF stands for Effects. "EF?" is thus a so-far unknown effect, something to be discovered.

A translator also needs to know what translation profile feature, in a given context, will lead to good, or intended, or desirable consequences:

TP? >>> +EF

where "+EF" stands for "a good effect". Exactly what is meant by "good" or "intended" (by whom?) or "desirable" (for whom?) is of course open to discussion and argument. (Below I will use "–EF" to symbolise "bad" effects.)

And a third kind of information for the translator can be symbolised thus:

CC? >>> TPx >>> +EF

That is, what are the Causal Conditions (CC) which tend to produce the kind of translation profile feature that gives rise to good effects?

Turning now to a second group of potential users: what does society as a whole want to know? And what does the client, as a member of a given society, want to know? As above, both:

TP? >>> +EF

and

CC? >>> TPx >>> +EF

but also, I think,

CC?>>> TPx>>> –EF

That is, what are the causes of translational features culminating in whole translations that have bad effects? Why are there so many bad translations around? A major element of translation discourse is composed, in fact, of complaints about translations. See newspaper letters to the editor, etc.

A third group of people concerned with translations are, of course, the teachers and trainers of translators. Their application needs could be listed as follows:

TP? >>> +EF (as above)
TP? >>> –EF (what features produce unwanted effects?)
CC? >>> TPx >>> +EF (as above: what conditions lead to translations that have good effects?)
CC? >>> TPx >>> –EF (as above: what conditions lead to bad effects, to be avoided?)
CCx >>> TPx >>> EF? (what will the effect be of a given condition?)

As for scholars of Translation Studies, their list of requirements is the longest, because they help to supply the information for the other mentioned groups. All the following relations seem relevant here:

TPx >>> EF?
TP? >>> +EF
TP? >>> –EF
CCx >>> TP? (given these conditions, what translation feature tends to occur?)
CC? >>> TPx (what conditions tend to give rise to this feature?)
CC? >>> TPx >>> +EF
CC? >>> TPx >>> –EF

CCx >>> TPx >>> EF? (given these conditions, and this resulting feature, what is the effect?)

Finally, note how this way of applying a causal model to user needs not only highlights the social relevance of translation research, but also offers a framework for research itself, in which hypotheses of various kinds can be formulated and tested. In particular, the importance of explanatory and predictive hypotheses is underlined. The aims of contemporary Translation Studies include:

- describing what translations are
- explaining why they are like that
- describing and explaining the effects they produce.

7. A Procrustean bed?

If we look at Translation Studies in this manner, using an explicit causal model, are we thereby forcing the discipline into the mould of the empirical hard sciences and neglecting its roots in philosophy, hermeneutics and literary studies? Are we exposing the field to accusations of essentialism? I think the answer to both these questions is "no".

In Section 4 above, I mentioned four basic kinds of hypotheses, starting with interpretive ones. These are the kind of hypotheses which are quite standard in any hermeneutic discipline. The aim is to understand a given phenomenon, and one does so by interpreting it in a way that sheds new light on it, in one way or another. For instance, by proposing a new metaphor or simile for the phenomenon in question (e.g. by suggesting that translation is performance, or cannibalism, or like sticking together the fragments of a broken vase), or by redefining a central term (e.g. by suggesting that equivalence can be understood as invariance, or as family resemblance, or as mapping ...). Any science has to acknowledge this interpretive basis; no definitions or concepts are theory-free. The contribution of hermeneutic approaches in translation research has been precisely to develop the conceptual apparatus that scholars use to make sense of the phenomenon of translation.

Such tools are justified by the balance of arguments and evidence for and against, and tested by the uses to which they can be put. Their added value is, in principle, that they allow us to think things we could not think before, or to make new claims, or to describe things in new and revealing ways. In other words, a proposed new conceptual tool should have consequences. (Note the causal model at work here too.) If there are no consequences, there seems little point in developing new conceptual tools, new interpretive hypotheses. So such hypotheses need not only to be argued about and their introduction justified in the first place, they must also be tested. That is, the academic community must try to work with these new concepts and see what their added value is.

However, in a field such as Translation Studies, which inevitably has a strong empirical dimension as well as a conceptual one, interpretive hypotheses are not enough. We are not doing conceptual analysis alone; we are also interested in making valid descriptive statements, hypotheses about translation(s), and in proposing and testing explanatory hypotheses, even predictive ones. In the history of the discipline it is surprising how much energy has gone into developing and arguing over conceptual tools in comparison to how little energy has gone into testing them. Both research and training would, I think, benefit if we spent more time investigating what we could do with our rich array of conceptual tools rather than admiring them or rearranging them on the shelf, as it were.

There is thus no necessary conflict here, between hard empiricists and soft hermeneuticists. Translation research needs both, since both contribute different kinds of hypotheses.

A second source of potential criticism has to do with the aims of empirical research to establish translation universals or laws of translation. On this view there are no valid grounds on which general descriptive, explanatory or predictive hypotheses can be posited at all, because all translations are always situation-bound, culture-bound and ideologically-bound. In other words, they are always particular, contingent.

There are several valid counter-arguments to such criticism. One is that translation universals and laws are never stated, to my knowledge, in absolute terms, but always in relative terms, as probabilistic tendencies. The statements in question attempt to capture regularities about what translators *tend* to do, what translations *tend* to be like. For instance, it has often been observed that translators tend to avoid, or reduce, repetition. This observation does not apply always, universally, to all translators, only perhaps to the majority. Furthermore, the observation itself does not create any necessity for any translator to follow this tendency.

Another counter-argument is that although all translations undoubtedly take place in unique circumstances, and are themselves unique, they are nevertheless all "translations" – presumably – and they are all produced by members of the same human race, who share genes and cognitive abilities, etc. to a surprising extent. The critics here are claiming simply that all translations are different. True, but trivial. On the other hand, no one is claiming that all translations are the same, either. But it is reasonable to claim that all translations may well share certain properties, and that all translators may also share certain properties. Empirical research is interested in what translations and translators have in common, as well as what makes each translation unique.

Finally, behind this kind of criticism may also lie the fear that claims are being made about the possibilities of determining human behaviour, especially as regards predictive hypotheses. Or, indeed, that attempts to state universals or causal laws are actually attempts to influence, to prescribe, to be authoritarian, to deprive translators of their free will and dignity. I think such fears are misplaced. Descriptive, explanatory and predictive hypotheses do not set out to prescribe, but to understand. What we do with any understanding is another question, and it is also another question why we want this understanding in the first place. Scholars may have all kinds of motivations for wanting to study translation.

It is worth repeating that the kind of causal, explanatory and predictive hypotheses that we can establish in Translation Studies are far from being deterministic. Human beings are not machines, and human behaviour cannot be predicted absolutely; but it is quite standard in, for example, sociology or economics or psychology to try to predict tendencies. The causal conditions which translation research is interested in vary enormously in causal degree: at one extreme we have the source text itself, which exerts considerable causal pressure; then we have the natural constraints and capabilities of human cognition; the purely linguistic possibilities of the target language; the strong pressure of the skopos and the absolute pressure of the deadline; the vaguer influence of the client, of the rate of pay, and perhaps the still vaguer influence of ideological and ethical factors, and so on. Altogether, translators work under many influences and pressures, which are all causal in a more or less loose sense; they are not deterministic, however, as the translator always retains a freedom of choice. (Another question of theoretical and practical interest is: under what conditions do translators seem to have more freedom of choice than others?)

Changes in causal conditions tend to produce changes in translations – which is precisely what many translation scholars are interested in. And as I have argued above, if we can build into our translator training courses an awareness about which causal conditions tend to produce good effects, etc., then we are surely helping to train good translators. After all, the training process itself is also a form of influence, but none the less acceptable and necessary for that.

The more we understand about translation, and the more we can transmit and develop this understanding in translator training, the more it should be possible for translators to feel masters of their craft, masters of the various conceptual and technical tools that they use. It is surely this feeling of expertise – of knowing what one is doing, how to do it, and why one is doing it in that way – that brings a sense of professional dignity and human value.

References

Arrojo, R. (1998). "The revision of the traditional gap between theory and practice and the empowerment of translation in postmodern times". *The Translator, 4*(1), 25–48.

Catford, J. C. (1965). *A Linguistic Theory of Translation.* Oxford: Oxford University Press.

Chesterman, A. (1997). *Memes of Translation.* Amsterdam and Philadelphia: John Benjamins.

Chesterman, A. (1998a). *Contrastive Functional Analysis.* Amsterdam and Philadelphia: John Benjamins.

Chesterman, A. (1998b). "Causes, translations, effects". *Target, 10*(2), 201–230.

Chesterman, A. (2000). "A causal model for translation studies". In Maeve Olohan (Ed.), *Intercultural Faultlines: Research Models in Translation Studies I: Textual and Cognitive Aspects* (pp. 15–17). Manchester: St. Jerome.

Gutt, E.-A. (1991). *Translation and Relevance. Cognition and Context.* Oxford: Blackwell.

Nida, E. A. (1964). *Toward a Science of Translation.* Leiden: Brill.

Nord, C. (1991). *Text Analysis in Translation.* Amsterdam: Rodopi.

Paloposki, O. (1996). "Originality in translation". In Riitta Oittinen, Outi Paloposki, & Jürgen Schopp (Eds.), *Aspectus varii translationis II* (Studia Translatologica, Ser. B., Vol. 2) (pp. 66–84). Tampere: Tampere University Publications.

Pym, A. (1997). *Pour une éthique du traducteur.* Arras: Artois Presses Universitaires.

Sager, J. C. (1994). *Language Engineering and Translations – Consequences of Automation.* Amsterdam and Philadelphia: John Benjamins.

Toury, G. (1995). *Descriptive Translation Studies and Beyond.* Amsterdam and Philadelphia: John Benjamins.

Venuti, L. (1995). *The Translator's Invisibility: A History of Translation.* London and New York: Routledge.

Vermeer, H. J. (1996). *A Skopos Theory of Translation.* Heidelberg: TEXTconTEXT.

Vinay, J.-P. & Darbelnet, J. (1958). *Stylistique comparée du français et de l'anglais.* Paris: Didier.

CHAPTER 10

Training functional translators

Christiane Nord

1. Introduction

Translator training institutions are shooting up like mushrooms all over the world, and even in the ordinary language classroom (e.g. at culture institutions like the British Council, Institut Français, Goethe-Institut or Instituto Cervantes) students are demanding some sort of basic training in (professional) translation. The problem is: Who is going to do the teaching? So far, there is no institutional training for translator trainers. Teachers of Mathematics or Philosophy are trained in their respective Faculties, Language Teachers are trained in Modern Language Departments or Faculties of Second Language Acquisition, but persons applying for a position as translator trainer in a Faculty of Translation and Interpreting need no particular formal qualification; and if they needed one, they would not know where to get it. This does not mean that they are all bad translator trainers, but maybe life would be a little easier for them (and for their students?) if they had had some kind of special instruction and were not forced to re-invent the wheel of translation pedagogy over and over again.

I went into translator training about 35 years ago, two weeks after graduating as a translator. I had a few very inspired trainers (some had been trained as translators, others as language teachers, others were "just" native speakers with a juridical or technical background), but did this qualify me for translator training? It didn't. At first I tried to imitate the teachers I had liked best in my own training, but then I felt this was not enough, and I started to develop my own teaching methodology. I presume that most novice translator trainers are still working along these lines today, and that, after years of practice, all their (positive or negative) experience and insights, their findings, their good ideas and original methods are oft interred with their bones.

To save my own insights and experience from this fate, I would like to present them for discussion in this chapter. After a brief outline of my theoretical starting-point, I will first analyse what I consider to be the groundwork of any translational skills – intercultural competence – and then proceed to discuss the relationship of practice and theory in translator training. The three sections that follow will tackle very practical aspects of translator training: the selection of learning material, teaching and learning methods, and quality assessment. To conclude, I will highlight a few areas where a co-operation between theory (i.e. research done by teachers or students) and practice (i.e. practising translators, commissioners, translation agencies, etc.) could be beneficial to both and help to make the training of the trainers a fully-fledged branch of applied Translation Studies.

2.   What is a "functional translator"?

Talking about a "functional translator" is a very abbreviated form of describing a professional translator who has the following characteristics.

S/he is aware of the fact that, in today's translation practice, translations are needed for a variety of communicative functions which are not always the same as the intended function of the corresponding source text (= professional knowledge). S/he knows that the selection of linguistic and non-linguistic signs which make up a text is guided by situational and cultural factors and that this principle applies to both source and target-cultural text production (= metacommunicative competence). S/he is able to spot the "rich points" (Agar 1991:168) where the behaviour of the representatives of a particular pair of cultures or diacultures in a given situation is so divergent that it may lead to communication conflicts or even breakdowns, and finds ways and means to solve cultural conflicts without taking sides (= intercultural competence). S/he knows that, due to culture-specific conventions, apparently similar or analogous structures of two languages are not always used with the same frequency or in the same situation (= distribution) by the respective culture communities and that the use of the wrong set of signs may severely interfere with the text's functionality. S/he has the ability to produce a target text serving the desired function, even though the source text may be badly written or poorly reproduced (= writing abilities) and knows how to use both traditional and modern (i.e. electronic) translation aids and knowledge sources (= media competence). S/he has a good general education and a better specific knowledge of the topic dealt with in the source text – or knows how to compensate efficiently for any lack of knowledge (= research competence). S/he works fast, cost-efficiently, and to perfection, even under high pressure (= stress resistance) and knows what her/his translations are worth (= self-assertion, from the practitioners' point of view and self-assurance or self-confidence, as the trainers see it).

This is the profile practitioners and theoreticians, or rather trainers, more or less agreed upon at a Conference on Translation Quality which took place in Leipzig in 1999. Of course, the practitioners uttered a few more requirements, such as skills in specific forms of translation (e.g. dubbing, voice-over, web-site translation, software localisation), management and leading competence, the ability to work in a team and to constantly adapt to changing working conditions, revision skills, and the like. There was no consensus as to whether they preferred the generalist or the specialist as far as factual knowledge was concerned. The trainers, however, maintained the view that university training programmes must be general enough to enable their graduates to take up a broad range of activities, and specific enough to lay the foundations for a fast acquisition of any kind of special skills after graduation. On the whole, a functional translator is obviously a very versatile animal.

3. Teaching intercultural competence: Pre-translational language activities

We have not mentioned linguistic and cultural competence, which, of course, should be perfect. It goes without saying that a solid linguistic and cultural competence in both source and target cultures is not the object of, but a prerequisite for, translator training. If translation is taught too early, i.e. before the students have reached a sufficient command of language and culture, translation classes will degenerate into language acquisition classes without the students – or the teachers – even realising it.

On the other hand, students entering translator training programmes do not normally come with sufficient language and culture competence; so they have to attend language classes before starting to translate. In order to save time and effort, however, the development of language and culture competence should be specifically designed for translator training. As we all know, it does make a difference whether somebody learns a language for such practical purposes as, for example, finding their way in a foreign country without starving or getting into all sorts of trouble, or in order to be able to translate from or into this language. Apart from the ability to communicate in the language (i.e. to understand texts that are read out or written and to produce texts which are apt to serve certain communicative purposes), translation requires a particular kind of metacommunicative competence, i.e. the knowledge about how the two languages and cultures work and where the differences lie that make it impossible just to "switch codes" in translation. Therefore, language teachers working in a translator training programme should be aware of the specificities of translational language use and take them into consideration.

It is a frequent complaint that translation students have an insufficient command of their own native language. Apart from the development of foreign-language proficiency, translation-oriented language classes may also lead to a better competence in the native language if the contrastive perspective is introduced at a rather early stage. This does not mean that I would like to revive the old tradition of using translation as a teaching tool in foreign-language acquisition, as was typical particularly of Latin and Greek classes. On the contrary, grammar translation or "philological translation" should definitely be banned from the translation-oriented language class. What is much more efficient is the contrastive analysis of authentic, real-life texts, which shows that similar communicative intentions are verbalised in different ways in the two cultures, even though the language system may allow the use of analogous structures. This is what I would like to call "contrastive style analysis": students should be made aware of the norms and conventions of communication in everyday settings before they start translating structure-by-structure or word-by-word.

Parallel to the development of native and foreign language competence, the students should gain some insight into the following aspects of general text competence:

- text production as a purposeful, culture-bound activity (text pragmatics)
- texts as means of communication used for specific purposes and addressees
- the importance of cultural and world knowledge for both text reception and production
- the extralinguistic restraints controlling text production (e.g. legal norms, corporate language, marketing policies)
- LSP and terminology as particular forms of communication in specific domains.

In order to achieve these insights, the following exercises may be found useful:

- analysis and comparison of texts and discourse

- produced for different audiences (women – men, children – students – adults, specialists – laypersons) or
- transmitted by different media (oral – written, written in traditional media – written in internet chatgroups)
- written at different times (i.e. diachronical differences) or in different places (i.e. diatopical differences within one language area)

- identification and evaluation of text strategies
- analysis and comparison of texts belonging to various text types or genres, identification of text-type conventions
- identification of function markers in texts or text segments
- spotting text defects
- revision of faulty or unfunctional texts, revision of translated or machine-translated texts, re-writing of deficient texts
- analysis of texts dealing with other cultures, identifying the methods used for providing cultural background information
- paraphrasing utterances and identifying the difference in use or communicative effect
- wordplay and punning, crossword puzzles ("creativity exercises")
- composing and structuring semantic fields, differentiating synonyms, defining word meaning and usage
- restructuring sentences (complex into simple, and vice versa)
- rewriting texts according to stylistic rules or instructions
- rewriting texts for other audiences, purposes, media, places etc. (= "intralingual translation")
- summarising or abstracting long texts
- converting nonverbal text elements (figures, tables, schematic representations, models) into verbal text (and vice versa), especially in technical communication
- producing written texts on the basis of oral information (or vice versa)
- revising deficient texts (= "quality management").

If training in these skills is offered in the native language first and then applied to the foreign languages, contrasting native and foreign texts in a third step, the students will have learned a lot about translation without having ever translated. At the same time, they will have developed their active and passive text competence both in the native and the foreign languages.

Contrastive text competence is the ability to analyse the culture-specific features of textual and other communicative conventions in two cultures. What is needed here is a number of general parameters that may have different forms in the source and the target culture. For example, we have textual macro-strategies or types of argument, i.e. how the material is organised rhetorically (e.g. proceeding from general to particular or vice versa, stating a position to take issue with it, what I term BPSE = background, problems, solution, evaluation); theme-rheme progression (focus, emphasis, as in cleft sentence structures); cohesive devices (e.g. linkages, signalling, structure markers); metadiscourse, i.e. discourse that refers overtly to itself (e.g. "As we saw earlier ...", "I will come back to this point later", also headings and subheadings indicating what is to follow in the text); attribution, i.e. the way things and phenomena are specified in the text (e.g. by an adjective, a prepositional phrase, a relative clause, a parenthesis); modalisation, i.e. implicit expressions of speaker attitudes (e.g. by subjunctive, modal particles, diminutives, word order), etc.

Text material should include mainly practice-oriented text types, such as business communication, computer manuals, software, product documentation, contracts, business and market reports, patents, image brochures, operating instructions, student textbooks or scholarly articles, "EU texts", and the like. Teaching methods include parallel text analysis, bilateral and multilateral translation criticism, rewriting and text revision again.

It is important to note that contrastive text competence is not based on systemic contrastive linguistics, but on a comparison of "language in action", where the focus is on the form, frequency, and distribution of communicative acts.

4.   From theory to practice and back to theory: The "pigtail method" in the translator-training curriculum

To train functional translators as described above, trainers need both practical and theoretical knowledge. They should know the skills and abilities that are required in the profession (= practical knowledge), and they should know how to describe them using the concepts and terms of some kind of theory (= theoretical knowledge). They need to learn means of identifying and recognising patterns of behaviour, relating them to a systematic framework, and to teach means of guiding students' attention towards relevant features, allowing them to discover the underlying regularities and giving names to the discovered phenomena.

There is often a debate on whether to start with theory (in a kind of land drill) or with practice (in a kind of swim-or-sink procedure). Personally, I am in favour of what I call "a pig-tail method": starting out with a small portion of theory, which is then applied to practice, where the need of more theory becomes obvious, which is then satisfied by another portion of theory, and so on.

The land-drill procedure soon becomes sterile because when the students start practising they will have forgotten what they have learnt in theory, and the swim-or-sink procedure has the great disadvantage of risking that the students acquire bad translation habits which have to be cured afterwards.

The curricular structure of our training programme for technical translators follows this pig-tail philosophy:[1]

- First to third semester: introduction to the theoretical and methodological concepts of intercultural communication and translation
- Fourth semester: introduction to translation practice of both general and specialised texts, into the native and into the foreign language, with constant references to the theoretical background
- Fifth semester: practical periods and/or university studies abroad
- Sixth and seventh semester: practice and theory of specialised translation, terminology, use of both traditional and electronic translation aids and tools, practical part of the final exams
- Eighth semester: diploma thesis and colloquium (i.e. theoretical part of the final exams).

The first theoretical phase includes the following activities: (1) development of a (contrastive) language and culture competence in two foreign languages and in the native language, including the ability to produce texts for a variety of situations and functions, see section three: "Teaching intercultural competence", (2) introduction to translation-relevant aspects of linguistics and pragmatics in order to provide the concepts and terms needed for text and discourse analysis and, (3) the basic concepts of intercultural communication and translation theory.

The introduction to translation theory is basically practice-oriented and deals with the most important aspects of professional translation, such as: translation as a purposeful activity, models of the translation process, communicative functions of texts and translations, translation typologies, the role of norms and conventions in translation, the translation brief, translational analysis of source texts and target-culture parallel texts, translation problems and strategies to solve them, translation aids (including dictionaries). Since the course is compulsory for all students, independent of the foreign languages they have chosen for their training, the main languages used for examples and illustration are German and English (which they all know), but frequent references to distant cultures (Asia, Latin America) have proved to be of advantage to make the students aware of cultural distance and of the culture-specificity of their own behaviour. Theoretical concepts can also be introduced (at least in part) in the pre-translational language courses.

5.   How to design a translation task: Source texts and target texts

Before entering the practical stage of translator training, we have to make sure that the students have reached an adequate level of language and culture competence, that they know how to use the main translation aids and tools, and that their theoretical knowledge of the basic concepts of translation and intercultural communication enables them to comment on translation procedures and strategies used by themselves or by others. If this is the case, translation practice – duly combined with back references to the theoretical groundwork, as suggested by the pig-tail model – should be geared towards a systematic development of transfer competence. This means that each translation task must be designed in such a way that it does not raise too many or too complicated translation problems. From the second translation task onward, the proportion of "familiar" translation problems that have been discussed before should be larger than, or at least equal to, the proportion of "new" translation problems.

The difficulty of a translation task is influenced by the following factors:

- the complexity and degree of specificity of the source text (= source-text qualities)
- the number and quality of the translation aids provided with the task or easily available (= available documentation)
- the translation brief which specifies the intended functions, addressees, medium, quality standard, etc. of the target text (= translation brief)
- the knowledge, resources, skills and abilities of the translating person (= student's level of competence).

If a translation task is to be feasible for a particular student or group of students, this means that: (1) the source text should be selected bearing the students' level of competence in mind (because a text which is too difficult is not likely to motivate the students but rather causes frustration and a feeling of failure), (2) every translation task should be accompanied by a translation brief (because it is easier to reach a well-defined goal than to poke about in the fog of what the teacher may have thought would be the target-text function), (3) translation aids and tools (parallel texts, dictionaries, glossaries, encyclopaedic material, internet search machines, etc.) should be available and accessible during the translation process and, (4) the time limit and the required quality standard of the target text should be geared to the degree of difficulty of the translation task.

All of these factors may be used to increase or reduce the overall degree of difficulty in order to achieve a slower or more rapid learning progression. They may be increased slowly but steadily (= "learning progression") by increasing the difficulty of one or more parameters, according to the learning stage. If, for example, in the initiating phase, the students have to translate a source text which is relatively complicated or of bad quality, there should at least be a sufficient amount of documentation available and the translation brief should not require a camera-ready equivalent translation but perhaps just a rough translation giving the main arguments of the text. In the advanced phase, however, the translation brief may ask for a perfect translation, even of a complex or badly written source text. But in addition to perfection, efficiency, too, is a factor that has to be taken into consideration: in a limited length of time, it is more efficient to produce a decent translation of the whole source text than a perfect rendering of only the first half.

On the whole, selecting texts for translation classes is not a matter of adhering to rigid principles, nor is it a matter of mere intuition. It is a fundamental requirement in translation teaching that only authentic texts should be used as material, i.e. real texts-in-situation, and that they should be practice-relevant. This means that in a culture like Germany, where newspaper articles are hardly ever translated because the big newspapers have their own correspondents all over the world, newspaper texts play a secondary role in translation classes, if any, although they may be quite useful when dealing with translation problems like culture-bound realities (realia) or citations. All source texts have to be presented to the students in such a way that as much information as possible is provided on the situation in which the original is or was used in order to make the task more realistic.

6.   Translation projects: Role-playing and acquiring responsibility

Many of us may remember translation classes where a text was translated sentence by sentence, discussing all or most of the participants' suggestions and questions and ending up – after a few weeks! – with a translation that more or less conformed to the teacher's ideas of a "good" (or "correct" or "adequate" or "equivalent" or whatever standard was preferred at the time) rendering (see Nord 1996:313). The main problem was that the text as a whole and as a purposeful instrument of communication never came into focus. Kiraly describes this situation as follows (1997:152):

> ... the traditional learning environment created for the teaching of translation skills ... essentially involves a didactic performance by the teacher, who believes that she has access to the 'correct' translation, and who goes about filling in gaps in the students' knowledge so that they can also come up with the 'correct' translation. In such a classroom, it is clearly the teacher's job to 'teach' – i.e. to pass on knowledge, and the students' job to 'learn', i.e. to absorb the teacher's knowledge.

In modern translation practice, team work and management skills are qualifications required of any professional translator, whether s/he works for a translation agency or free-lance (mostly in a group of colleagues) or for a company. In the traditional translation classroom, these qualifications cannot be acquired. Therefore, translation practice during training should, at least in part, be organised in projects where each student has the chance to play various roles: that of client, of revisor, of terminologist, of documentation assistant, of free-lancer, of in-house translator working for a translation company, etc. The teacher's role is that of a monitor and fire-brigade, but students learn to manage their translation projects autonomously, and – to a certain degree – they may even learn how to negotiate working conditions, fees or deadlines. In some exceptional cases, students may even work on real translation jobs required by real clients and receive real money for it. The Magdeburg students spend their fifth semester abroad, working as interns in some kind of intercultural setting; many of them even have to perform translation jobs.

Of course, if we want to teach within a project framework, the traditional university schedule (i.e. spending a certain amount of classroom hours per week, say Tuesday from 2 to 4 p.m., on a particular task) has to be abandoned. Professional practice does not consist of spending two hours per week on one translation job, and two more hours on another, and so on, until ten little jobs have been finished after three or four months. Professional practice means deadline pressure, working through nights and Sundays, and having half a day off on Thursday, if you are lucky. It is not necessary to organise translator training completely by projects, but each student should at least have had the experience of some project training, preferably in the advanced phases of the programme. One advantage of project teaching is that source texts may be longer (and thus more realistic!) than those dealt with in a classroom setting.

7.   Quality control: Monitoring the learning progress

Along the lines of norms like ISO 9000ff. (1992) or DIN 2345 (1998), "quality control" and "quality management" are modern buzzwords in professional translation settings (see Schmitt 1998:395) which should also be considered – at least to a certain extent – in translator training. In the translation projects, one role might be that of quality manager: in the classroom, students have to become acquainted with the procedures of proof-reading and revising their own translations and those produced by other translators making use of the linguistic and translatological concepts they have learned in the preparatory course in order to justify their judgements.

Monitoring takes various forms in the different stages of the learning process. Using a top-down strategy which proceeds from situational macrostructures to linguistic microstructures, pragmatic adequacy is more important than linguistic correctness in the introductory phase, whereas violations of stylistic and linguistic conventions and norms will carry more weight in the advanced phases of the training programme. The grading of cultural and linguistic errors depends on the influence they have on the function of the target text (see Nord 1997a:76f.). If a missing comma or a spelling mistake leads to an inadequate interpretation of any of the intended functions, it is no longer a mere deviation from a linguistic norm but has pragmatic consequences (see Schmitt 1997:306). In a translation where the referential function is predominant, the information given in the source text would have priority over any other function or sub-function. But in a translation where the appellative function is predominant, one might be justified in playing down or even omitting certain information if it obstructs the intended appellative function.

Another criterion for the grading of mistakes might be the amount of time required in the revision process (see Schmitt 1997:307). A wrong term which has been used consistently and can be corrected by a mere search-replace procedure of the text processing programme, may be considered less relevant than an inappropriate sentence structure reproduced from the source language which does not conform to target-culture style conventions and can only be corrected by restructuring the whole paragraph.

8. From practice to theory and back to practice: Application-oriented research in translator-training institutions

As I have mentioned before, translator trainers usually come from various backgrounds. They may have been language teachers or self-made translators or even bilingual engineers. This is not a bad thing in itself, and it may even be an inspiring contribution to the methodological discussions among the staff of a translator training department if the profession is looked at from a variety of perspectives. But for translator training it is not sufficient just to produce good translations, nor is it enough to know everything about language, pragmatics and linguistics – or even Translation Theory. The interplay of theory and practice may be more important in this area than anywhere else. Although translating as an activity has been around for more than two thousand years, Translation Studies is still striving for its recognition as a discipline in its own right. Therefore, the "pig-tail" procedure may also render good results for trainers: practitioners should not despise theory, and theoreticians might benefit from a "sabbatical" in a translation company, which could lead them to more specific theoretical insights.

Moreover, in order to achieve the learning aims described in Section 3, "Teaching intercultural competence," we cannot rely on a large number of publications studying all the aspects of language-bound and contrastive text competence. Thus, there is a great need for application-oriented research in translator training, especially with regard to corpus-based, descriptive comparative studies on what is usually called "norms and conventions". Here is just a small glimpse into an extremely rewarding field of investigation and a selection of the studies that have been realised or are now being worked on in translator training institutions so far:

- text-type conventions, e.g. titles and headings in German, English, French and Spanish (Nord 1993, 1994a, 1995)
- scientific and technical texts in German and English (Göpferich 1995)
- academic rhetoric in English and Finnish (Mauranen 1993)
- pharmaceutical package inserts in Spanish and German (Nord 1999)
- style conventions, e.g. for the expression of modality in French and German (Feyrer 1997), for attribution, reported speech, cohesion etc. in Spanish and German (Nord 2003)
- conventions for the verbalisation of certain communicative (sub)functions, e.g. for metacommunication in German, French and Spanish university manuals (see Nord 2000), topic-comment structures in German

and French encyclopaedic texts (Hirsch 1995), intertextuality (see Nord 1993:189ff.; Waismayer 2000), or references to realities of another culture (see Odenthal 1995)
- conventions of non-verbal behaviour in real-life or fictitious situations, e.g. nonverbal or paraverbal behaviour in *Alice in Wonderland* and some of its translations into German, French, Spanish, Italian and Brazilian Portuguese (Nord 1994b, 1997b)
- translational conventions, e.g. how translators deal with proper names or quotations, whether – in which cases and how often – they prefer source-culture reproduction to target-culture adaptations, etc.

9. Conclusion

There are questions to study and corpora to analyse for many generations of students and teachers. Today's critical students no longer silently agree if you tell them that this or that is the way "you" or "people" express a particular function in a particular text type or situation; they find their own ways of expressing something just as appropriate, or even better. And it is really not very motivating to play the "age card" (the teacher is always older than the students, and therefore s/he is right!). Moreover, conventions are subject to change, so perhaps the students are right and your own way of expressing yourself is completely obsolete or at least hopelessly old-fashioned.

Therefore, the best method to motivate students – and trainers – for taking up application-oriented research is to discuss the norms and conventions of any kind of verbal or nonverbal behaviour and let them see for themselves what they are like. And if the results of these studies, however limited their range may be, flow back directly into training, they will make better students and better trainers, and translation classes will be more efficient.

Note

1. The following details refer to the four-year Programme for "Specialised Communication" at the University of Applied Sciences (Fachhochschule) of Magdeburg-Stendal, Germany, which started in 1994 and leads to a German Diploma degree corresponding to a British Bachelor Honours or a Spanish Licenciatura.

References

Agar, M. (1991). "The biculture in bilingual". *Language in Society, 20*, 167–181.

DIN 2345 (1998). *Übersetzungsaufträge.*

Feyrer, C. (1997). *Modalität im Kontrast: Ein Beitrag zur übersetzungsorientierten Modalpartikelforschung anhand des Deutschen und des Französischen.* Frankfurt am Main: Peter Lang.

Göpferich, S. (1995). *Textsorten in Naturwissenschaft und Technik: Pragmatische Typologie – Kontrastierung – Translation* [Forum für Fachsprachenforschung 27]. Tübingen: Narr.

Hirsch, C. (1995). Die Thema-Rhema-Gliederung in deutschen und französischen Fachtexten am Beispiel von Sachwörterbuchartikeln. Unpubl. Diploma Thesis. University of Hildesheim, Germany.

ISO 9000ff. (1992). *Qualitätsmanagement und Elemente eines Qualitätssicherungssystems –* Teil 2: Leitfaden für Dienstleistungen.

Kiraly, D. C. (1997). "Collaborative learning in the translation practice classroom". In E. Fleischmann, W. Kutz, & P. A. Schmitt (Eds.), *Translationsdidaktik* (pp. 152–158). Tübingen: Narr.

Mauranen, A. (1993). *Cultural Differences in Academic Rhetoric.* Frankfurt am Main: Peter Lang.

Nord, C. (1993). *Einführung in das funktionale Übersetzen. Am Beispiel von Titeln und Überschriften* [*utb 1734*]. Tübingen: Francke.

Nord, C. (1994a). "Functional units in translation". In A. Mauranen & T. Puurtinen (Eds.), *Translation – Acquisition – Use* (pp. 41–50). Jyväskylä: University Press.

Nord, C. (1994b). "It's tea-time in Wonderland: Culture-markers in fictional texts". In H. Pürschel et al. (Eds.), *Intercultural Communication* (pp. 523–538). Frankfurt am Main: Peter Lang.

Nord, C. (1995). "Text-functions in translation. Titles and headings as a case in point". *Target, 7*, 261–284.

Nord, C. (1996). "Wer nimmt denn mal den ersten Satz?" In A. Lauer et al. (Eds.), *Translationswissenschaft im Umbruch. Festschrift für Wolfram Wilss* (pp. 313–327). Tübingen: Narr.

Nord, C. (1997a). *Translating as a Purposeful Activity.* Manchester: St. Jerome.

Nord, C. (1997b). "Alice Abroad: Dealing with descriptions and transcriptions of paralanguage in literary translation". In F. Poyatos (Ed.), *Nonverbal Communication and Translation* (pp. 107–129). Amsterdam and Philadelphia: John Benjamins.

Nord, C. (1999). "Der Adressat – das unbekannte Wesen? Möglichkeiten und Grenzen der Adressatengerechtheit beim Übersetzen". In Alberto Gil et al. (Eds.), *Modelle der Translation* (pp. 192–207). Frankfurt am Main: Peter Lang.

Nord, C. (2000). "Das hinkende Beispiel und andere Merk-Würdigkeiten. Metakommunikation in deutschen, spanischen und französischen Lehrbuchtexten". In Gerd Wotjak (Ed.), *Akten der IV. Internationalen Tagung zum romanisch-deutschen und innerromanischen Sprachvergleich Leipzig 1999* (pp. 329–340). Leipzig.

Nord, C. (2003). *Kommunikativ handeln auf Spanisch und Deutsch. Übersetzungsorientierter Sprach- und Stilvergleich.* Wilhelmsfeld: Gottfried Egert.

Odenthal, C. (1995). Die Übersetzung spanischer Realienbezeichnungen ins Deutsche. Eine textsortenspezifische Untersuchung. Unpubl. Diploma Thesis. University of Hildesheim, Germany.

Schmitt, P. A. (1997). "Evaluierung von Fachübersetzungen". In G. Wotjak & H. Schmidt (Eds.), *Modelle der Translation – Models of Translation* (pp. 301–332). Frankfurt am Main: Vervuert.

Schmitt, P. A. (1998). "Qualitätsmanagement". In Mary Snell-Hornby et al. (Eds.), *Handbuch Translation* (pp. 394–399). Tübingen: Stauffenburg.

Waismayer, M. (2000). Intertextualität in deutschen und britischen Pressetexten. Unpubl. Diploma Thesis. University of Vienna.

CHAPTER 11

The ethics of translation in contemporary approaches to translator training*

Rosemary Arrojo

The training of translators has been one of the most crucial research interests of scholars devoted to the development of Translation Studies as a discipline in its own right. Particularly during the last decade we have witnessed the publication of several texts claiming to offer new insights into this difficult task. The main goal of this chapter is to examine the ways in which some of these approaches implicitly and explicitly treat translation as a profession. In other words, into what kind of professional image will aspiring translators be able to reflect themselves as they try to learn their skills, and what kind of professional attitude and ethics do contemporary theories and conceptions of translation end up teaching them? The objects of my analysis are three representative books which can still be linked to a predominantly essentialist theoretical foundation: Baker's *In Other Words: A Coursebook on Translation* (1992), Kussmaul's *Training the Translator* (1995), and Hatim and Mason's *The Translator as Communicator* (1997). As a brief conclusion, I intend to concentrate on some of their valuable arguments and reflect on how they could be incorporated into an approach to teaching which would fully accept the far-reaching implications of the inevitably ideological basis of the translator's task.

1. Tradition and essentialism

In the last fifteen years or so it has been my contention that most of the prevalent clichés involving translators and their work are a necessary consequence of a pervading essentialism which has dominated our conceptions of language and text, as well as our thoughts about translation for at least twenty centuries. By essentialism I mean a world view that relies on the possibility of forever stable meanings safely kept in language and texts which could transcend history and ideology, as well as the psychology of those involved in processing it. It is only from this perspective – which sees the so-called original as an immutable entity present to itself – that one can think of translation as the ideally neutral reproduction of a text across different languages, cultures and times, irrespective of the translator's conscious and unconscious circumstances, motivations, and goals.

The image of the word, the text, or of any language fragment as a reliable container which could allegedly protect frozen, untouched meaning from difference is central to most conceptions of language and translation, whether they find themselves in common sense or in formalised, academic theories. For example, one can point to Nida's well-known comparison of the words of a sentence to a series of freight cars that he uses as an illustration of his argument, according to which what is important in translation is to make sure that all meaning is safely transported from one language to another, no matter the order in which it is rearranged (1975: 190). In traditional terms the translator's task has generally been described as a code-switching operation, as is made clear, for instance, in Catford's classic definition: translation is "the replacement of textual material in one language (SL) by equivalent material in another language (TL)" (1965: 20). Equivalence and translation are in fact often taken to be almost synonyms, as the following excerpt from Koller illustrates:

> There exists equivalence between a given source text and a given target text if the target text fulfils certain requirements with respect to these frame conditions. The relevant conditions are those having to do with such aspects as content, style and function. The requirement of equivalence thus has the following form: quality (or qualities) X in the SL text must be preserved. This means the source-language content, form, style, function, etc. must be preserved, or at least that the translation must seek to preserve them as far as possible.   (1979: 187, quoted in Nord 1997: 7)

If one conceives of translation as a process which involves the accurate recovery of stable meaning from a text and, subsequently, the safe transportation of such meaning to another language, another culture, another time and another place – that is, if one thinks of translation as an idealised form of equivalence – then one must agree that it is mostly a mechanical activity which does not involve specific skills apart from the adequate knowledge of the pair of languages involved in any given instance of meaning transferral. This is a conclusion which has far-reaching consequences for the practice of translation. It is implicitly taken for granted, for instance, by the usual remuneration offered to professionals, who are generally paid by the number of words or pages translated. We can also attribute to such notions the underlying frustration associated with the alleged "imperfections" and "impossibilities" of translation which is recurrent among laypeople and specialists who share the pre-babelic desire that language can be non-arbitrary and can offer the possibility of perfect repetition. Usually viewed as a task which never quite fulfils its intended goal, the translator's work always seems to be promising – and failing to deliver – the original in its almost absolute integrity. As Dollerup points out, for example:

> In relation to a non-native language, the translator will, in terms of mastery move along an axis from 0 to perhaps 90% proficiency. And in relation to the native language, *the mastery will, in translation, be perhaps 95–97% but, once again, never complete*, because the source text will at all levels constitute a constraint, perhaps an unconscious one, but nevertheless a limitation in terms of the realisations in the target language, in the translator's mind: *it is part of the awareness of translation, and hence competent teaching of translation, to be fully conscious of the impossibility of the perfect translation.*
>
> (1995:23–24, my emphasis)

As an activity which is usually associated with imprecision, translation has not become the object of serious, systematic academic attention until recently when it began to emerge as a discipline in its own right. The resistance to view translation as an academic discipline, however, is still quite strong, for example, among professional translators who fail to see any relevant connection between their practice and most theoretical statements associated with academic research.[1]

Undoubtedly, within such a scenario, in spite of the fact that translation is generally recognised as a fundamental instrument for any level of interaction between different nations and peoples, we are dealing with a peculiar profession which is, nevertheless, still associated with failure and frustration. Sometimes described as unwelcome intermediaries, translators generally agree to practice an activity which perversely associates excellence with invisibility and, thus, openly proposes for its practitioners a bizarre professional ethics: a successful translator is allegedly the one who gives readers the illusion of his or her non-interference in the writing he or she actually produces. It is not by chance, though, that the profession is said to attract people with "weak egos." Kussmaul gives the example of a professional translator who maintains that there is a close relationship between the practice of translation and "weak personality structures":

> what [such a professional] meant was that translators were not adventurous, dynamic, vigorous, in short not self-confident. In his opinion, the translating profession attracted such personalities. One reason for this may be that translating and interpreting are "serving" professions, and serving does not usually go together with a well developed ego.
>
> (Cf. Bühler 1993:97f., quoted in Kussmaul 1995:32)

2.   The emergence of Translation Studies and the interests of linguistics in the 1990s: Baker, Hatim and Mason, and Kussmaul

Since the emergence of Translation Studies as a relatively independent discipline was officially proclaimed in the 1980s there has been a clear, explicit effort on the part of scholars to anchor translation on an objectively minded, academic basis. This was generally associated with contemporary developments in mainstream linguistics, which would allegedly free translations from their frequent associations of amateurism and improvisation.[2] As a consequence, the training of translators would find a legitimate place in academic institutions and universities and would provide the area with a much desired specificity, as well as a universality, and would definitively establish the study of translation as an institutionalised area of research.

From this perspective, the academic basis of Translation Studies needed a methodology that would direct and discipline the training of aspiring professionals world-wide.[3] Such a methodological basis would be found in contemporary linguistics. According to scholars such as Baker, Basil Hatim, Ian Mason and Kussmaul, this methodological basis has greatly progressed since the early attempts at building an interface between translation and linguistics were made by linguists such as Georges Mounin, J. C. Catford and even Eugene Nida.

Hatim and Mason, for instance, claim to take "a fairly broad view of text linguistics and incorporate insights from various other disciplines such as stylistics, rhetoric, exegesis, discourse analysis, ethnomethodology, as well as from recent attempts at developing text grammars within a science of texts" (1997:179). For Baker, modern linguistics "no longer restricts itself to the study of language per se but embraces such sub-disciplines as textlinguistics (the study of text as a communicative event rather than as a shapeless string of words and structures) and pragmatics (the study of language in use rather than language as an abstract system)" (1992:4–5). Thus, her well-known book "attempts to explore some areas in which modern linguistic theory can provide a basis for training translators and can inform and guide the decisions they have to make in the course of performing their work" (1992:5). As Kussmaul's approach claims to fit in "with this newer, method-oriented tradition," he "still draws predominantly on linguistics," relying "more specifically on psycholinguistics and textlinguistics". From psycholinguistics he uses such notions as "bottom-up and top-down processing, activation of semantic features, prototypes, and scenes and frames". At the same time, "the notion of text linguistics [that he favours] includes the pragmatic dimension, that is to say, the relation of the text to the author and to the reader of the text. Special emphasis is laid on the methods and models of descriptive stylistics, speech act theory, text-typology and functional sentence perspective" (1995:203).

Far from those who have attempted to ground translation theory on traditional language theories, Baker, Kussmaul and Hatim and Mason claim to resort to a brand of linguistics which goes beyond the merely linguistic, supposedly taking into account cultural and ideological aspects which would entail a conception of reading and interpretation and, consequently, of translation in which the reader, the interpreter, and the translator play a fundamental role. According to Baker (1992:219):

> The ability to make sense of a stretch of language depends on the hearer's or reader's expectations and experience of the world. Different societies, and indeed different individuals and groups of individuals within the same society, have different experiences of the world and different views on the way events and situations are organised or related to each other. A network of relations which is valid and makes sense in one society may not be valid in another. This is not just a question of agreeing or disagreeing with a certain view of the world but of being able to make sense of it in the first place. Whether a text is judged as acceptable or not does not depend on how closely it corresponds to some state of affairs in the world, but rather on whether the reader finds the presented version of reality believable, homogeneous, or relevant.

As she aptly recognises, such a conception of the relationship between language and the "world" has fundamental implications for translation. If, for example, as Baker points out, coherence is more a matter of the reader's judgment of the text, rather than the text itself, then the inherent difficulties in translation would reflect less the source text than "the significance of the translated text for its readers as members of a certain culture, or of a sub-group within that culture, with the constellation of knowledge, judgment and perception they have developed from it" (Snell-Hornby 1988:42, quoted in Baker 1992:222).

Hatim and Mason also recognise that "textual strategy is closely bound up with cultural beliefs, values and expectations". As they claim, from the perspective of linguistics, "all use of language reflects a set of users' assumptions which are closely bound up with attitudes, beliefs and value systems" (1997:143–144). From such a stance, they define ideology together with Simpson: "as the tacit assumptions, beliefs and value systems which are shared collectively by social groups" (1993:5, quoted in Hatim & Mason 1997:144). "Closely associated to this" is their use of the term "discourse" "as institutionalised modes of speaking and writing which give expression to particular attitudes towards areas of socio-cultural activity". Again, the consequences for translation are fundamental and far-reaching: For Hatim and Mason, translation cannot be "a neutral activity". To the extent that the translator "acts in a social context and is part of that context," his/her task "is, in itself, an ideological activity" (1997:144–146).

In a similar vein, Kussmaul argues, for instance, that "ever since J. L. Austin delivered his famous lectures 'How to do things with words' (Austin 1962), linguists have become more and more aware of the fact that saying something means performing actions" (1995:61). An important consequence of such an insight is the conclusion that "our process of comprehension is interpretive" (Kussmaul 1995:61). If any level of language use implies the performing of actions, there can be no level of understanding or communication which could take place without some kind of interference on the part of those involved. Furthermore, as Kussmaul also observes, "the things we say, imply or allude to are not only determined by situation and by our intentions, but also by the culture we live in [...]. The influence of situation and culture on what we say or write may sometimes be so strong that they determine the form of texts" (1995:55). Again, the implications for translation are clear. According to Kussmaul, to translate is first and foremost an "interpretive use of language" (1995:61). As he suggests, such a conclusion is further complicated by the fact that translation involves an act of communication which "takes place between the writer of a source text and the reader of a target text, that is, between members of two different cultures" (1995:64).

If we were to take such conclusions and insights to their last consequences, we would certainly come to a conception of translation and to a pedagogical approach which should be drastically different from the ones fully recognised and subscribed to by tradition. First of all, we would have to agree that what is involved in translation is definitely more related to a transformation of textual material – controlled by the circumstances which, both implicitly and explicitly, both consciously and unconsciously, guide the translator's work –

than to a process of neutral meaning transferral resulting in an ideal form of inherent equivalence between the so-called original and its translation.[4] In other words, if we truly accepted the full implications of language theories which claim to go beyond the merely linguistic and to take into account the ideological, historical, and cultural basis of meaning, we would have to recognise the translator's inescapable authorial interference in the process of translation and would have to review most of the clichés which consider it as a "serving" profession.

If translation were fully recognised to be an ideologically marked activity which depends directly on the attitudes, beliefs and value systems which constitute the translator's cultural and ideological universe, such a recognition would have to be clearly reflected in the pedagogical approaches which claim to entertain such notions. One might expect, for instance, that the academic training of translators proposed by the scholars discussed above would focus on an ethics of translation which took into account the translator's inevitable visibility in the work he or she does. If translation is an interpretive task that cannot be in any sense neutral or above ideological and historical constraints, it seems logical that translation students should be taught the responsibilities involved in being active interpreters and writers of translated texts.

Yet this is not exactly the road taken by Baker, Hatim and Mason, or Kussmaul in their well-known books. In spite of their apparent defence of a conception of translation which would contemplate the full implications of the intimate relationship that binds together language, culture and ideology, their overall views on the translator's task and the pedagogical approaches they propose are still very much committed to essentialism.

2.1 Mona Baker: *In Other Words: A Coursebook on Translation*

Mona Baker's book is basically about equivalence, in which "equivalence" seems to be viewed as a linguistic or a textual property which does not really depend on the circumstances which have allowed a certain text, or a text fragment, at a certain point in time, to be considered as "equivalent" to another one. Even though Baker illustrates her discussion with useful examples of actual translation fragments, involving English and several other languages (Arabic, Spanish, German, Italian, Portuguese, Japanese, Chinese), she grounds such examples on a theoretical basis which does not seem to take into account her own conclusions regarding the intimate relationship between language and perspective. As is implied in an epigraph taken from a text written in the early 1960s, the conception of translation which seems to give real support to her comments is fully located within tradition:

> even the simplest, most basic requirement we make of translation cannot be met without difficulty: one cannot always match the content of a message in language A by an expression with exactly the same content in language B, because what can be expressed and what must be expressed is a property of a specific language in much the same way as how it can be expressed.
>
> (Winter 1961:98,quoted in Baker 1992:82)

To the extent that equivalence is treated as a textual property which does not really depend on the translator's or the reader's circumstances, Baker "assumes" that the translator's goal is to convince the reader "to accept a given translation as a text in its own right, if possible without being unduly alerted to the fact that is a translation" (1992:112).

Such a perspective also touches on two fundamental, inescapable and intimately related implications which have important consequences for the teaching of translation. The first one is the impossible, doubtful ethics of the invisible translator, and the second is the underlying negativity which often colours any discourse on translation and which is often expressed by the notion of the resilient difficulty, or even the impossibility, of translation as a profession. Or, what is even worse, by the frequent desire to do away with translation altogether. Another epigraph in Baker's book is an exemplary illustration of just that:

> The great pest of speech is frequency of translation. No book was ever turned from one language into another, without imparting something of its native idiom; this is the most mischievous and comprehensive innovation; single words may enter by thousands, and the fabrick of the tongue continue the same, but new phraseology changes much at once; it alters not the single stones of the building, but the order of the columns. If an academy should be established for the cultivation of our style, ... let them, instead of compiling grammars and dictionaries, endeavour, with all their influence, to stop the licence of translators, whose idleness and ignorance, if it be suffered to proceed, will reduce us to babble a dialect of France.
>
> (Samuel Johnson, Preface to the Dictionary 1755:xii,
> quoted in Baker 1992:46)

What seems to be prevalent in Baker's discussion is the basic notion that meaning is actually in the text and because it is in the text – and not in the context, or in history, or in social conventions – it can allegedly be stable and forever protected from ideology or any other form of difference or change. As she clearly states, the translator's task is to "attempt to perceive the meanings of words and utterances very precisely in order to render them into another language" (1992: 17). Therefore, if one is hoping to find some ethical guidance in what is implicitly and explicitly proposed in her book, it seems to be the belief that it is indeed possible for a translator to be invisible and to recover meaning from a text and transfer it elsewhere without the interference of the circumstances involved in the process. Any form of "visibility" for translators is, thus, the result of conscious decisions or, at most, signs of linguistic ignorance.

2.2 Hatim and Mason: *The Translator as Communicator*

A similar gap between the defence of a supposedly contemporary conception of translation and the acceptance of the age-old traditional notions that have informed thought on the subject can also be found in Hatim and Mason's *The Translator as Communicator* (1997). As a brief illustration of my argument, I will comment on one of the subitems of their important chapter on ideology, appropriately entitled "The translation of ideology." Here they use as an illustration "one of the few existing studies of translation from the point of view of critical discourse analysis" (1997: 146), viz. an analysis by Knowles and Malmkjær of four English translations of Hans Christian Andersen's fairy tale *Den Standhaftige Tinsoldat* (*The Steadfast Tin Soldier*) (Knowles and Malmkjær 1989). According to Hatim and Mason, "the analysis shows that variant translations at many points in the text reflect with varying degrees of explicitness the ideology of Andersen's text world" (1997: 147). One of such points is the "use of recurrence (of the adjective *nydeligt*, 'pretty', with pejorative connotations of superficiality), retained throughout in one translation but variously translated as "pretty", "lovely", "charming", "enchanting", "graceful" in the others" (1997: 147). At the same time, however, the authors remind the reader that:

> the decision, say, to translate all instances of the source text term *nydeligt* by the target language item "pretty" may reflect either a concern to relay the ideological value implicit in the use of the cohesive device of recurrence or, more simply, a general orientation towards literal translating, in the sense of selecting the nearest lexical 'equivalent' wherever possible. It is only when evidence of this kind is part of a discernible trend, reflected in the way a whole range of linguistic features are treated in a particular translation that the analyst may claim to detect an underlying motivation or orientation on the part of the translator. In effect, the discernible trend may be seen in terms

of degrees of mediation, that is, the extent to which translators intervene in the transfer process, feeding their own knowledge and beliefs into their processing of a text.   (1997:147)

The treatment of ideology which Hatim and Mason seem to suggest here presupposes that some language users, at least in some circumstances, are immune to the influence of "the attitudes, beliefs and value systems" in which they find themselves. One such "user" is, without a doubt, the "analyst" of translations for whom Hatim and Mason intend to establish objective patterns of analysis that will indicate when a certain textual device or characteristic should be seen as "an underlying motivation or orientation on the part of the translator" (1997:147). Thus, the translator's work presents "degrees of mediation" which indicate the "extension" of his or her "intervention" in the process of transferring meaning from one text to another. At the same time they believe that authors use "devices" – such as the repetition of a certain adjective – which have implicit "ideological value," while the task of the analyst, as absolutely impartial arbiter and judge, seems to transcend such "limitations." Furthermore, just as there are "users" who are immune to ideology, there are, also, translation options which may, or may not, reflect "a concern to relay [...] ideological value" (1997:147).

If, as Hatim and Mason claim, "all use of language reflects a set of users' assumptions which are closely bound up with attitudes, beliefs and value systems" (1997:144), how can they justify, for instance, their conclusion according to which a certain translation option does not have any "ideological value"? Wouldn't the "general orientation towards literal translating," pointed out by the authors in the text in question, be also (and inevitably) marked by ideological values? Similarly, how can we account for the privileged position they attribute to the "critical analyst" of translated texts?[5]

On one level it appears that they work with a definition of translation which seems to recognise the "differences" brought about not only by the translator, but also by the language and the culture in which he or she is producing the target text – that is, as "an act of communication which attempts to relay, across cultural and linguistic boundaries, another act of communication (which may have been invented for different purposes and different readers/hearers)" (1997:1). Yet, Hatim and Mason tend to view the translator as someone whose ethical task is basically restricted to the reproduction of the original's supposedly definitive, forever present meaning. In their book, texts can be, for instance, perfectly stable and the translator's interference, as in Baker's model, is at most an optional possibility. According to Hatim and Mason, for instance, there are "textual occurrences":

> which display maximal cohesion and consequently maximal coherence, where intertextuality is least intricate, intentionality least opaque, situationality least cumbersome and informativity sparingly used. At the other extreme, there will be local- and global-level textual occurrences where cohesion is not straightforward and where coherence is problematical to retrieve. In such cases, values yielded by other factors such as intentionality and intertextuality become slightly less transparent.   (1997:27)

On the basis of this conclusion, they propose different "translation strategies" and different degrees of interference for translators:

> Where a source text is situated towards the stable end of the scale, a fairly literal approach may and often will be appropriate. That is, least intervention on the part of the translator is called for – unless the brief for the job includes different requirements. On the other hand, where the source text displays considerable degrees of dynamism, the translator is faced with more interesting challenges and literal translation may no longer be an option.
>   (1997:30–31)

Within such a theoretical framework, which seems to rephrase traditional clichés in a more contemporary jargon, visibility and interference are, again, merely conscious options for translators. Whatever Hatim and Mason read in the texts that they discuss and analyse is, for them, definitely in those texts. In other words, in their privileged position as "critical analysts," they seem to be above ideology and history and, thus, implicitly claim to have access to readings, or to interpretations, which are not biased or interfering. As a whole, under an allegedly different, culturally-minded approach to translation, what is actually being proposed in Hatim and Mason's book is an overall conception of language which keeps intact most of the essentialist notions that are so dear to tradition. Among them, the belief in the possibility of a neutral, perfectly objective "critical analysis" of the translator's work is perhaps the one most detrimental to students truly interested in understanding the ethical implications of translation. It is conceivable, then, that Hatim and Mason may implicitly teach students that if only they make an effort and come up with the right choices, they can hope to produce a translation which could be fully acceptable in any circumstances.

2.3   Paul Kussmaul: *Training the Translator*

In Kussmaul's book (1995) we find a similar tension between a notion of translation which supposedly contemplates the translator's basically interpretive vocation and an underlying allegiance to the traditional conception of the translator's task as that of an ideally invisible mediator in charge of rescuing meaning from the original and transferring it elsewhere. As I have pointed out above, Kussmaul repeatedly suggests that translation is basically an interpretive task. Furthermore, he openly associates interpretation, and even comprehension, with creativity. At the same time, he coherently compares the translator's task with that of a writer:

> We usually associate creativity with production. Thus within the field of language, saying things, writing and translating texts are typical creative activities. But what about comprehension? Is there not something like creative comprehension? We sometimes even talk of creative miscomprehension. It is a commonplace that when rereading a text after some time we understand it in a different way. When we read Shakespeare's great tragedies as adolescents and when we read them again after twenty or thirty years we certainly arrive at different interpretations of these plays. Comprehension [...] is not only guided by what we hear or read but also by our personal knowledge and experience. Understanding is not merely a receptive but also a productive process.   (1995:41)

As he appropriately reminds us interpretation – or comprehension – mediates or "guides" what we hear or read, including of course the reading of translations. Therefore, "translators have to be aware of the fact that readers' expectations, their norms and values, are influenced by culture and that their comprehension of utterances is to a large extent determined by these expectations, norms and values" (1995:70).

Yet, such insights do not seem to be taken too seriously when Kussmaul explicitly relates the translator's decision-making process to the following quote from Gutt: "what the translator has to do in order to communicate successfully is to arrive at the intended interpretation of the original, and then determine in what respects his translation should interpretively resemble the original in order to be consistent with the principle of relevance for his target audience with its particular cognitive environment" (1990:157, quoted in Kussmaul 1995:65). Thus, even though Kussmaul's proposal does contemplate the need to reconcile both the function of the translated text and the goal of the translation with the interests of the target audience, he still seems to believe in the possibility of "arriving at the intended interpretation of the original."

If, as Kussmaul also defends, our reading of texts is directly related to our own circumstances, which do not remain forever the same, how can we possibly determine, once and for all, the "intended interpretation" of any text? If we believe, as he declares, that "understanding is not merely a receptive but also a productive process" (1995:41) and if our "comprehension of utterances is to a large extent determined by [... our] expectations, norms and values" (1995:70), we will have to accept that the space in which the translator works – both as a "productive" interpreter and as a writer of translated texts – is inevitably marked by all the circumstances (expectations, norms and values) which constitute it. Consequently, if different translators, in different circumstances, translate the "same" text they will certainly have different views on what the "intended interpretation of the original" might be. Thus, we will have to accept that the translated text will inevitably bear the marks of the circumstances and the context which have made its writing possible and acceptable. In other words, translation can never be the neutral, invisible activity which tradition expects it to be. From such a stance, one of the main questions related to translator training remains unanswered in Kussmaul's book: if translators are inevitably reflected in their work, what is a professional to do when he or she accepts this delicate, complex mission which is still viewed as an allegedly impersonal mediation between languages and cultures?

Kussmaul does, however, seem to be often close to approaching such a question. He acknowledges, for example, that translation is not merely a mechanical activity. According to him:

> translation is not only a skill but also a problem-solving process. If translation were a skill like, say, driving a car, professionalism could be achieved once and for all. The correct actions for driving can be internalized, and then normal driving situations are mastered without any conscious mental effort. With problem-solving activities like translating, internalization of strategies and techniques is only part of the process.   (1995:9)

What he calls a "problem-solving" activity also involves a decision-making process which necessarily depends on the kind of reading of the source text that the translator actually proposes to implement in his or her translation. Such a "creative" or "productive" aspect of translating is, as Kussmaul himself has recognised, very similar to original writing and, thus, cannot be mastered simply by applying a certain method or a collection of rules. According to him:

> [since] communicative acts are part of a culture ... translators have had to decide ... [for instance] if names of people or institutional terms not known

in the target culture had to be explained or adapted, if allusions had to be made explicit or even dropped in the translation. There are no hard and fast rules for these decisions, although some may think there are.   (1995:65)

Therefore, if there are no rules that could exempt translators from making their own authorial decisions, "there is no other way for [them] but taking the trouble to start a chain of reflections, as it were, considering the function of the text-element within the overall text and the embeddedness of the text within its culture" (1995:65).

Kussmaul's functionalist emphasis on the reader of translated texts seems to distract him from the fact that translators are also readers and thus inevitably embedded in their own culture. It is only on the basis of such a "distraction" that we may understand why he seems to rely so much on research based on Think-Aloud Protocol (TAPs) which is, according to him "a new process-oriented approach ... developed recently in order to gain more immediate access to that notorious black box, the translator's mind." As he explains it:

> By adopting introspective methods from psychology, experiments have been carried out in which translators were asked to utter everything that went on in their minds while they were translating, and these monologues were tape recorded. These monologues are referred to as think-aloud protocols (TAPs). Such protocols have been analysed in order to classify translation strategies, with the pedagogical (diagnostic) aim of observing difficulties encountered by the students.   (1995:7)

What seems to be implied in this kind of research is the belief that the translator's "mind," – some secretive "black box," – can in fact reveal something about the mechanisms of translation which would bring universally valid insights to be used in translator training. To the extent that, as Kussmaul himself states elsewhere, "culture is the most comprehensive aspect when we make our decisions as translators" (1995:71), whatever conclusions he may arrive at through his TAPs research will only have a limited, local scope.

3.   A non-essentialist approach to translator training: A brief illustration

As I have tried to show, some of our most representative translation scholars today are beginning to recognise the intimate relationship which binds together meaning and culture and, therefore, also meaning and ideology, meaning and interest, meaning and perspective. However, they do not seem ready to accept all the implications of such a relationship both for the study and the teaching of translation. At the basis of their conceptions of translation and, thus, at the roots of the teaching approaches they implicitly and explicitly propose, there is an underlying belief in the possibility of translation as absolute equivalence. As a consequence, they still contemplate the translator's ideal role as that of an invisible mediator equally serving both the target and the source texts, as well as the languages and the cultures they represent. Their notions of science and theory still seem to be embedded in what we might view as a modern ideal of knowledge: the construction of a body of allegedly objective data which could be systematised and universally applied, regardless of the peculiarities, the interests and the circumstances of those involved. Using Lyotard's notion of "modernity," we could say that Translation Studies today is still an emerging discipline generally pursuing a scientific ideal that could legitimise it on the basis of contemporary, basically essentialist, linguistics as its totalising metadiscourse.[6]

My main purpose in this section is to illustrate how translator training could focus on the consequences of a conception of language and text which takes the conventionality of meaning to its last consequences. This is a perspective generally associated with post-modern, post-structuralist, or even post-colonial notions of language and the subject which have as a common ground a disbelief in the possibility of any level of neutral, purely objective meaning. If meaning is viewed as an inevitable product of the individual and the context and the social environment which produce and accept it as legitimate, and if individuals, contexts and social groups are not themselves forever stable or predictable, we will certainly have to review all of our traditional notions concerning the translator's craft.

In the limited space which I have here I would like to reflect on a brief practical example in order to show how we might help students become aware of the translator's inescapably interfering role in the production of the translated text. I believe this can be an efficient way to teach students about the complexity of translation and, above all, about the responsibility involved in agreeing to perform such a task.

This example is a translation exercise originally proposed in an article I wrote in 1985 and one which still seems appropriate. Initially students are invited to translate a short, rather informal text which is supposed to be a note left by an American guest to his Brazilian host: "This is just to say I have eaten the plums that were in the icebox and which you were probably saving for breakfast. Forgive me, they were delicious: so sweet and so cold." As translators of a simple personal note, whose context and function have been clearly established by the teacher, students in general do not hesitate to reproduce the information they allegedly find in the original. After they finish their assignment, however, they are introduced to the fact that the fragment they have just translated is in reality a poem by William Carlos Williams:

> This is just to say
> I have eaten
> the plums
> that were in
> the icebox
>
> and which
> you were probably
> saving
> for breakfast
>
> Forgive me
> they were delicious
> so sweet and so cold
>
> (quoted in Bradley, S. et al. (Eds.) 1974: 1618–1619)

As they learn that the "same" fragment is now rather different and that their new assignment is to produce a Portuguese version of this well-known poem, whatever was prosaic and simple about it becomes poetic and complex. To the extent that they are educated readers, i.e. members of a cultural community which accepts this "new" fragment as a poem and which is familiar with the prevalent conventions generally guiding the reading of poetry, they must accept the challenge of interpreting it "poetically," that is, they must attribute to each element of the poem a function and a meaning which should transcend those which they originally saw in the note.

What students can learn from the confrontation of these two "different" texts, which are in fact verbally identical, is first of all the notion that what makes a text temporarily stable in a certain context is precisely the circumstances within which it is framed and the way it is read. Thus, whether a text is literary or not, whether it is a poem or not, does not really depend on something which is intrinsically found in its language or in its structure but, rather, on the conventional interpretive strategies which readers activate in order to (literally) make sense of it.[7] We can imagine, for instance, that for those who are familiar with Williams' poem and who have learned to accept and read it as such, the fragment could never be seen as a simple, informal note.

The implications for the translator's task are of course fundamental: to the extent that the so-called original only comes to life as it is actually read or interpreted by someone, in certain circumstances and with certain goals and constraints, a translation will inevitably be faithful to the translator's reading of the source text, and never to the original as a closed, forever stable textual container of its author's meanings and intentions. Therefore, it is the translator's first inescapable task and responsibility to be as fully aware as possible of the kind of interpretation of the original he or she produces and brings to the translated text.

In the case of Williams' poem, seen within the pedagogical context outlined above, we can read it, for example, from the perspective of an interpretation proposed by Culler who views the text as an opposition "between the eating of plums and the social rules which this violates". According to him,

> the poem as note becomes a mediating force, recognising the priority of rules by asking forgiveness but also affirming, by the thrust of the last few words, that immediate sensuous experience also has its claims and that the order of personal relations (the relationship between the 'I' and the 'you') must make a place for such experience.   (1975: 175)

If a translator decides to elaborate on this reading, he or she will have to deal with the problem of translating "plums," for instance, which certainly becomes a key element as it is directly associated with the transgressive, sensuous experience that is at the centre of such an interpretation. In order for a translation to be faithful to this reading, it is essential that the associations developed around "plums" find equivalents in the translated text. Since these associations bring to mind a sensuous experience, it is certainly meaningful that such a fruit – desired and eaten by the "I" of the poem and specially reserved for breakfast by the "you" – is sweet, juicy, soft-skinned; and in its shape and colour, it probably reminds one of the forbidden fruit of the Garden of Eden.

When we translate "plums" into the Portuguese "ameixas," however, the spectrum of associations may change radically, particularly if one considers the original context and the circumstances in which this exercise was proposed. When I wrote the article about the poem while in São Paulo in the 1980s, fresh plums were imported and, thus, very expensive and difficult to find. When in class discussions, my students and I talked about "ameixas" in that context, the tendency was to think of "prunes" rather than "plums". To the extent that prunes are dried and wrinkled and, ironically, usually associated with some relief for constipation, particularly when consumed at breakfast, "ameixas" could hardly be related to a sensuous experience and, thus, might not be an acceptable choice.

Such considerations touch other fundamental issues. If plums were difficult to find in São Paulo in the 1980s, should we consider whether plums were
also rare in Rutherford, New Jersey, Williams' hometown, in the mid 1930s
when the poem was written? Were plums usually part of a breakfast in his
context? If they were not, we might conclude that the sensuous experience referred to in the poem is something quite special, out of the ordinary. In other
words, should our translation of "plums" take into account the circumstances
in which we imagine Williams might have written his poem? Should we try to
be faithful to an interpretation that tries to recover the original context and circumstances of the poem, or should we try to produce a version of the poem that
works in our context in the same way we imagine it did in the poet's? Would it
be appropriate, for instance, not to translate "plums" literally and to look for
other equivalents which might convey some of the associations that we have
privileged in our interpretation? Thus, would it be acceptable to choose equivalents such as "pêssegos" ("peaches"), or even "sapotis" ("sapodilla," a Brazilian
native fruit)?

As I look back at some of these questions related to the translation of
"plums," it is also appropriate to consider how the passing of time (almost
two decades) has solved most of the translation problems involved for reasons
which are quite prosaic. Now that plums are easy to find in São Paulo and that
"ameixas" would not immediately remind us of "prunes," a literal translation
may be an adequate choice for our version. However, we are still left with
other related issues to think about. Let's imagine, for example, that the poem
would be part of a collection of American poetry in translation to be published
by a major publishing house with branches all over the country as well as
abroad. Would our choice also work in other Brazilian regions or even in other
countries such as Portugal or Mozambique? Should, then, our translation of
the poem aim at reaching a larger public? Would that be possible? Would it be
possible for our translation to be equally as acceptable in the classroom where
it has been discussed and produced as in other countries where Portuguese
is spoken? Furthermore, students should also be stimulated to think about
more general issues such as the implications of translating such a poem
into Portuguese. For instance, how would it relate to Brazilian contemporary
poetry? Or, even, why should it be translated at all? There should also be a
discussion about the impact of the classroom, or the role of the teacher (as the
one who initiates the exercise and who even proposes a basic reading for the
text) on the students' translations. Hopefully, this might lead to an important
reflection on evaluation and, thus, also on translation criticism. According to

which criteria would the students' work be evaluated? What would such an evaluation reflect?

As students are guided to reflect on these and other related questions, they will learn that it is impossible for them (and their circumstances) to be "invisible" in their translated texts. As they are stimulated to experience the intimate relationship which is established between their readings – as well as their conceptions on how translation and poetry should be dealt with – and the translated texts they will finally produce, they are also learning to take their job as seriously as professionals who know the scope and the importance of their craft.

As we try to stimulate students to acknowledge what they bring to their translation work, we could also teach them, for instance, the full implications of Kussmaul's appropriate association between translation and Austin's notion of the performative (Kussmaul 1995:61). If any use of language implies the performing of actions, translating cannot be, by any means, an innocent activity, merely at the service of a client or of the languages and cultures involved. As students of translation begin to recognise the power relations involved in their future profession, they also begin to realise how influential and complex it is. Thus, as they begin to conceive of a different version for the translator's usually marginal and inadequate professional profile, they are preparing to face the challenges involved in accepting their "visibility" and in taking responsibility for the work they do.

Notes

* This chapter is part of a research project sponsored by Brazil's National Council for Research (Conselho Nacional de Desenvolvimento Científico e Tecnológico, CNPq).

1. See, for example, Baker (1992:3) and Kussmaul (1995:1).

2. See, for example, Baker (1992:4).

3. See also Kussmaul (1995:1–2).

4. This notion of translation as a form of regulated transformation is related, of course, to a definition by Jacques Derrida: "In the limits to which it is possible, or at least *appears* possible, translation practices the difference between signified and signifier. But if this difference is never pure, no more so is translation, and for the notion of translation we would have to substitute a notion of *transformation*: a regulated transformation of one language by another, of one text by another. We will never have, and in fact have never had, to do with some 'transport' of pure signifieds from one language to another, or within one and the same language, that the signifying instrument would leave virgin and untouched" (1987:20).

5. I have also discussed Hatim and Mason's notion of the 'critical analyst' in Arrojo (1998).

6. For Lyotard, "modern" refers to "any science that legitimates itself with reference to a [totalising] metadiscourse making an explicit appeal to some grand narrative, such as the dialectics of Spirit, the hermeneutics of meaning, the emancipation of the rational or working subject, or the creation of wealth" (1984:xxiii).

7. My proposal of such an exercise in the 1980s was directly influenced by my reading of Fish's work and, particularly, of his essay 'How to recognize a poem when you see one' (1980:322–337).

References

Arrojo, R. (1998). "Os 'Estudos da Tradução' como Área de Pesquisa Independente: Dilemas e Ilusões de uma Disciplina em (Des)Construção". *D.E.L.T.A.*, Pontifícia Universidade Católica de São Paulo, *14*(2), 423–454.

Austin, J. J. (1962). *How to Do Things with Words*. Oxford: Claredon Press.

Baker, M. (1992). *In Other Words: A Coursebook on Translation*. London and New York: Routledge.

Bassnett, S. & Trivedi, H. (Eds.). (1999). *Post-Colonial Translation*. London and New York: Routledge.

Bradley, S. et al. (Eds.). (1974). *The American Tradition in Literature*. New York: Grosset and Dunlap.

Bühler, H. (1993). "Vom Wert der Übersetzung und vom Selbstwertgefühl der Übersetzenden." In J. Holz-Mänttäri & C. Nord (Eds.), *Traducere Navem. Festschrift für Katharina Reiss zum 70 Geburtstag*, Studia translatologica ser. A, Vol. 3 (pp. 91–102). Tampere: University of Tampere.

Catford, J. C. (1965). *A Linguistic Theory of Translation: An Essay in Applied Linguistics*. London: Oxford University Press.

Culler, J. (1975). *Structuralist Poetics: Structuralism, Linguistics, and the Study of Literature*. Ithaca: Cornell University Press.

Derrida, J. (1987). *Positions*. A. Bass (Trans.). London: The Athlone Press.

Dollerup, C. (1995). "The emergence of the teaching of translation". In C. Dollerup & Vibeke Appel (Eds.), *Teaching Translation and Interpreting 3* (pp. 19–30). Amsterdam and Philadelphia: John Benjamins.

Fish, S. (1980). "How to recognize a poem when you see one." In *Is There a Text in This Class? The Authority of Interpretive Communities*. Cambridge: Harvard University Press.

Gutt, E. A. (1990). "A theoretical account of translation – Without a translation theory." *Target, 2*(2), 135–164.

Hatim, B. & Mason, I. 1997. *The Translator as Communicator*. London and New York: Routledge.

Johnson, S. (1755). *A Dictionary of the English Language*, 2 vols. London: Knapton.

Knowles, M. & Malmkjær, K. (1989). "Translating ideology: Language, power and the world of the tin soldier." *Language and Ideology, ELR Journal, 3*, 205–241.

Koller, W. (1979). *Einführung in die Übersetzungswissenschaft*. Heildelberg: Quelle & Meyer. English translation in A. Chesterman (Ed., 1989), *Readings in Translation* (pp. 99–104). Helsinki: Oy Finn Lectura Ab.

Kussmaul, P. (1995). *Training the Translator*. Amsterdam and Philadelphia: John Benjamins.

Lyotard, J. F. (1984). *The Postmodern Condition: A Report on Knowledge*. G. Bennington & B. Massumi (Trans.). Manchester: Manchester University Press.

Nida, E. (1975). *Language Structure and Translation*. Stanford: Stanford University Press.

Nord, C. (1997). *Translating as a Purposeful Activity: Functionalist Approaches Explained*. Manchester: St. Jerome.

Simpson, P. (1993). *Language, Ideology and Point of View*. London and New York: Routledge.

Snell-Hornby, M. (1988). *Translation Studies: An Integrated Approach*. Amsterdam and Philadelphia: John Benjamins.

Winter, W. (1961). "Impossibilities of Translation." In W. Arrowsmith & R. Shattuck (Eds.), *The Craft and Context of Translation*. New York: Anchor.

PART IV

Epilogue

CHAPTER 12

Deschooling translation
Beginning of century reflections on teaching translation and interpreting

Michael Cronin

In 1754 the pupils studying at the Oratorian College in Saint-Omer rioted. Their principal grievance, they explained, was that they had to speak Latin during school hours. The authorities eventually relented and, as in many other schools and colleges throughout eighteenth-century France, Latin was henceforth taught as a language to be understood not spoken (Waquet 1998: 21). The schoolbooks reflected the changing conditions and the anthologies of Latin lexical exotica and idioms were replaced by *Selecta*, collections of passages especially chosen for use in *version* classes. The change in pedagogical emphasis would have profound implications for translation teaching. Translation into the vernacular language in the Age of Enlightenment now became the primary activity in the teaching of Latin, and the prestige of the language of Cicero, Livy, Horace remained immense despite the advances of vernacular languages during the Reformation period. Thus, translation was inextricably linked with the learning of Latin and the dominant paradigm here was close, faithful, exact rendition of source text where competence in and understanding of the source text was paramount. Translation was used to teach language and punish deviance. Bassnett speaks of this use of translation as a pedagogical instrument (1996: 19):

> Translation in the classroom had to be assessed, and hence the notion of faithfulness to the source text was a crucial one. In the age of dictionaries, the bilingual dictionary as a tool for translators posited the idea of equivalence as sameness across linguistic frontiers. Difference was elided in this view of translation; whatever was said in one language could and should be rendered into another, and the success of that rendering was gauged in terms of the faithfulness of the copy to the original. School text books presupposed a

binary relationship between languages, with translation as a servile activity designed to show the competence of the student in understanding the source and rendering it into an acceptable version in the target language.

The decline of Latin did not lead to paradigm shift. Translation between vernacular languages throughout much of the twentieth century followed the traditional Latin model of the teacher-centred, source text-oriented, grammatically obsessive translation practice that Ladmiral dubbed the *performance magistrale* (Ladmiral 1977).

The persistence of this practice might seem curious in that it was the practical needs of the translation profession that led to the establishment of many translation schools from the 1940s onwards. Distinctive courses for translators must surely have produced distinctive approaches to teaching. This, by and large, was not the case. Why? One answer provides the topic of this chapter, namely, that it was not until the 1990s, at the end of the twentieth century, that serious monographs began to appear which looked at the teaching of translation not only as a practical but as a *theoretical* problem. In other words, translation pedagogy needed a theory not only because teaching itself is a worthy object of theoretical speculation but because good theory makes for more effective teaching. Translation theoreticians had in previous decades tended to neglect translation pedagogy for considerations of translation, text, history, abstracted from the teaching process. Presentations on pedagogy at translation conferences were devoted either to a scornful repudiation of theory in the name of experience or to thought-deadening outlines of course syllabi which told one little if anything about how courses were delivered or what their deeper theoretical underpinnings were.

1.   The pedagogical gap

Gregory M. Shreve in his Foreword to Kiraly's *Pathways to Translation: Pedagogy and Process* deplores the absence of a theoretically self-aware translation didactics, "A translation pedagogy without a theoretical basis will be a blind pedagogy. It will fail to set reasonable objectives, will be unable to create and apply methods appropriate to the learning task, will be unable to measure and evaluate results, and will ultimately fail to create the effective translators our society demand" (Kiraly 1995:x). Not surprisingly, Kiraly agrees and points to the "pedagogical gap" (1995:5) in translation teaching where a lack of clear objectives, curricular materials and teaching methods means that students blunder

along with no sense of incremental progress. He is withering on traditional approaches to translation teaching. Kiraly, in common with many other thinkers
on translation in the 1990s, sees translation primarily as process rather than
product and stresses the importance of translation as a socially-grounded act
of intercultural communication. Think-aloud protocols (TAP) appeal because
they provide (with all their imperfections) some way of getting to know what
goes on in the translator's head and therefore allow us to formulate, however
tentatively, a psychologically valid description of the act of translation. Firth's
linguistic theory and in particular the notion of context of situation provides
the social foundation for the pedagogical theory developed. The case studies
in *Pathways to Translation* are not particularly illuminating in terms of giving
us unusual or unknown insights into the translator's psyche, but they do con-
firm in a more rigorous fashion the insights of many translation instructors,
namely that students tend to translate at the level of the word and that they do
not often factor social variables into the cognitive translation task.

To provide a more complex picture of the psycholinguistic processes and
strategies of the translator, Kiraly along with most other commentators on
translation pedagogy argues that more empirical data is needed (1995:2). As
Kussmaul puts it, "translation teaching ought to be based on data-based research" (1995:5). A similar plea has gone out time and time again from interpreting scholars, notably Gile (1995b). It is a scholarly truism to point out
the complexity of the translating and interpreting process, but it is a truism that puts theoreticians of translation pedagogy in a peculiar predicament
for two reasons. Firstly, there is the problem of *critical mass in research*. The
last two decades have seen a substantial growth in the number of training
courses, journals, publications and scholars in the field of Translation Studies. However, as the field expands so also does the number of areas to be
investigated. Among the subject categories listed in the annual *Bibliography
of Translation Studies* are translation theory, interpreting, history of translation, corpus-based translation studies, translation and gender, translation and
cultural identity, translator/interpreter training, bible translation, specialised
translation, contrastive linguistics, machine(-aided) translation, localisation,
audiovisual translation and terminology/lexicography (Bowker et al. 1999).
Riccardi in a debate on the interaction between research and training in conference interpreting claims that,

> [t]rainers need to have a background in a variety of research areas if they are
> to be effective in dealing with individual student problems. The areas include:
> sociolinguistics, psycholinguistics, neurolinguistics, text linguistics, transla-

tion studies, cognitive linguistics and sciences, neurophysiology, semantics, pragmatics and communication theory.   (1997:94)

Even allowing for overlap, fragmentation of attention is obvious. The result is that a relatively small number of scholars is available to work in any one area. On a macro-level, even in countries with a strong translation studies tradition like Canada, the numbers of scholars working in the area of Translation Studies is much inferior to the number of colleagues working in physics, English, French, computer science, to name but a few disciplines. At a micro-level, many different branches of Translation Studies lay claims on the attentions of potential researchers. Thus, the number of researchers available to undertake the research envisaged by Kiraly, Kussmaul, Gile and others is limited. As Kiraly and Kussmaul demonstrate, even modest case studies with a relatively small number of subjects, are extremely labour-intensive. As vital as basic scientific research is to develop psychologically valid theories for translation pedagogy, results of such investigations are always at least partially compromised by small research bases.

A second, related difficulty in translation pedagogy research is the tension between the desire for the inductive certainties of science and the deductive necessities of providing a rationale for a course. Kussmaul's *Training the Translator* basically uses a functional text-linguistic approach to translation and invokes scenes and frames theory, functional sentence perspective, speech act theory and *skopos* theory where felt appropriate. Although Kussmaul refers to various TAP studies, including his own, it is never entirely clear what processes described in the work are inductively extrapolated from observable phenomena and therefore incorporated into an empirically verifiable theory of translation pedagogy and what are processes derived deductively from theories of language that seem to be a good fit with his own experience of teaching translation. The theoretical uncertainty surrounding Kussmaul's project is not a matter of an individual failing but of a disciplinary dilemma. If the quantity of empirical research is affected by problems to which we have already referred, the translation pedagogue for the foreseeable future is going to have to effect a type of *bricolage* between theories of language and culture that appear to give a reasonable account of how translation operates in the real world and insights from psycholinguistics and cognitive psychology as to what actually goes on in the black box when the translator shifts from one language-world to the other.

2.   Revolution in the classroom

A danger for researchers in translation teaching is that emphasis on translation can lead to a neglect of teaching, and undue concern with teaching can lead to a neglect of the specificity of the subject taught, to wit, translation. In the area of teaching Kiraly (1995) is right to express indignant surprise that as late as the mid-nineties the communicative revolution seemed to have passed translation teaching by. The stress on language function, communicative competence, creativity and active student participation are central tenets of the communicative approach to foreign language pedagogy (Krashen 1982) but were slow in coming to the world of translation didactics. The attention has now shifted in the field of foreign-language pedagogy to the concepts of autonomy (Little 1992) and Computer-Assisted Language Learning (CALL). The stress by translation theorists in the 1990s on the development of the autonomy and self-confidence of the student translator (Gile 1995a; Kussmaul 1995; Kiraly 1995; Robinson 1997) is thus in keeping with the pedagogical spirit of the age with its aim to "deschool" education and hand the learning initiative over to the learner and move away from top-down, teacher-centred approaches to pedagogy. The benefits of techniques like tandem-teaching for translator training are obvious, allowing students, for example, in different countries through e-mail to comment on or edit each other's translations in the native or foreign language.

If the insights of foreign-language pedagogy are stimulating and liberatory for translation didactics, the reception must always be vigilant. Like other areas of the social and human sciences, second-language acquisition is no stranger to ideological fashion. The postwar behaviourist vogue informed the use of language drills and the language laboratory; the post-68 counter-culture inspired the communicative *aggiornamento*; and the free market philosophy of Reaganomics in the 1980s was crucial in the emergence of the student as the autonomous consumer of educational product, a notion that sits easily with the autonomous learner at the work station. Each shift in language pedagogy tends to be presented as the revaluation of all values until another paradigm comes along and captures the pedagogic imagination. Translation Studies is not immune to ideological shifts either, but translation pedagogy should avoid isolating pedagogic techniques from larger changes in *Weltanschauung*.

The contextualisation of translation pedagogy indeed needs to be pursued more vigorously if theoretical models are to have any purchase on teaching realities. Kiraly mentions teaching activities suggested by Skerritt for the translation classroom which include getting-to-know-you activities, learning cells, small-group work, simulations and role playing (Kiraly 1995: 23–24). The pedagogic value of these activities would appear undisputed, but the material infrastructure they presuppose is infinitely more problematic. Small-group work with a group of 48 students in a 90-minute translation class can rapidly become unmanageable in terms of any worthwhile feedback or evaluation, yet they were the constraints under which I worked in a second-year *thème* class in a French university in the early 1980s. Access to new technology throughout the world is starkly uneven. Only 3% of the world's population have the use of a personal computer (Cronin 2000), and when I lectured in Belgrade at the *Fédération Internationale des Traducteurs* (FIT) Congress in 1990 on the advantages of information technology in overcoming geographical disadvantage, I was taken aside after the lecture by a Serbian translator who pointed out that most of her colleagues were still sharing typewriters rather than comparing the merits of FAX cards and Integrated Services Digital Network (ISDN) lines (Cronin 1991). In other words, there is a *geopolitics of pedagogy* which if it is ignored can lead to the ritualised hypocrisy of teaching conferences where speakers preach one thing and are forced to practise another.

The problem in pedagogy is that some translators are more visible than others and the visible translators are almost invariably those from developed Western countries. In the collection of conference papers edited by Israel (1998) under the suggestive title *Quelle formation pour le traducteur de l'an 2000?*, Seleskovitch is fulsome in her praise of the international dimension to the 1996 conference on translator training hosted by ESIT (École supérieure d'interprètes et de traducteurs),

> International au vrai sens du terme puisqu'une trentaine de pays sont effec-tivement représentés ici et puisque nous espérons, non seulement avoir dit un certain nombre de choses pour ce qui est des doctrines de l'ESIT, mais aussi avoir reçu bon nombre de suggestions, d'interventions, d'observations qui permettent une meilleure interprétation de ce que, les uns et les autres, nous disons.
>
> International in the true sense of the word because around thirty countries are represented here and because we hope, not only to have said a number of things about the teachings of ESIT, but also to have listened to a good number of suggestions, comments and observations that will improve our understanding of what each of us is saying.   (Seleskovitch 1998:287–288)

The praise is justified by the attendance list, not by the publication. There were indeed translators and translator trainers from many parts of the world but over 90% of the published interventions come from speakers based in Western Europe and North America (Israel 1998). It is often unfair to blame conference organisers for this phenomenon as they are frequently victims of the particular

politics and economics of international gatherings (travel costs, visas, communication problems), but the result is that certain voices are rarely heard and
pedagogic models rooted in certain material circumstances are universalised
in classic diffusionist models of globalisation (Robertson 1992). Translation
pedagogy would be greatly enhanced not just by genuinely international perspectives but by the institution of a number of ethnographic field studies which
would examine the overall material and institutional context in which translation is taught. The advantage of such studies is that translation pedagogy
could then be elaborated in a manner that was appropriate and sensitive to
local conditions and therefore would have a much greater likelihood of being
effective. In the absence of a holistic vision of context there is the danger of re-
ductionist teaching "recipes" being delivered in a piecemeal fashion in wholly
inappropriate circumstances.

3. Pedagogy and metalanguage

Kussmaul is not shy in embracing the heritage of the Enlightenment. Any claim
to legitimacy is founded ultimately in reason, "It is the rational approach which
distinguishes the expert from the non-expert" (Kussmaul 1995:4). The analytical procedures used in looking at texts in his work, guided primarily by
text linguistics, are detailed and sometimes complex, which is not surprising
as texts and translations are complex objects of study. Kussmaul anticipates
the objections, "All these rationalisations are often very time-consuming", but
his belief is that self-awareness makes for coherence, effectiveness and quality
and that over time the strategies learnt at the training stage will become "inter-
nalized and automatized by frequent use" (1995:150). Ballard in his "L'apport
du comparatisme à la formation du traducteur" shows how a detailed knowledge of the formal changes possible in English-French translation can allow
for a more effective and creative understanding of the notion of translation
unit (1998:33–49). In the interface between theory and practice, time devoted
to rationalisation can certainly be an issue (too much talk, too little translation). However, there is a further problem which has to do with the language
of rationalisation itself.

In order to talk or theorise about phenomena, one inevitably uses a
language that is in effect a metalanguage, a special instance of language that
allows the theorist to stand back and describe what is happening. The purpose
of the metalanguage is to facilitate understanding and allow the results of
research to be communicated to others in the field in a mutually intelligible

discourse. The difference between stamp collecting and science is that science seeks significant patterns, simpler ways of explaining complex phenomena and is not content with merely aligning one fact after the other. Thus, it is perfectly understandable why translation theory should use its own metalanguage. The difficulty is not the lazy demagogy of conference lounge lizards denouncing "theory" but the manner in which for students the language itself can become its own end. For instance, one of the signal merits of comparative stylistics is that it is a way of alerting students to the possibilities of transformations, to the enormous potential of shifting operations in translation as a way of developing translational fluency in the target language. To explain how certain translation choices are definitely possible and others less likely often involves detailed formal descriptions of source and target languages (a task greatly complicated by the increasingly poor grasp of grammar of school leavers, a casualty of the communicative revolution). Students will, however, frequently lose themselves in the analytic detail of the metalanguage and devote their energies to mastering the language itself rather than looking beyond it to its ultimate use as a tool in developing effective translation strategies.

Jean Delisle asks a timely question in *Quelle formation* when he wonders, "si on accepte qu'il faut un métalangage pour tenir un discours sur la traduction et faciliter l'enseignement, à quel moment doit s'enseigner ce métalangage? Est-ce dans un cours de théorie distinct, ou est-ce dans les cours pratiques, au fur et à mesure des besoins?" [if we accept the necessity of a metalanguage to talk about and to teach translation, at what point should we teach this metalanguage? Should this be done in a separate theory course, or should it be done in translation practice classes, as the need arises?] (Israel 1998:27). The difficulty in teaching the metalanguage of theory separately is that it becomes divorced from its purpose and is seen as a procession of rootless abstractions, while integrating metalanguage and practice has not only time implications but the balance between analysis and action is not always easy to achieve.

4.   Games translators play

Kiraly acknowledges in his discussion of the implications of his case study that "translation pedagogy must more and more focus on ways to maximize intuitive processing" (1995:109), and Kussmaul devotes a whole chapter to creativity in translation, looking at notions of divergent production, parallel-activity techniques and the role of sexual desire. Robinson, for his part, in *Becoming a Translator* argues for a shift from a "pedagogy that places primary emphasis on conscious analysis to a pedagogy that balances conscious analysis with subliminal discovery and assimilation" (1997:2). To this end, he uses ideas and techniques from suggestopedia, learning-styles theory, brain science and neurolinguistic programming. Translation pedagogy theorists are correct to stress the importance of the creative and the intuitive or what we have described elsewhere as the crucial role of *hinting* in translation teaching (Cronin 2000:142–144). However, there is an inevitable epistemic dilemma. On the one hand, as Kiraly (1995) and Gile (1995b) stress, there are recurrent difficulties with examining translation process at the sub-conscious level as the evidence is not directly observable. On the other, if – as in the works of Kussmaul and Robinson – theories are imported from other disciplines to attempt to explain creativity and intuition in translation, the theories might seem to make for a good intuitive fit and make for some impressive results in the classroom; but the question still remains as to whether they accurately describe the *specific* nature of creativity and the operation of intuition in translation as opposed to other areas of human activity and reflection.

Strangely absent in theoretical speculation on translation teaching have been theories of play and game in language. This is all the more surprising in that any attempt to theorise intuition in thought and creativity in language must surely take into account the enormous cognitive contribution of play in human development (Bruner et al. 1976). Volkovitch, for example, gives an eloquent and enthusiastic description of his approach to teaching writing skills on the post-graduate course in Literary Translation in Paris VII University. Central to his pedagogic practice is the use of techniques developed by the Oulipo group of French experimental writers where the emphasis is on playing around with words, syntax, generic conventions and text types (Oulipo 1973, 1981). Volkovitch offers the following rationale for his ludic approach (1998:242):

> L'ambiance dans laquelle se déroule ce travail est évidemment primordiale. N'oublions pas l'adage de Queneau: 'On n'écrit pas' (et on ne traduit pas non plus, ajouterai-je) 'pour emmieller le monde!' Il s'agit de mettre la notion de *plaisir* au premier plan – et pour cela, commencer par installer une ambiance fondée sur le jeu et la bonne humeur. Il s'agit de *débloquer*, dans tous les sens du terme, et croyez-moi, il y a des moments où ça débloque sérieusement! Je dis 'sérieusement', car cet aspect ludique n'exclut pas du tout la rigueur, même quand elle se cache par pudeur ou calcul.   (Author's emphasis)

> The atmosphere in which this work takes place is of the utmost importance. We must not forget Queneau's motto, 'One does not write' (and I might add, one does not translate) to get on people's nerves!' The idea is to foreground the notion of pleasure – and to do that, to begin by creating a playful and good-

humoured atmosphere. We're talking about *release* here, in every sense of the word, because, believe you me, seriously, there are times when we let it all hang out! I say 'seriously' because the ludic dimension is in no way incompatible with rigour, even if the latter is hidden by way of modesty or by design.

Kiraly mentions Sager on role-playing and Skerritt on role-play and simulation in the translation classroom (1995:22–24). Kussmaul notes that "in the protocols, especially during incubation, when relaxation was part of the game, [...] a certain amount of laughter and fooling around took place among the subjects if they did not find the solutions at once" (1995:48). There is an awareness, therefore, of ludic potential in translation pedagogy, but the actual theorisation of play itself is almost wholly absent from speculation (see Cronin 1995).

The work of Reynolds (1976) on simulative mode in play, of Bateson (1978) on metacommunication, of Koestler (1989) on bisociative thinking, of Carse (1987) on metaphor and of Bruss (1977) on formal game theory and literature, to mention but a few writers on play, greatly add to our understanding of how human beings use play to interact creatively with language. Since the point is repeatedly stressed by a wide variety of translation theoreticians that creativity is at the heart of the translation process, it would seem only logical that translation didactics would benefit greatly from full engagement with ludicity, not just at a practical but at a theoretical level.

5.   Translators as readers

Manguel in *A History of Reading* speaks of the special role of reading in the emergence of the educated subject, "The child learning to read is admitted into the communal memory by way of books, and thereby becomes acquainted with a common past which he or she renews, to a greater or lesser degree, in every reading" (1997:71). Theorists of translation pedagogy agree in signalling the primacy for translation of the act of understanding through reading. Kiraly claims that, "A flaw in most translation programs is the lack of emphasis on reading and using parallel texts in the L_2" (1995:110). The neglect by students of the translation possibilities of paraphrasing is attributed by Kussmaul to their mistaken belief that text analysis and translation are two separate activities, "It could be seen from our protocols that the phase of understanding the source text is linked up with the phase of producing via paraphrasing" (1995:31). No one disputes the importance of reading for translation, but what about our students as readers? Seleskovitch senses that there is a problem of

literacy, "Nous constatons la dégradation de la qualité d'expression des étudi-
ants" [We note the decline in our students' powers of expression] (1998:288)
but sees terminology as the solution.

The history of reading is a history of change, and changes in our age may
in fact be radical with long-term consequences for how we teach translation.
An assumption made in much translation pedagogy is that while theories may
change and disciplinary models come into or drop out of vogue, students are
always and everywhere the same. In other words, the student is an invariant,
transhistorical subject who is, to all intents and purposes, indistinguishable
from his or her counterpart in the seventeenth, eighteenth or nineteenth century. We have noted this difficulty earlier with respect to the failure of translation pedagogy to take into account synchronic, geopolitical differences in
the student body and teaching profession, but there is the further issue of the
diachronic evolution of students over time, which directly impacts on what theories will be appropriate in pedagogic settings. One of the anomalies of translation as an activity in the modern age is that it is primarily about the production
and reception of the written word. However, a salient characteristic of modernity has been the exponential growth of orality in its various forms in our lives.
Ong speaks of the electronic age as one of "secondary orality" where the "orality of telephones, radio and television" is dominant (1982:3). Secondary orality
is distinct from the primary orality of pre-literate societies in that the former
is strongly marked by the practices and mindset of print culture. Be that as it
may, phone calls are now made where letters would have been sent previously
and even when e-mails are sent, the form of communication is more akin to
oral than written forms of communication. Television programmes, cinema,
popular music, talk radio constitute a constant oral presence for students in
developed countries from a very early age.

Encounters with the written word outside the set tasks of formal schooling
are becoming increasingly rare. Ritual complaints about students' "ignorance"
may flatter the vanity of teachers but it crucially misses the point. What
we are experiencing is a fundamental shift in our culture which has moved
away from an age of high literacy to an era of generalised orality. Debray has
dubbed this transformation the movement from graphosphere to videosphere
(2000:51). It might be countered that the Internet is the saviour of print
and that Web pages and e-mails are instances of written production and
consumption experienced by many students in the West on a quasi-daily basis.
Birkerts in *The Gutenberg Elegies: The Fate of Reading in an Electronic Age* is
not convinced (1996). For Birkerts, reading on the screen is an exacerbated
example of a process set in motion by the printing press itself. If readers

before 1750 read a small number of books over and over again (most notably in the West the Bible), from the mid-eighteenth century onwards, they read more and more, everything from pamphlets and newspapers to periodicals and books, but only once. The shift was from intensive to extensive reading (Darnton 1990). The Information Age has brought with it a proliferation of textual sources, "Awed and intimidated by the availability of texts, faced with the all but impossible task of discriminating among them, the reader tends to move across surfaces, skimming, hastening from one site to the next without allowing the words to resonate inwardly. The inscription is light but it covers vast territories: quantity is elevated over quality" (Birkerts 1996:72). The superficial, extensive reading described here is of course a necessary part of the translator's approach to text. The Web offers translators an unparalleled source of contemporaneous information by way of parallel texts, background cultural knowledge, technical data and terminological access. As Robinson is quick to point out, speed is everything for the professional translator and getting and assimilating information rapidly often makes the difference between poverty and solvency (1997:2). The problem for translation teachers is the establishment of what might be termed *hyper-extensive* reading as the dominant and exclusive mode with consequent effects for general literacy and competent textual production. Birkerts argues that deep, vertical reading is difficult (1996:76):

> What is true of art is true of serious reading as well. Fewer and fewer people, it seems, have the leisure or the inclination to undertake it. And true reading is hard. Unless we are practised, we do not just crack the covers and slip into an alternate world. We do not get swept up as readily as we might be by the big-screen excitements of the film. But if we do read perseveringly we make available to ourselves, in a most portable form, an ulterior existence. We hold in our hands a way to cut against the momentum of the times. We can resist the skimming tendency and delve; we can restore, if only for a time, the vanishing assumption of coherence.

The assumption made hitherto is that the tendency of students to adopt a word-for-word approach to translation is the result of a baleful literalism inherited from foreign-language learning (Kiraly 1995:1). This fear underlines the refusal of ESIT to engage in foreign-language instruction on its translation and interpreting programmes. However, it is equally plausible to argue that a failure to consider translation units larger than words or word-strings and the inability to situate texts in their social and communicative context results primarily from the abandonment of deep reading and the increasingly rare opportunities for formal written communication in lives mediated by an omnipresent orality. In other words, if we do not take account of the culture our students are born into, we run the risk of a mistaken etiology in diagnosing their problems and theorising their difficulties.

Cultural changes can of course provide the pretext for a grim millenari-anism where translation teachers lament the decay of learning and evoke an improbable Golden Age (when they were young). It is more useful to fore-ground reading as a specific area of difficulty and institute reading courses as part of translation programmes. There is little point in exhorting students to read if they neither know how to nor have any incentive (other than duty) to do so. Debates on translation pedagogy frequently concentrate on demand-side factors such as the emergence of new markets, the demand for different skills, the significance for translators of the latest technologies or the relative importance of particular language groups. It is time to pay more attention to supply-side factors and in particular to how our students, as much as transla-tors and translations, are bound up with the history of their own time.

6. Translators in society

A recurrent theme in the writings of those theorists identified with the cultural turn in Translation Studies over the last twenty-five years has been the central importance of translators themselves as active shapers of their texts and histor-ical subjects (Gentzler 1993; Venuti 1995). Theorists of translation teaching in the past decade, from Lederer to Gile to Kussmaul, Kiraly and Robinson have in turn stressed the significance of the individual identity of the translator, albeit in a different manner. A crucial component of translator performance is self-confidence and a positive self-image, and this positive self-image is based on the knowledge that s/he is "un spécialiste de l'expression et de la compréhension" [a specialist in expression and understanding] (Israel 1998: 129) or as Kussmaul puts it, "Others may be experts in law, engineering and business; translators are experts in languages and cultures and in the production of texts" (1995: 146). The value of professional self-confidence for translators is obvious, and it is the possession of a particular expertise that confers legitimacy on their work and justifies the existence of a specific training. However, if we are to train trans-lators, a narrow sense of professional expertise should not be allowed to limit their wider cultural impact. In other words, translators need to be taught from a very early stage to translate texts, but they need also to be made aware of the fact that precisely because the activity of translation makes them, "experts in languages and cultures", they have a contribution to society and culture that goes beyond the strictly professional activity of translation itself.

Castells in *The Rise of the Network Society*, the first volume in his *The Information Age: Economy, Society and Culture* trilogy, unwittingly indicates what that contribution might be (1996:3):

> In a world of global flows of wealth, power, and images, the search for identity, collective or individual, ascribed or constructed, becomes the fundamental source of social meaning. This is not a new trend, since identity, and particularly religious and ethnic identity, have been at the roots of meaning since the dawn of human society. Yet identity is becoming the main, and sometimes the only, source of meaning in a historical period characterized by widespread destructuring of organisations, delegitimation of institutions, fading away of major social movements, and ephemeral cultural expressions.

Translators and interpreters, in both history (Delisle & Woodsworth 1995) and in the contemporary world (viz. localisation industry), are crucial agents in facilitating "global flows of wealth, power, and images" around the planet. Yet, they have also been major figures in the establishment of ethnic identities, national languages and religious affiliations (see Cronin 1996 for the specific case of Ireland). A core feature of post-Fordist economic activity is the rise in what are sometimes termed "postmodern goods"; these are objects which "possess a substantial aesthetic component (such as pop music, cinema, leisure, magazines, video and so on)" (Lash & Urry 1994:4). More generally, we witness the growing centrality of "design"-intensive production and the increasing importance of the "expressive component" in the manufacture and delivery of goods and services (Lash & Urry 1994:111–144). Thus, cultural content and aesthetic mediation are at the heart of the new economic paradigm, the globalised network of flexible production units responding rapidly to changes in taste and fashion through computerised, small-batch production techniques (Harvey 1990).

Translators, as experts in languages and cultures, are ideally placed to make a significant contribution to our understanding of the contemporary world, particularly in apprehending the cultural impact of economic change. Their contribution is all the more important in that they are constantly moving backwards and forwards between languages and are therefore sensitive to the liminal, in-between zones that increasingly characterise contemporary consciousness and global cultural evolution. It can be argued therefore that translation pedagogy must not only concern itself with issues relating to the socio-cultural insertion of texts, the functional appropriateness of translation practices and rational self-possession based on the acquisition of procedural expertise but must positively enable the translator as an active and vocal participant in the political, cultural and intellectual life of his or her society. To this end, it may be necessary to go beyond the more traditional translation theory courses and offer "Translator in Society" courses that would be a hybrid of political science, sociology, economics, and translation history and which would offer students the conceptual tools and historical knowledge to become *visible* not only as signatories of translation texts but as fully-fledged intellectuals in their own right. If historians (Foucault), sociologists (Giddens), philosophers (Nussbaum) can enter the public sphere and use their expertise to engage in debates on the cultural, political and educational choices of societies, there is no reason, given the particular sets of knowledge and skills that they have at this moment in human history, why translators cannot do the same. We would be remiss in our teaching mission if we did not at least offer our students (at undergraduate and postgraduate level) the wherewithal to do so.

Cassandra Reilly, the heroine of Wilson's *Gaudí Afternoon* is on a trip back to Barcelona. Cassandra, born in the United States, holder of an Irish passport, makes her living translating Latin American novels from Spanish into English. Her lover, Carmen, is annoyed with Cassandra's frequent absences but Cassandra's reply is immediate, "That's what life in the translation business is all about, Carmen. Speed, violence, sex, mystery. Translators come and they go, you can't count on them. You should never count on a translator" (Wilson 1990: 171). Theorists of translation pedagogy encounter their own fair share of speed (the "accelerated course" of Robinson), violence (what students do to texts), sex (the "coital furor" of creative illumination (Kussmaul 1995: 48)) and mystery (what exactly does go on inside the translator's head?) in their research. In an age where the activities of translators are being redefined by the use of tools like translation memories and speech recognition software, where there is an exponential growth in Web localisation and an increasingly widespread use of often low-level MT software, translators cannot be counted on to remain unaffected. They will be both victims and agents of change and the need will be as great as ever for appropriate theory to inform their education as professionals in the marketplace and as citizens of the world.

References

Ballard, M. (1998). "L'apport du comparatisme à la formation du traducteur". In Fortunato Israel (Ed.), *Quelle formation pour le traducteur de l'an 2000?* (pp. 33–49). Paris: Didier.

Bassnett, S. (1996). "The meek or the mighty: Reappraising the role of the translator". In Roman Álvarez & M. Carmen-África Vidal (Eds.), *Translation, Power, Subversion* (pp. 10–24). Clevedon: Multilingual Matters.

Bateson, G. (1978). *Steps to an Ecology of Mind*. London: Paladin.

Birkerts, S. (1996). *The Gutenberg Elegies. The Fate of Reading in an Electronic Age*. London: Faber & Faber.

Bowker, L., Kenny, D., & Pearson, J. (Eds.). (1999). *Bibliography of Translation Studies*. Manchester: St. Jerome.

Bruner, J. S., Jolly, A., & Sylva, K. (Eds.). (1976). *Play. Its Role in Development and Evolution*. Harmondsworth: Penguin.

Bruss, E. (1977). "The game of literature and some literary games". *New Literary History, 9*(1), 153–172.

Carse, J. (1987). *Finite and Infinite Games*. Harmondsworth: Penguin.

Castells, M. (1996). *The Rise of the Network Society*. Oxford: Blackwell.

Cronin, M. & Nolan, J. (1991). "Language, technology and the network-based economy: A peripheral perspective". In Mladan Jovanovic (Ed.), *Translation, a creative profession/La traduction, une profession créative* (pp. 320–324). Belgrade: Previdolac.

Cronin, M. (1995). "Keeping one's distance: Translation and the play of possibility". *TTR, 8*(2), 227–243.

Cronin, M. (1996). *Translating Ireland: Translation, Languages, Cultures*. Cork University Press.

Cronin, M. (2000). *Across the Lines. Travel, Language, Translation*. Cork: Cork University Press.

Darnton, R. (1990). *The Kiss of Lamourette*. New York: W.W. Norton and Co.

Debray, R. (2000). *Introduction à la médiologie*, Paris: Presses Universitaires de France.

Delisle, J. & Woodsworth, J. (Eds.). (1995). *Translators through History*. Amsterdam and Philadelphia: John Benjamins.

Gentzler, E. (1993). *Contemporary Translation Theories*. London and New York: Routledge.

Gile, D. (1995a). *Basic Concepts and Models for Interpreter Training*. Amsterdam and Philadelphia: John Benjamins.

Gile, D. (1995b). *Regards sur la recherche en interprétation de conférence*. Lille: Presses Universitaires de Lille.

Harvey, D. (1990). *The Condition of Postmodernity*. Oxford: Blackwell.

Israel, F. (Ed.). (1998). *Quelle formation pour le traducteur de l'an 2000?* Paris: Didier.

Kiraly, D. C. (1995). *Pathways to Translation. Pedagogy and Process*. Kent, OH: Kent State University Press.

Koestler, A. (1989). *The Act of Creation*. London: Arkana.

Krashen, S. D. (1982). *Principles and Practice in Second Language Acquisition*. Oxford: Pergamon Press.

Kussmaul, P. (1995). *Training the Translator*. Amsterdam and Philadelphia: John Benjamins.

Ladmiral, J. R. (1977). "La traduction dans le cadre de l'institution pédagogique". *Die Neuren Sprachen, 76*, 489–516.

Lash, S. & Urry, J. (1994). *Economies of Signs and Space*. London: Sage.

Little, D. (1992). *Learner Autonomy. 1: Definitions, Issues, and Problems*. Dublin: Authentik.

Manguel, A. (1997). *A History of Reading*. London: Flamingo.

Ong, W. J. (1982). *Orality and Literacy. The Technologizing of the Word*. London and New York: Routledge.

Oulipo (1973). *La littérature potentielle*. Paris: Gallimard.

Oulipo (1981). *Atlas de littérature potentielle*. Paris: Gallimard.

Reynolds, P. C. (1976). "Play, language and human evolution". In J. S. Bruner, A. Jolly, & K. Sylva (Eds.), *Play: Its Role in Development and Evolution* (pp. 620–626). Harmondsworth: Penguin.

Riccardi, A. (1997). "Conference interpreting: The background to research and training". In Y. Gambier, D. Gile, & C. Taylor (Eds.). *Conference Interpreting. Current Trends in Research*. Amsterdam and Philadelphia: John Benjamins.

Robertson, R. (1992). *Globalization. Social Theory and Global Culture*. London: Sage.

Robinson, D. (1997). *Becoming a Translator. An Accelerated Course*. London and New York: Routledge.

Seleskovitch, D. (1998). "Allocution de clôture". In Fortunato Israel (Ed.), *Quelle formation pour le traducteur de l'an 2000?* (pp. 287–291). Paris: Didier.

Venuti, L. (1995). *The Translator's Invisibility*. London and New York: Routledge.

Volkovitch, M. (1998). "Une idée neuve en Europe". In Fortunato Israel (Ed.), *Quelle formation pour le traducteur de l'an 2000?* (pp. 235–244). Paris: Didier.

Waquet, F. (1998). *Le Latin ou l'empire d'un signe xvie-xxe siècle*. Paris: Albin Michel.

Wilson, B. (1990). *Gaudí Afternoon*. Seattle: Seal Press.

Index

In the series *Benjamins Translation Library* the following titles have been published thus far or are scheduled for publication:

36 **SCHMID, Monika S.:** Translating the Elusive. Marked word order and subjectivity in English-German translation. 1999. xii, 174 pp.

37 **TIRKKONEN-CONDIT, Sonja and Riitta JÄÄSKELÄINEN (eds.):** Tapping and Mapping the Processes of Translation and Interpreting. Outlooks on empirical research. 2000. x, 176 pp.

38 **SCHÄFFNER, Christina and Beverly ADAB (eds.):** Developing Translation Competence. 2000. xvi, 244 pp.

39 **CHESTERMAN, Andrew, Natividad GALLARDO SAN SALVADOR and Yves GAMBIER (eds.):** Translation in Context. Selected papers from the EST Congress, Granada 1998. 2000. x, 393 pp.

40 **ENGLUND DIMITROVA, Birgitta and Kenneth HYLTENSTAM (eds.):** Language Processing and Simultaneous Interpreting. Interdisciplinary perspectives. 2000. xvi, 164 pp.

41 **NIDA, Eugene A.:** Contexts in Translating. 2002. x, 127 pp.

42 **HUNG, Eva (ed.):** Teaching Translation and Interpreting 4. Building bridges. 2002. xii, 243 pp.

43 **GARZONE, Giuliana and Maurizio VIEZZI (eds.):** Interpreting in the 21st Century. Challenges and opportunities. 2002. x, 337 pp.

44 **SINGERMAN, Robert:** Jewish Translation History. A bibliography of bibliographies and studies. With an introductory essay by Gideon Toury. 2002. xxxvi, 420 pp.

45 **ALVES, Fabio (ed.):** Triangulating Translation. Perspectives in process oriented research. 2003. x, 165 pp.

46 **BRUNETTE, Louise, Georges BASTIN, Isabelle HEMLIN and Heather CLARKE (eds.):** The Critical Link 3. Interpreters in the Community. Selected papers from the Third International Conference on Interpreting in Legal, Health and Social Service Settings, Montréal, Quebec, Canada 22–26 May 2001. 2003. xii, 359 pp.

47 **SAWYER, David B.:** Fundamental Aspects of Interpreter Education. Curriculum and Assessment. 2004. xviii, 312 pp.

48 **MAURANEN, Anna and Pekka KUJAMÄKI (eds.):** Translation Universals. Do they exist? 2004. vi, 224 pp.

49 **PYM, Anthony:** The Moving Text. Localization, translation, and distribution. 2004. xviii, 223 pp.

50 **HANSEN, Gyde, Kirsten MALMKJÆR and Daniel GILE (eds.):** Claims, Changes and Challenges in Translation Studies. Selected contributions from the EST Congress, Copenhagen 2001. 2004. xiv, 320 pp. [EST Subseries 1]

51 **CHAN, Leo Tak-hung:** Twentieth-Century Chinese Translation Theory. Modes, issues and debates. 2004. xvi, 277 pp.

52 **HALE, Sandra Beatriz:** The Discourse of Court Interpreting. Discourse practices of the law, the witness and the interpreter. 2004. xviii, 267 pp.

53 **DIRIKER, Ebru:** De-/Re-Contextualizing Conference Interpreting. Interpreters in the Ivory Tower? 2004. x, 223 pp.

54 **GONZÁLEZ DAVIES, Maria:** Multiple Voices in the Translation Classroom. Activities, tasks and projects. 2004. x, 262 pp.

55 **ANGELELLI, Claudia V.:** Revisiting the Interpreter's Role. A study of conference, court, and medical interpreters in Canada, Mexico, and the United States. 2004. xvi, 127 pp.

56 **ORERO, Pilar (ed.):** Topics in Audiovisual Translation. 2004. xiv, 227 pp.

57 **CHERNOV, Ghelly V.:** Inference and Anticipation in Simultaneous Interpreting. A probability-prediction model. Edited with a critical foreword by Robin Setton and Adelina Hild. 2004. xxx, 268 pp. [EST Subseries 2]

58 **BRANCHADELL, Albert and Lovell Margaret WEST (eds.):** Less Translated Languages. 2005. viii, 416 pp.

59 **MALMKJÆR, Kirsten (ed.):** Translation in Undergraduate Degree Programmes. 2004. vi, 202 pp.

60 **TENNENT, Martha (ed.):** Training for the New Millennium. Pedagogies for translation and interpreting. 2005. xxv, 274 pp.

61 **HUNG, Eva (ed.):** Translation and Cultural Change. Studies in history, norms and image-projection. xvi, 188 pp. + index. *Expected Spring 2005*

62 **POKORN, Nike K.:** Challenging the Traditional Axioms. Translation into a non-mother tongue. xii, 158 pp. + index. [EST Subseries 3] *Expected Spring 2005*

A complete list of titles in this series can be found on www.benjamins.com/jbp